*M*odern *B*uddhism

Also by Geshe Kelsang Gyatso

Meaningful to Behold
Clear Light of Bliss
Heart of Wisdom
Universal Compassion
Joyful Path of Good Fortune
Guide to Dakini Land
The Bodhisattva Vow
Heart Jewel
Great Treasury of Merit
Introduction to Buddhism
Understanding the Mind
Tantric Grounds and Paths
Ocean of Nectar
Essence of Vajrayana
Living Meaningfully, Dying Joyfully
Eight Steps to Happiness
Transform Your Life
The New Meditation Handbook
How to Solve Our Human Problems
Mahamudra Tantra

Profits received by Tharpa Publications from
the sale of this book will be donated to the
NKT-IKBU International Temples Project
A Nonprofit Buddhist Organization
Building for World Peace
www.kadampa.org/temples

GESHE KELSANG GYATSO

$\mathcal{M}$odern $\mathcal{B}$uddhism

THE PATH OF COMPASSION AND WISDOM

THARPA PUBLICATIONS
US UK CANADA
AUSTRALIA HONG KONG

Tharpa Publications US
47 Sweeney Road
Glen Spey, NY 12737
USA

Tharpa Publications UK
Conishead Priory
Ulverston, Cumbria
LA12 9QQ, England

Tharpa Publications has offices around the world, and our books are available in most major languages. See page 411 for more information.

Hardcover ISBN 978-1-61606-005-3
Paperback ISBN 978-1-61606-006-0

Library of Congress Control Number: 2010932058

Printed in the United States of America on acid-free paper.

FSC
Mixed Sources
Product group from well-managed forests and other controlled sources

Cert no. SW-COC-002283
www.fsc.org
© 1996 Forest Stewardship Council

Contents

Illustrations

Preface

The instructions given in this book are scientific methods for improving our human nature and qualities through developing the capacity of our mind. In recent years our knowledge of modern technology has increased considerably, and as a result we have witnessed remarkable material progress, but there has not been a corresponding increase in human happiness. There is no less suffering in the world today, and there are no fewer problems. It could even be said that there are now more problems and greater dangers than ever before. This shows that the cause of happiness and the solution to our problems do not lie in knowledge of material things. Happiness and suffering are states of mind, and so their main causes cannot be found outside the mind. If we want to be truly happy and free from suffering, we must learn how to control our mind.

When things go wrong in our life and we encounter difficult situations, we tend to regard the situation itself as our problem, but in reality whatever problems we experience come from the side of the mind. If we responded to difficult situations with a positive or peaceful mind they would not be problems for us; eventually, we might even regard them as challenges or opportunities for growth and development. Problems arise only if we respond to difficulties with a negative state of mind. Therefore, if we want to be free from problems, we must transform our mind.

Buddha taught that the mind has the power to create all pleasant and unpleasant objects. The world is the result of the karma, or actions, of the beings who inhabit it. A pure world is the result of pure actions and an impure world is the result of impure actions. Since all actions are created by mind, ultimately everything, including the world itself, is created by mind. There is no creator other than the mind.

Normally we say, "I created such and such," or "He or she created such and such," but the actual creator of everything is the mind. We are like servants of our mind—whenever it wants to do something we have to do it without any choice. Since beginningless time until now we have been under the control of our mind, without any freedom; but if we sincerely practice the instructions given in this book, we can reverse this situation and gain control over our mind. Only then will we have real freedom.

Through studying many Buddhist texts we may become a renowned scholar; but if we do not put Buddha's teachings into practice, our understanding of Buddhism will remain hollow, with no power to solve our own or others' problems. Expecting intellectual understanding of Buddhist texts alone to solve our problems is like a sick person hoping to cure his or her illness through merely reading medical instructions without actually taking the medicine. As Buddhist Master Shantideva says:

We need to put Buddha's teachings, the Dharma, into
  practice
Because nothing can be accomplished just by reading
  words.
A sick man will never be cured of his illness
Through merely reading medical instructions!

Each and every living being has the sincere wish to avoid all
suffering and problems permanently. Normally we try to do this by
using external methods, but no matter how successful we are from a
worldly point of view—no matter how materially wealthy, powerful, or highly respected we become—we will never find permanent
liberation from suffering and problems. In reality, all the problems
we experience day-to-day come from our self-cherishing and self-
grasping—misconceptions that exaggerate our own importance.
However, because we do not understand this, we usually blame
others for our problems, and this just makes them worse. From
these two basic misconceptions all our other delusions arise, such as
anger and attachment, causing us to experience endless problems.

I pray that everyone who reads this book may experience deep
inner peace, or peace of mind, and accomplish the real meaning
of human life. I particularly would like to encourage everyone to
read specifically the chapter "Training in Ultimate Bodhichitta."
Through carefully reading and contemplating this chapter again and
again with a positive mind, you will gain very profound knowledge,
or wisdom, which will bring great meaning to your life.

Geshe Kelsang Gyatso

PART ONE

Sutra

Buddha Shakyamuni

Preliminary Explanation

WHAT IS BUDDHISM?

*B*uddhism is the practice of Buddha's teachings, also called *Dharma*, which means "protection." By practicing Buddha's teachings, living beings are permanently protected from suffering. The founder of Buddhism is Buddha Shakyamuni, who showed how to accomplish the ultimate goal of living beings, the attainment of enlightenment, at Bodh Gaya in India in 589 BC. At the request of the gods Indra and Brahma, Buddha then began to expound his profound teachings, or *turned the Wheel of Dharma*. Buddha gave eighty-four thousand teachings, and from these precious teachings Buddhism developed in this world.

Today we can see many different forms of Buddhism, such as Zen and Theravada Buddhism. All these different aspects are practices of Buddha's teachings, and all are equally precious; they are just different presentations. In this book I will explain about Buddhism according to the Kadampa tradition, which I have studied and practiced, and the lineage of this tradition is below. This explanation is not given for the purpose of intellectual understanding, but for gaining profound realizations through which we can solve our daily problems of delusions and accomplish the real meaning of our human life.

There are two stages to the practice of Buddha's teachings—the practices of Sutra and Tantra—both of which are explained in this book. Although the instructions presented here come from Buddha Shakyamuni, and Buddhist Masters such as Atisha, Je Tsongkhapa, and our present Teachers, this book is called *Modern Buddhism* because its presentation of Dharma is designed especially for the people of the modern world.

If everyone sincerely practices the path of compassion and wisdom, all their problems will be solved. I guarantee this.

My intention in writing this book is to give the reader strong encouragement to develop and maintain compassion and wisdom. If everyone sincerely practices the path of compassion and wisdom, all their problems will be solved and never arise again; I guarantee this.

We need to practice Buddha's teachings because there is no other real method to solve human problems. For example, because modern technology often causes more suffering and dangers, it cannot be a real method to solve human problems. Although we want to be happy all the time we do not know how to do this, and we are always destroying our own happiness by developing anger, negative views, and negative intentions. We are always trying to escape from problems, even in our dreams, but we do not know how to liberate ourself from suffering and problems. Because we do not understand the real nature of things, we are always creating our own suffering and problems by performing inappropriate, or non-virtuous, actions.

The source of all our daily problems is our delusions such as attachment. Since beginningless time, because we have been so attached to the fulfillment of our own wishes, we have performed various kinds of non-virtuous actions—actions that harm others. As a result we continually experience various kinds of suffering and miserable conditions in life after life without end. When our wishes are not fulfilled we usually experience unpleasant feelings, such as unhappiness or depression; this is our own problem because we are so attached to the fulfillment of our wishes. When we lose a close friend we experience pain and unhappiness, but this is only because of our attachment to this friend. When we lose our possessions, position, or reputation we experience unhappiness and depression because we are so attached to these things. If we had no attachment there would be no basis to experience these problems. Many people are engaged in fighting, criminal actions, and even warfare; all these actions arise from their strong attachment to the fulfillment of their own wishes. In this way we can see that there is not a single problem experienced by living beings that does not come from their attachment. This proves that unless we control our attachment our problems will never cease.

The method for controlling our attachment and other delusions is the practice of Buddha's teachings. By practicing Buddha's teachings on renunciation, we can solve our daily problems that arise from attachment; by practicing Buddha's teachings on universal compassion, we can solve our daily problems that arise from anger; and by practicing Buddha's teachings on the profound view of emptiness, ultimate truth, we can solve our daily problems that arise from ignorance. How to develop renunciation, universal compassion, and the wisdom realizing emptiness will be explained in this book.

The root of attachment and of all our suffering is self-grasping ignorance, ignorance about the way things actually exist. Without relying on Buddha's teachings we cannot recognize this ignorance; and without practicing Buddha's teachings on emptiness we cannot abandon it. Therefore we will have no opportunity to attain liberation from suffering and problems. Through this explanation we can understand that, since all living beings, whether human or non-human, Buddhist or non-Buddhist, wish to be free from suffering and problems, they all need to practice Dharma. There is no other method to accomplish this goal.

We should understand that our problems do not exist outside of ourself, but are part of our mind that experiences unpleasant feelings. When our car, for example, has a problem we usually say, "I have a problem," but in reality it is the car's problem and not our problem. The car's problem is an outer problem, and our problem, which is our own unpleasant feeling, is an inner problem. These two problems are completely different. We need to solve the car's problem by repairing it, and we need to solve our own problem by controlling our attachment to the car. Even if we keep solving the car's problems, if we are unable to control our attachment to the car we will continually experience new problems related to the car. It is the same with our house, our money, our relationships, and so forth. Due to mistakenly believing that outer problems are their own problems, most people seek ultimate refuge in the wrong objects. As a result, their suffering and problems never end.

As long as we are unable to control our delusions such as attachment, we will have to experience suffering and problems continually, throughout this life and in life after life without end. Because we are bound tightly by the rope of attachment to *samsara*, the cycle of impure life, it is impossible for us to be free from suffering and problems unless we practice Dharma. Understanding this we should develop and maintain the strong wish to abandon the root of suffering—attachment and self-grasping ignorance. This wish is called *renunciation*, and arises from our wisdom.

Buddha's teachings are scientific methods to solve the problems of all living beings permanently. By putting his teachings into practice we will be able to control our attachment, and because of this we will be permanently free from all our suffering and problems. From this alone we can understand how precious and important his teachings, the Dharma, are for everyone. As mentioned above, because all our problems come from attachment, and there is no method to control attachment other than Dharma, it is clear that only Dharma is the actual method to solve our daily problems.

BUDDHIST FAITH

For Buddhists, faith in Buddha Shakyamuni is their spiritual life; it is the root of all Dharma realizations. If we have deep faith in Buddha we will naturally develop the strong wish to practice his teachings. With this wish we will definitely apply effort in our Dharma practice, and with strong effort we will accomplish permanent liberation from the suffering of this life and countless future lives.

The attainment of permanent liberation from suffering depends on effort in our Dharma practice, which depends on the strong wish to practice Dharma, which in turn depends on deep faith in Buddha. Therefore we can understand that if we truly want to experience great benefit from our practice of Buddhism, we need to develop and maintain deep faith in Buddha.

How do we develop and maintain this faith? First, we should know why we need to attain permanent liberation from suffering. It is not enough just to experience temporary liberation from a particular suffering; all living beings, including animals, experience temporary liberation from particular sufferings. Animals experience temporary liberation from human suffering, and humans experience temporary liberation from animal suffering. At the moment we may be free from physical suffering and mental pain, but this is only temporary. Later in this life and in our countless future lives, we will have to experience unbearable physical suffering and mental pain, again and again without end. In the cycle of impure life, samsara, no one has permanent liberation; everyone has to experience the sufferings of sickness, aging, death, and uncontrolled rebirth continually, in life after life without end.

Buddha is actually liberating us by revealing the wisdom path that leads us to the ultimate goal of human life.

Within this cycle of impure life there are various realms or impure worlds into which we can be reborn: the three lower realms—the animal, hungry ghost, and hell realms—and the three higher realms—the god, demi-god, and human realms. Of all impure worlds, hell is the worst; it is the world that appears to the very worst kind of mind. The world of an animal is less impure, and the world that appears to human beings is less impure than the world that appears to animals. However, there is suffering within every realm. When we take rebirth as a human being we have to experience human suffering, when we take rebirth as an animal we have to experience animal suffering, and when we take rebirth as a hell being we have to experience the suffering of a hell being. Through contemplating this we will realize that just experiencing a temporary liberation from particular sufferings is not good enough; we definitely need to attain permanent liberation from the sufferings of this life and all our countless future lives.

How can we accomplish this? Only by putting Buddha's teachings into practice. This is because only Buddha's teachings are the actual methods to abandon our self-grasping ignorance, the source of all our suffering. In his teaching called *King of Concentration Sutra*, Buddha says:

> A magician creates various things
> Such as horses, elephants, and so forth.
> His creations do not actually exist;
> You should know all things in the same way.

This teaching alone has the power to permanently liberate all living beings from their suffering. Through practicing and realizing this teaching, which is explained more fully in the chapter "Training in Ultimate Bodhichitta" we can permanently eradicate the root of all our suffering, our self-grasping ignorance. When this happens we will experience the supreme permanent peace of mind, known as *nirvana*, permanent liberation from suffering, which is our deepest wish and the real meaning of human life. This is the main purpose of Buddha's teachings.

Through understanding this we will deeply appreciate the great kindness of Buddha to all living beings in giving profound methods to achieve permanent freedom from the cycle of suffering of sickness, aging, death, and rebirth. Even our mother does not have the compassion that wishes to liberate us from these sufferings;

only Buddha has this compassion for all living beings without exception. Buddha is actually liberating us by revealing the wisdom path that leads us to the ultimate goal of human life. We should contemplate this point again and again until we develop deep faith in Buddha. This faith is the object of our meditation; we should transform our mind into faith in Buddha, and maintain it single-pointedly for as long as possible. By continually practicing this contemplation and meditation we will maintain deep faith in Buddha day and night, throughout our life.

One of Buddha's main functions is to bestow mental peace on each and every living being by giving blessings. By themselves, living beings are unable to cultivate a peaceful mind; it is only through receiving Buddha's blessings on their mental continuum that living beings, including even animals, can experience peace of mind. When their minds are peaceful and calm they are really happy; but if their minds are not peaceful they are not happy, even if their external conditions are perfect. This proves that happiness depends on mental peace, and since this depends on receiving Buddha's blessings, Buddha is therefore the source of all happiness. Understanding and contemplating this we should develop and maintain deep faith in Buddha, and generate the strong wish to practice his teachings in general and Kadam Lamrim in particular.

WHO ARE THE KADAMPAS?

Ka refers to Buddha's teachings, and *dam* refers to Atisha's instructions on Lamrim (the "Stages of the Path to Enlightenment," also known as *Kadam Lamrim*). *Kadam* therefore refers to the union of Buddha's teachings and Atisha's instructions, and sincere practitioners of Kadam Lamrim are called *Kadampas*. There are two

Kadampa traditions, the ancient and the new. Practitioners of the ancient Kadampa tradition appeared to emphasize the practice of Kadam Lamrim of Sutra more than the practice of Tantra. Later, Je Tsongkhapa and his disciples emphasized the practice of Kadam Lamrim of both Sutra and Tantra equally. This new tradition founded by Je Tsongkhapa is called the new Kadampa tradition.

Kadampas sincerely rely on Buddha Shakyamuni because Buddha is the source of Kadam Lamrim; they sincerely rely on Avalokiteshvara, the Buddha of Compassion, and on the Wisdom Dharma Protector, indicating that their main practice is compassion and wisdom; and they sincerely rely on Arya Tara because she promised Atisha that she would take special care of Kadampa practitioners in the future. For this reason, these four enlightened holy beings are called the "Four Kadampa Guru Deities."

The founder of the Kadampa tradition is the great Buddhist Master and scholar, Atisha. Atisha was born in AD 982 as a prince in East Bengal, India. His father's name was Kalyanashri (Glorious Virtue) and his mother's name was Prabhavarti Shrimati (Glorious Radiance). He was the second of three sons and when he was born he was given the name Chandragarbha (Moon Essence). The name Atisha, which means Peace, was given to him later by the Tibetan king Jangchub Ö because he was always calm and peaceful.

When he was still a child, Chandragarbha's parents took him to visit a temple. All along the way thousands of people gathered to see if they could catch a glimpse of the prince. When he saw them Chandragarbha asked, "Who are these people?" and his parents replied, "They are all our subjects." Compassion arose spontaneously in the prince's heart and he prayed, "May all these people enjoy good fortune as great as my own." Whenever he met anyone the wish arose naturally in his mind, "May this person find happiness and be free from suffering."

Even as a small boy Chandragarbha received visions of Arya Tara, a female enlightened being. Sometimes, while he was on his mother's lap, blue upali flowers would fall from the sky and he would begin to speak, as if to the flowers. Yogis later explained to his mother that the blue flowers she had seen were a sign that Tara was appearing to her son and speaking to him.

When the prince was older his parents wanted to arrange a marriage for him, but Tara advised him: "If you become attached to your kingdom you will be like an elephant when he sinks into mud and cannot lift himself out again because he is so huge and heavy. Do not become attached to this life. Study and practice Dharma. You have been a Spiritual Guide in many of your previous lives and in this life also you will become a Spiritual Guide." Inspired by these words Chandragarbha developed a very strong interest in studying and practicing Dharma and he became determined to attain all the realizations of Buddha's teachings. He knew that to accomplish his aim he would need to find a fully qualified Spiritual Guide. At first he approached a famous Buddhist Teacher called Jetari, who lived nearby, and requested Dharma instructions on how to find freedom from samsara. Jetari gave him instructions on refuge and bodhichitta, and then told him that if he wanted to practice purely he should go to Nalanda and learn from the Spiritual Guide Bodhibhadra.

When he met Bodhibhadra, the prince said, "I realize that samsara is meaningless and that only liberation and full enlightenment are really worthwhile. Please give Dharma instructions that will lead me quickly to the state beyond sorrow, nirvana."

Bodhibhadra gave him brief instructions on generating bodhichitta and then advised, "If you wish to practice Dharma purely you should seek the Spiritual Guide Vidyakokila." Bodhibhadra knew that Vidyakokila was a great meditator who had gained a perfect realization of emptiness and was very skillful in teaching the stages of the profound path.

Vidyakokila gave Chandragarbha complete instructions on both the profound path and the vast path and then sent him to study with the Spiritual Guide Avadhutipa. Avadhutipa did not give guidance immediately but told the prince to go to Rahulagupta to receive instructions on *Hevajra* and *Heruka Tantras* and then to return to him to receive more detailed instructions on Tantra, or Secret Mantra. Rahulagupta gave Chandragarbha the secret name Janavajra (Indestructible Wisdom) and his first empowerment, which was into the practice of Hevajra. Then he told him to go home and obtain the consent of his parents.

If I practice Dharma purely, I will be able to repay the kindness of all living beings.

Although the prince was not attached to worldly life it was still important for him to have his parents' permission to practice in the way he wished. So he returned to his parents and said, "If I practice Dharma purely, then as Arya Tara has predicted, I will be able to repay your kindness and the kindness of all living beings. If I can do this my human life will not have been wasted. Otherwise, even though I may spend all my time in a glorious palace, my life will be meaningless. Please give me your consent to leave the kingdom and dedicate my whole life to the practice of Dharma." Chandragarbha's father was unhappy to hear this and wanted to prevent his son from giving up his prospects as the future king, but his mother was delighted to hear that her son wished to dedicate his life to Dharma. She remembered that at his birth there had been marvelous signs, such as rainbows, and she remembered miracles like the blue upali flowers falling from the sky. She knew that her son was no ordinary prince and she gave her permission without hesitation. Eventually the king also granted his son's wish.

Chandragarbha returned to Avadhutipa and for seven years he received instructions on Secret Mantra. He became so accomplished that on one occasion he developed pride, thinking, "I probably know more about Secret Mantra than anyone else in the whole world." That night in his dream Dakinis came and showed him rare scriptures that he had never seen before. They asked him, "What do these texts mean?" but he had no idea. When he awoke, his pride was gone.

Later, Chandragarbha began to think that he should imitate Avadhutipa's way of practicing and strive to attain enlightenment quickly as a layman by practicing Mahamudra depending on an action mudra; but he received a vision of Heruka who told him that if he were to take ordination he would be able to help countless beings and spread Dharma far and wide. That night he dreamed that he was following a procession of monks in the presence of Buddha Shakyamuni, who was wondering why Chandragarbha had not yet taken ordination. When he awoke from his dream he resolved to become a monk. He received ordination from Shilarakshita, and was given the name Dhipamkara Shrijana.

From the Spiritual Guide Dharmarakshita, Dhipamkara Shrijana received extensive instructions on the *Seven Sets of Abhidharma* and the *Ocean of Great Explanation*—texts written from the point of view of the Vaibhashika system. In this way he mastered the Hinayana teachings.

Still not satisfied, Dhipamkara Shrijana went to receive detailed instructions at Bodh Gaya. One day he overheard a conversation between two women who were actually emanations of Arya Tara. The younger asked the elder, "What is the principal method for attaining enlightenment quickly?" and the elder replied, "It is bodhichitta." Hearing this, Dhipamkara Shrijana became determined to attain the precious bodhichitta. Later, while he was circumambulating the great stupa at Bodh Gaya, a statue of Buddha Shakyamuni spoke to him, saying, "If you wish to attain enlightenment quickly you must gain experience of compassion, love, and the precious bodhichitta." His desire to realize bodhichitta then became intense. He heard that the Spiritual Guide Serlingpa, who lived far away in a place called Serling, in Sumatra, had attained a very special experience of bodhichitta and was able to give instructions on the *Perfection of Wisdom Sutras*.

It took Dhipamkara Shrijana thirteen months to sail to Sumatra. When he arrived there he offered Serlingpa a mandala and made his requests. Serlingpa told him that the instructions would take twelve years to transmit. Dhipamkara Shrijana stayed in Sumatra for twelve years and finally gained the precious realization of bodhichitta. Then he returned to India.

By relying on his Spiritual Guides, Atisha gained special knowledge of the three sets of Buddha's teachings—the set of moral discipline, the set of discourses, and the set of wisdom; and of the four classes of Tantra. He also mastered arts and sciences such as poetry, rhetoric, and astrology, was an excellent physician, and was very skilled in crafts and technology.

Atisha also gained all the realizations of the three higher trainings: training in higher moral discipline, training in higher concentration, and training in higher wisdom. Since all the stages of Sutra, such as the six perfections, the five paths, the ten grounds; and all the stages of Tantra, such as generation stage and completion stage, are included within the three higher trainings, Atisha therefore gained all the realizations of the stages of the path.

There are three types of higher moral discipline: the higher moral discipline of the Pratimoksha vows, or vows of individual liberation; the higher moral discipline of the Bodhisattva vow; and the higher moral discipline of the Tantric vows. The vows to abandon two hundred and fifty-three downfalls, undertaken by a fully ordained monk, are among the Pratimoksha vows. Atisha never broke any one of these. This shows that he possessed very strong mindfulness and very great conscientiousness. He also kept purely the Bodhisattva vow to avoid eighteen root downfalls and forty-six secondary downfalls, and he kept purely all his Tantric vows.

The attainments of higher concentration and higher wisdom are divided into common and uncommon. A common attainment is one that is gained by practitioners of both Sutra and Tantra, and an uncommon attainment is one that is only gained by practitioners of Tantra. By training in higher concentration Atisha gained the common concentration of tranquil abiding, and based on that, clairvoyance, miracle powers, and the common virtues. He also attained uncommon concentrations such as the concentrations of generation stage and completion stage of Secret Mantra. By training in higher wisdom Atisha gained the common realization of emptiness, and the uncommon realizations of example clear light and meaning clear light of Secret Mantra.

Atisha mastered the teachings of both Hinayana and Mahayana and was respected by Teachers of both traditions. He was like a king, the crown ornament of Indian Buddhists, and was regarded as a second Buddha.

Before Atisha's time, the thirty-seventh king of Tibet, Trisong Detsen (AD circa 754–97), had invited Padmasambhava, Shantarakshita, and other Buddhist Teachers from India to Tibet, and through their influence pure Dharma had flourished; but some years later, a Tibetan king called Lang Darma (AD circa 836) destroyed the pure Dharma in Tibet and abolished the Sangha. Until that time most of the kings had been religious, but it was a dark age in Tibet during Lang Darma's evil reign. About seventy

The king wept when he thought of the purity of Dharma in former times compared with the impure Dharma now being practiced.

years after his death, Dharma began to flourish once again in the upper part of Tibet through the efforts of great Teachers such as the translator Rinchen Sangpo, and it also began to flourish in the lower part of Tibet through the efforts of a great Teacher called Gongpa Rabsel. Gradually, Dharma spread to central Tibet.

At that time, there was no pure practice of the union of Sutra and Tantra. The two were thought to be contradictory, like fire and water. When people practiced Sutra they abandoned Tantra, and when they practiced Tantra they abandoned Sutra, including even the rules of the Vinaya. False teachers came from India wishing to procure some of Tibet's plentiful gold. Pretending to be Spiritual Guides and Yogis they introduced perversions such as black magic, creating apparitions, sexual practices, and ritual murder. These malpractices became quite widespread.

A king called Yeshe Ö and his nephew Jangchub Ö, who lived in Ngari in western Tibet, were greatly concerned about what was happening to the Dharma in their country. The king wept when he thought of the purity of Dharma in former times compared with the impure Dharma now being practiced. He was grieved to see how hardened and uncontrolled the minds of the people had become. He thought, "It would be wonderful if pure Dharma could flourish once again in Tibet to tame the minds of our people." To fulfill this wish he sent Tibetans to India to learn Sanskrit and train in Dharma, but many of these people were unable to endure the hot climate. The few who survived learned Sanskrit and trained very well in Dharma. Among them was the translator Rinchen Sangpo, who received many instructions and then returned to Tibet.

Since this plan had not met with much success, Yeshe Ö decided to invite an authentic Teacher from India. He sent a group of Tibetans to India with a large quantity of gold and gave them the task of seeking out the most qualified Spiritual Guide in India. He advised them all to study Dharma and gain perfect knowledge of Sanskrit. These Tibetans suffered all the hardships of climate and travel in order to accomplish his wishes. Some of them became famous translators. They translated many scriptures and sent them to the king, to his great delight.

When these Tibetans returned to Tibet they informed Yeshe Ö, "In India there are many very learned Buddhist Teachers, but the most distinguished and sublime of all is Dhipamkara Shrijana. We would like to invite him to Tibet, but he has thousands of disciples in India." When Yeshe Ö heard the name "Dhipamkara Shrijana" he was pleased and became determined to invite this Master to

Tibet. Since he had already used most of his gold and more was now needed to invite Dhipamkara Shrijana to Tibet, the king set off on an expedition to search for more gold. When he arrived at one of the borders, a hostile non-Buddhist king captured him and threw him into prison. When the news reached Jangchub Ö he considered, "I am powerful enough to wage war on this king, but if I do this many people will suffer and I will have to commit many harmful, destructive actions." He decided to make an appeal for his uncle's release, but the king responded by saying, "I will release your uncle only if you either become my subject or bring me a quantity of gold as heavy as your uncle's body." With great difficulty Jangchub Ö managed to gather gold equal in weight to his uncle's body, less the weight of his head. Since the king demanded the extra amount, Jangchub Ö prepared to go in search of more gold, but before he set out he visited his uncle. He found Yeshe Ö physically weak but in a good state of mind. Jangchub Ö spoke through the bars of the prison, "Soon I will be able to release you because I have managed to collect almost all the gold." Yeshe Ö replied, "Please do not treat me as if I were important. You must not give the gold to this hostile king. Send it all to India and offer it to Dhipamkara Shrijana. This is my greatest wish. I will give my life joyfully for the sake of restoring pure Dharma in Tibet. Please deliver this message to Dhipamkara Shrijana. Let him know that I have given my life to invite him to Tibet. Since he has compassion for the Tibetan people, when he receives this message he will accept our invitation."

Jangchub Ö sent the translator Nagtso together with some companions to India with the gold. When they met Dhipamkara Shrijana they told him what was happening in Tibet and how the people wanted to invite a Spiritual Guide from India. They told him how much gold the king had sent as an offering and how many Tibetans had died for the sake of restoring pure Dharma. They told him how Yeshe Ö had sacrificed his life to bring him to Tibet. When they had made their request, Dhipamkara Shrijana considered what they had said and accepted their invitation. Although he had many disciples in India and was working very hard there for the sake of Dharma, he knew that there was no pure Dharma in Tibet. He had also received a prediction from Arya Tara that if he went to Tibet he would benefit countless living beings. Compassion arose in his heart when he thought how many Tibetans had died in India, and he was especially moved by the sacrifice of Yeshe Ö.

Dhipamkara Shrijana had to make his way to Tibet in secret, because if his Indian disciples had known that he was leaving India they would have prevented him. He said that he was making a pilgrimage to Nepal, but from Nepal he crossed into Tibet. When his Indian disciples eventually realized that he was not going to return, they protested that the Tibetans were thieves who had stolen their Spiritual Guide!

Since it was customary in those days, as it is today, to greet an honored guest in style, Jangchub Ö sent an entourage of three hundred horsemen with many eminent Tibetans to the border to welcome Atisha and offer him a horse to ease the difficult journey to Ngari. Atisha rode at the center of the three hundred horsemen, and by means of his miracle powers he sat one cubit above his horse's back. When they saw him, those who previously had no respect for him developed very strong faith, and everyone said that the second Buddha had arrived in Tibet.

When Atisha reached Ngari, Jangchub Ö requested him: "O Compassionate Atisha, please give instructions to help the Tibetan people. Please give advice that everyone can follow. Please give us special instructions so that we can practice all the paths of Sutra and Tantra together." To fulfill this wish Atisha composed and taught *Lamp for the Path to Enlightenment*, the first text written on the stages of the path, Lamrim. He gave these instructions first in Ngari and then in central Tibet. Many disciples who heard these teachings developed great wisdom.

THE PRECIOUSNESS OF KADAM LAMRIM

Atisha wrote the original Kadam Lamrim based on *Ornament of Clear Realization* by Buddha Maitreya, which is a commentary to the *Perfection of Wisdom Sutras* that Buddha Shakyamuni taught on Massed Vultures Mountain in Rajagriha, India. Later, Je Tsongkhapa wrote his extensive, middling, and condensed Kadam Lamrim texts as commentaries to Atisha's Kadam Lamrim instructions, and through this the precious Buddhadharma of Kadam Lamrim flourished in many countries in the East and now in the West. The Kadam Lamrim instructions, the union of Buddha's teachings and Atisha's special instructions, are presented in three stages: the instructions on the stages of the path of a person of initial scope; the instructions on the stages of the path of a person of intermediate scope; and the instructions on the stages of the path of a person of great scope.

All Buddha's teachings, both Sutra and Tantra, are included within these three instructions. Buddha's teachings are the supreme medicine that permanently cures both physical sickness and the sickness of delusions. Just as doctors give different medicine for different sicknesses, so Buddha gave different Dharma medicine according to people's different capacities. He gave simple teachings to those of initial scope, profound teachings to those of intermediate scope, and very profound teachings to those of great scope. In practice, all these teachings are part of Kadam Lamrim, which is the main body of Buddha's teachings; there is not a single teaching of Buddha that is not included within Kadam Lamrim. For this reason, Je Tsongkhapa said that when we listen to the entire Lamrim we are listening to all Buddha's teachings and when we practice the entire Lamrim we are practicing all Buddha's teachings. Kadam Lamrim is the condensation of all Buddha's teachings; it is very practical and suitable for everyone and its presentation is superior to other instructions.

Everyone, both Buddhist and non-Buddhist, needs permanent liberation from suffering, and pure and everlasting happiness.

Through gaining experience of Lamrim we will understand that none of Buddha's teachings are contradictory, we will put all Buddha's teachings into practice, we will easily realize Buddha's ultimate view and intention, and we will become free from all mistaken views and intentions. Everyone, both Buddhist and non-Buddhist, needs permanent liberation from suffering, and pure and everlasting happiness. This wish will be fulfilled through Lamrim practice; therefore it is the real wishfulfilling jewel.

In general, all Buddha's teachings, the Dharma, are very precious, but Kadam Dharma or Lamrim is a very special Buddhadharma that is suitable for everyone without exception. The great Master Dromtonpa said, "Kadam Dharma is like a mala made of gold." Just as everyone, even those who do not use a mala (or prayer beads), would be happy to accept a gift of a gold mala because it is made of gold, in a similar way, everyone, even non-Buddhists, can receive benefit from Kadam Dharma. This is because there is no difference between Kadam Dharma and people's everyday experiences. Even without studying or listening to Dharma, some people often come to conclusions similar to those explained in Kadam Dharma teachings through looking at newspapers or television and understanding the world situation. This is because Kadam Dharma accords with people's daily experience; it cannot be separated from daily life. Everyone needs it to make their lives happy and meaningful, to solve their human problems temporarily, and to enable them ultimately to find pure and everlasting happiness through controlling their anger, attachment, jealousy, and especially ignorance.

In this spiritually degenerate time there are five impurities that are increasing throughout the world: (1) our environment is becoming increasingly impure because of pollution; (2) our water, air, and food are becoming increasingly impure, also because of pollution; (3) our body is becoming increasingly impure because sickness and disease are now more prevalent; (4) our mind is becoming increasingly impure because our delusions are getting stronger and stronger; and (5) our actions are becoming increasingly impure because we have no control over our delusions.

Because of these five impurities, suffering, problems, and dangers are increasing everywhere. However, through Lamrim practice we can transform our experience of all these impurities into the spiritual path that leads us to the pure and everlasting happiness of liberation and enlightenment. We can use all the difficulties that we see in the world as spiritual teachings that encourage us to develop renunciation, the wish to liberate ourself from the cycle of impure life; compassion, the wish that others may be liberated permanently from the cycle of impure life; and the wisdom that realizes that all these impurities are the results of our non-virtuous actions. In this way, through Lamrim practice we can transform all adverse conditions into opportunities for developing realizations of the spiritual path that will bring us pure and everlasting happiness.

Whenever Lamrim practitioners experience difficulties and suffering they think, "Countless other living beings experience greater suffering and difficulties than I do," and in this way they develop or increase their compassion for all living beings, which leads them quickly to the supreme happiness of enlightenment. Kadam Lamrim is the supreme medicine that can permanently cure all the sufferings of sickness, aging, death, and rebirth; it is the scientific method to improve our human nature and qualities, and to solve our daily problems. Kadam Lamrim is the great mirror of Dharma in which we can see the way things really are; and through which we can see what we should know, what we should abandon, what we should practice, and what we should attain. And it is only by using this mirror that we can see the great kindness of all living beings.

The Path of a Person of Initial Scope

*I*n this context, a *person of initial scope* refers to someone who has an initial capacity for developing spiritual understanding and realizations.

THE PRECIOUSNESS OF OUR HUMAN LIFE

The purpose of understanding the preciousness of our human life is to encourage ourself to take the real meaning of our human life and not to waste it in meaningless activities. Our human life is very precious and meaningful, but only if we use it to attain permanent liberation and the supreme happiness of enlightenment. We should encourage ourself to accomplish the real meaning of our human life through understanding and contemplating the following explanation.

Many people believe that material development is the real meaning of human life, but we can see that no matter how much material development there is in the world, it never reduces human suffering and problems. Instead, it often causes suffering and problems to increase; therefore it is not the real meaning of human life. We should know that we have now reached the human world for just a brief moment from our former lives, and we have the opportunity to attain the supreme happiness of enlightenment by practicing Dharma. This is our extraordinary good fortune. When we attain enlightenment we will have fulfilled our own wishes, and we can fulfill the wishes of all other living beings; we will have liberated ourself permanently from the sufferings of this life and countless future lives, and we can directly benefit each and every living being every day. The attainment of enlightenment is therefore the real meaning of human life.

Enlightenment is the inner light of wisdom that is permanently free from all mistaken appearance, and its function is to bestow mental peace on each and every living being every day. Right now we have obtained a human rebirth and have the opportunity to attain enlightenment through *We should encourage ourself* Dharma practice, so if we waste this *to accomplish the real meaning* precious opportunity in meaningless *of our human life.* activities there is no greater loss and no greater foolishness. This is because in the future such a precious opportunity will be extremely hard to find. In one Sutra, Buddha illustrates this by giving the following analogy. He asks his disciples, "Suppose there existed a vast and deep ocean the size of this world, and on its surface floated a golden yoke, and at the bottom of the ocean lived a blind turtle who surfaced only once in every one hundred thousand years. How often would that turtle raise its head through the middle of the yoke?" His disciple, Ananda, answers that it would be extremely rare indeed.

In this context, the vast and deep ocean refers to samsara—the cycle of impure life that we have experienced since beginningless time, continually in life after life without end—the golden yoke refers to Buddhadharma, and the blind turtle refers to us. Although we are not physically a turtle, mentally we are not much different; and although our physical eyes may not be blind, our wisdom eyes are. For most of our countless previous lives we have remained at the bottom of the ocean of samsara, in the three lower realms—the animal, hungry ghost, and hell realms—surfacing only once in every one hundred thousand years or so as a human being. Even when we briefly reach the upper realm of samsara's ocean as a human being, it is extremely rare to meet the golden yoke of Buddhadharma: the ocean of samsara is extremely vast, the golden yoke of Buddhadharma does not remain in one place but moves from place to place, and our wisdom eyes are always blind. For these reasons, Buddha says that in the future, even if we obtain a human rebirth, it will be extremely rare to meet Buddhadharma again; meeting Kadam Dharma is even more rare than this. We can see that the great majority of human beings in the world, even though they have briefly reached the upper realm of samsara as human beings, have not met Buddhadharma. This is because their wisdom eyes have not opened.

What does "meeting Buddhadharma" mean? It means entering into Buddhism by sincerely seeking refuge in Buddha, Dharma, and Sangha, and in this way having the opportunity to enter and make progress on the path to enlightenment. If we do not meet Buddhadharma we have no opportunity to do this, and therefore we have no opportunity to accomplish the pure and everlasting happiness of enlightenment, the real meaning of human life. In conclusion, we should think:

I have now briefly reached the human world and have the opportunity to attain permanent liberation from suffering and the supreme happiness of enlightenment through putting Dharma into practice. If I waste this precious opportunity in meaningless activities there is no greater loss and no greater foolishness.

With this thought we make the strong determination to practice the Dharma of Buddha's teachings on renunciation, universal compassion, and the profound view of emptiness now, while we have the opportunity. We then meditate on this determination again and again. We should practice this contemplation and meditation every day in many sessions, and in this way encourage ourself to take the real meaning of our human life.

We should ask ourself what we consider to be most important—what do we wish for, strive for, or daydream about? For some people it is material possessions, such as a large house with all the latest luxuries, a fast car, or a well-paid job. For others it is reputation, good looks, power, excitement, or adventure. Many try to find the meaning of their life in relationships with their family and circle of friends. All these things can make us superficially happy for a short while, but they will also cause us much worry and suffering. They will never give us the real happiness that all of us, in our hearts, long for. Since we cannot take them with us when we die, if we have made them the principal meaning of our life they will eventually let us down. As an end in themselves worldly attainments are hollow—they are not the real meaning of human life.

We should ask ourself what we consider to be most important— what do we wish for, strive for, or daydream about?

With our human life we can attain the supreme permanent peace of mind, known as *nirvana*, and enlightenment by putting Dharma into practice. Since these attainments are non-deceptive and ultimate states of happiness they are the real meaning of human life. However, because our desire for worldly enjoyment is so strong, we have little or no interest in Dharma practice. From a spiritual point of view, this lack of interest in Dharma practice is a type of laziness called the *laziness of attachment*. As long as we have this laziness, the door to liberation will be closed to us, and consequently we will continue to experience misery and suffering in this life and in countless future lives. The way to overcome this laziness, the main obstacle to our Dharma practice, is to meditate on death.

We need to contemplate and meditate on our death again and again until we gain a deep realization of death. Although on an intellectual level we all know that eventually we are going to die, our awareness of death remains superficial. Since our intellectual knowledge of death does not touch our hearts, each and every day we continue to think, "I will not die today, I will not die today." Even on the day of our death, we are still thinking about what we will do tomorrow or next week. This mind that thinks every day, "I will not die today" is deceptive—it leads us in the wrong direction and causes our human life to become empty. On the other hand, through meditating on death we will gradually replace the deceptive thought, "I will not die today," with the non-deceptive thought, "I may die today." The mind that spontaneously thinks each and every day, "I may die today" is the realization of death. It is this realization that directly eliminates our laziness of attachment and opens the door to the spiritual path.

In general, we may die today or we may not die today—we do not know. However, if we think each day, "I may not die today," this thought will deceive us because it comes from our ignorance. If instead we think each day, "I may die today," this thought will not deceive us because it comes from our wisdom. This beneficial thought will prevent our laziness of attachment, and will encourage us to prepare for the welfare of our countless future lives or to put great effort into entering the path to liberation and enlightenment. In this way, we will make our present human life meaningful. Until now we have wasted our countless former lives without any meaning; we have brought nothing with us from our former lives except delusions and suffering.

WHAT DOES OUR DEATH MEAN?

Our death is the permanent separation of our body and mind. We may experience many temporary separations of our body and mind, but these are not our death. For example, when those who have completed their training in the practice known as *transference of consciousness* engage in meditation, their mind separates from their body. Their body remains where they are meditating, and their mind goes to a Pure Land and then returns to their body. At night, during dreams, our body remains in bed but our mind goes to various places of the dream world and then returns to our body. These separations of our body and mind are not our death because they are only temporary.

At death, our mind separates from our body permanently. Our body remains at the place of this life but our mind goes to various places of our future lives, like a bird leaving one nest and flying to another. This clearly shows the existence of our countless future lives, and that the nature and function of our body and mind are very different. Our body is a visual form that possesses color and shape, but our mind is a formless continuum that always lacks color and shape. The nature of our mind is empty like space, and its function is to perceive or understand objects. Through this we can understand that our brain is not our mind. The brain is simply a part of our body that, for example, can be photographed, while our mind cannot.

We may not be happy to hear about our death, but contemplating and meditating on death is very important for the effectiveness of our Dharma practice. This is because it prevents the main obstacle to our Dharma practice—the laziness of attachment to the things of this life—and it encourages us to practice pure Dharma right now. If we do this we will accomplish the real meaning of human life before our death.

HOW TO MEDITATE ON DEATH

First we engage in the following contemplation:

I will definitely die. There is no way to prevent my body from finally decaying. Day by day, moment by moment, my life is slipping away. I have no idea when I will die—the time of death is completely uncertain. Many young people die before their parents, some die the moment they are born—there is no certainty in this world. Furthermore, there are so many causes of untimely death. The lives of many strong and healthy people are destroyed by accidents. There is no guarantee that I will not die today.

Having repeatedly contemplated these points, we mentally repeat over and over again, "I may die today, I may die today," and concentrate on the feeling it evokes. We transform our mind into this feeling "I may die today" and remain on it single-pointedly for as long as possible. We should practice this meditation repeatedly until we spontaneously believe each and every day "I may die today." Eventually we will come to a conclusion: "Since I will soon have to leave this world, there is no point in my becoming attached to the things of this life. Instead, from now on I will devote my whole life to practicing Dharma purely and sincerely." We then maintain this determination day and night.

During the meditation break, we should apply effort to our Dharma practice without laziness. Realizing that worldly pleasures are deceptive, and that they distract us from using our life in a meaningful way, we should abandon attachment to them. In this way, we can eliminate the main obstacle to pure Dharma practice.

THE DANGERS OF LOWER REBIRTH

The purpose of this explanation is to encourage us to prepare protection from the dangers of lower rebirth. If we do not do this now, while we have a human life with its freedoms and endowments and we have the opportunity to do so, it will be too late once we have taken any of the three lower rebirths; and it will be extremely difficult to obtain such a precious human life again. It is said to be easier for human beings to attain enlightenment than it is for beings such as animals to attain a precious human rebirth. Understanding this will encourage us to abandon non-virtue, to practice virtue, and to seek refuge in Buddha, Dharma, and Sangha (the supreme spiritual friends)—this is our actual protection.

Performing non-virtuous actions is the main cause of taking lower rebirth, while practicing virtue and seeking refuge in Buddha, Dharma, and Sangha are the main causes of taking a precious human rebirth—a rebirth in which we have the opportunity to attain permanent liberation from all suffering. Heavy non-virtuous actions are the main cause of rebirth as a hell being, middling non-virtuous actions are the main cause of rebirth as a hungry ghost, and lesser non-virtuous actions are the main cause of rebirth as an animal. There are many examples given in Buddhist scriptures of how non-virtuous actions lead to rebirth in the three lower realms.

There was once a hunter whose wife came from a family of animal farmers. After he died he took rebirth as a cow belonging to his wife's family. A butcher then bought this cow, slaughtered it, and sold the meat. The hunter was reborn seven times as a cow belonging to the same family, and in this way became food for other people.

In Tibet there is a lake called Yamdroktso, where many people from the nearby town used to spend their whole lives fishing. At one time a great Yogi with clairvoyance visited the town and said, "I see the people of this town and the fish in this lake are continually switching their positions." What he meant was that the people of the town who enjoyed fishing were reborn as the fish, the food of other people, and the fish in the lake were reborn as the people who enjoyed fishing. In this way, changing their physical aspect, they were continually killing and eating each other. This cycle of misery continued from generation to generation.

HOW TO MEDITATE ON THE DANGERS OF LOWER REBIRTH

First we engage in the following contemplation:

When the oil of an oil lamp is exhausted, the flame goes out because the flame is produced from the oil; but when our body dies our consciousness is not extinguished, because consciousness is not produced from the body. When we die our mind has to leave this present body, which is just a temporary home, and find another body, similar to a bird leaving one nest to fly to another. Our mind has no freedom to remain and no choice about where to go. We are blown to the place of our next rebirth by the winds of our actions or karma (our good fortune or misfortune). If the karma that ripens at our death time is negative, we will definitely take a lower rebirth. Heavy negative karma causes rebirth in hell, middling negative karma causes rebirth as a hungry ghost, and lesser negative karma causes rebirth as an animal.

It is very easy to commit heavy negative karma. For example, simply by swatting a mosquito out of anger we create the cause to be reborn in hell. Throughout this and all our countless previous lives we have committed many heavy negative actions. Unless we have already purified these actions by practicing sincere confession, their potentialities remain in our mental continuum, and any one of these negative potentialities could ripen when we die. Bearing this in mind, we should ask ourself: "If I die today, where will I be tomorrow? It is quite possible that I will find myself in the animal realm, among the hungry ghosts, or in hell. If someone called me a stupid cow today, I would find it difficult to bear, but what will I do if I actually become a cow, a pig, or a fish—the food of human beings?"

Having repeatedly contemplated these points and understood how beings in the lower realms, such as animals, experience suffering, we generate a strong fear of taking rebirth in the lower realms.

This feeling of fear is the object of our meditation. We then hold this without forgetting it; our mind should remain on this feeling of fear single-pointedly for as long as possible. If we lose the object of our meditation we renew the feeling of fear by immediately remembering it or by repeating the contemplation.

During the meditation break we try never to forget our feeling of fear of taking rebirth in the lower realms. In general fear is meaningless, but the fear generated through the above contemplation and meditation has immense meaning, because it arises from wisdom and not from ignorance. This fear is the main cause of seeking refuge in Buddha, Dharma, and Sangha, which is the actual protection from such dangers, and helps us be mindful and conscientious in avoiding non-virtuous actions.

GOING FOR REFUGE

In this context, *going for refuge* means seeking refuge in Buddha, Dharma, and Sangha. The purpose of this practice is to protect ourself permanently from taking lower rebirth. Right now because we are human, we are free from rebirth as an animal, hungry ghost, or hell being, but this is only temporary. We are like a prisoner who gets permission to stay at home for a week, but then has to return to prison. We need permanent liberation from the sufferings of this life and countless future lives. This depends on entering, making progress on, and completing the Buddhist path to liberation, which in turn depends on entering Buddhism.

We enter Buddhism through the practice of going for refuge. For our practice of refuge to be qualified, while visualizing Buddha in front of us we should verbally or mentally make the promise to seek refuge in Buddha, Dharma, and Sangha throughout our life. This promise is our refuge vow, and is the gateway through which we enter Buddhism. For as long as we keep this promise we are inside Buddhism, but if we break this promise we are outside. By entering and remaining inside Buddhism we have the opportunity to begin, make progress on, and complete the Buddhist path to liberation and enlightenment.

We should never give up our promise to seek refuge in Buddha, Dharma, and Sangha throughout our life. Going for refuge to Buddha, Dharma, and Sangha means that we apply effort to receiving Buddha's blessings, to putting Dharma into practice, and to receiving help from Sangha. These are the three principal commitments of the refuge vow. Through maintaining and sincerely practicing these three principal commitments of refuge we can fulfill our final goal.

The main reason why we need to make the determination and promise to seek refuge in Buddha, Dharma, and Sangha throughout our life is because we need to attain permanent liberation from suffering. We may now be free from physical suffering and mental pain, but as mentioned earlier this freedom is only temporary. Later in this life and in our countless future lives we will have to experience unbearable physical suffering and mental pain continually, in life after life without end.

When our life is in danger or we are threatened by someone, we usually seek refuge in the police. Of course, sometimes the police can protect us from a particular danger, but they cannot give us permanent liberation from death. When we are seriously ill we seek refuge in doctors. Sometimes doctors can cure a particular illness, but no doctor can give us permanent liberation from sickness. What we really need is permanent liberation from all sufferings, and as human beings we can achieve this by seeking refuge in Buddha, Dharma, and Sangha.

Buddhas are *awakened*, which means that they have awakened from the sleep of ignorance and are free from the dreams of samsara, the cycle of impure life. They are completely pure beings who are permanently free from all delusions and mistaken appearance. As mentioned earlier, Buddha's function is to bestow mental peace on each and every living being every day by giving blessings. We know that we are happy when our mind is peaceful, and unhappy when it is not. It is therefore clear that our happiness depends on our having a peaceful mind and not on good external conditions. Even if our external conditions are poor, if we maintain a peaceful mind all the time we will always be happy. Through continually receiving Buddha's blessings we can maintain a peaceful mind all the time. Buddha is therefore the source of our happiness. Dharma is the actual protection through which we are permanently released from the sufferings of sickness, aging, death, and rebirth. And Sangha are the supreme spiritual friends who guide us to correct spiritual paths. Through these three precious wishfulfilling jewels, Buddha, Dharma, and Sangha—known as the *Three Jewels*—we can fulfill our own wishes as well as the wishes of all living beings.

Every day, from the depths of our heart we should recite requesting prayers to the enlightened Buddhas, while maintaining deep faith in them. This is a simple method for us to receive the Buddhas' blessings continually. We should also join group prayers, known as *pujas*, organized at Buddhist Temples or Prayer Halls, which are powerful methods to receive Buddha's blessings and protection.

HOW TO MEDITATE ON GOING FOR REFUGE

First we engage in the following contemplation:

I want to protect and liberate myself permanently from the sufferings of this life and countless future lives. I can accomplish this only by receiving Buddha's blessings, putting Dharma into practice, and receiving help from Sangha—the supreme spiritual friends.

Thinking deeply in this way, we first make the strong determination and then the promise to seek refuge sincerely in Buddha, Dharma, and Sangha throughout our life. We should meditate on this determination every day and maintain our promise continually for the rest of our life. As the commitments of our refuge vow, we should always apply effort to receive Buddha's blessings, to put Dharma into practice, and to receive help from Sangha, our pure spiritual friends including our Spiritual Teacher. This is how we go for refuge to Buddha, Dharma, and Sangha. Through this we will accomplish our goal—permanent liberation from all the sufferings of this life and countless future lives, the real meaning of our human life.

To maintain our promise to go for refuge to Buddha, Dharma, and Sangha throughout our life, and so that we and all living beings may receive Buddha's blessings and protection, we recite the following refuge prayer every day with strong faith:

I and all sentient beings, until we achieve enlightenment,
Go for refuge to Buddha, Dharma, and Sangha.

WHAT IS KARMA?

The purpose of understanding and believing in karma is to prevent future suffering and to establish the basic foundation for the path to liberation and enlightenment. Generally, *karma* means "action." From non-virtuous actions comes suffering, and from virtuous actions comes happiness—if we believe this, we believe in karma. Buddha gave extensive teachings that prove the truth of this statement, and many different examples that show the special connection between the actions of our former lives and our experiences of this life, some of which are explained in *Joyful Path of Good Fortune*.

In our previous lives we performed various kinds of non-virtuous actions that caused others suffering. As a result of these non-virtuous actions, various kinds of miserable conditions and situations arise and we experience endless human suffering and problems. This is the same for all other living beings.

We should judge whether or not we believe that the main cause of suffering is our non-virtuous actions and the main cause of happiness is our virtuous actions. If we do not believe this we will never apply effort to accumulating virtuous actions, or merit, and we will never purify our non-virtuous actions, and because of this we will experience suffering and difficulties continually, in life after life without end.

Every action we perform leaves an imprint on our very subtle mind, and each imprint eventually gives rise to its own effect. Our mind is like a field, and performing actions is like sowing seeds in that field. Virtuous actions sow seeds of future happiness and non-virtuous actions sow seeds of future suffering. These seeds remain dormant in our mind until the conditions for them to ripen occur, and then they produce their effect. In some cases, this can happen many lifetimes after the original action was performed.

The seeds that ripen when we die are very important because they determine what kind of rebirth we will take in our next life.

The purpose of understanding and believing in karma is to prevent future suffering.

Which particular seed ripens at death depends on the state of mind in which we die. If we die with a peaceful mind, this will stimulate a virtuous seed and we will experience a fortunate rebirth. However, if we die with an unpeaceful mind, such as in a state of anger, this will stimulate a non-virtuous seed and we will experience an unfortunate rebirth. This is similar to the way nightmares are triggered by our being in an agitated state of mind just before falling asleep.

All inappropriate actions, including killing, stealing, sexual misconduct, lying, divisive speech, hurtful speech, idle chatter, covetousness, malice, and holding wrong views, are non-virtuous actions. When we abandon non-virtuous actions and apply effort to purifying our previous non-virtuous actions we are practicing moral discipline. This will prevent us from experiencing future suffering and from taking a lower rebirth. Examples of virtuous actions are training in all the meditations and other spiritual practices presented in this book. Meditation is a virtuous mental action that is the main cause for experiencing mental peace in the future. Whenever we practice meditation, whether or not our meditation is clear, we are performing a virtuous mental action that is a cause of our future happiness and peace of mind. We are normally concerned mainly about bodily and verbal actions, but in reality mental actions are more important. Our bodily and verbal actions depend on our mental action, on our mentally making a decision.

Whenever we perform virtuous actions such as meditation or other spiritual practices we should have the following mental determination:

> While riding the horse of virtuous actions
> I will guide it onto the path of liberation with the reins of renunciation;
> And through urging this horse forward with the whip of effort,
> I will quickly reach the Pure Land of liberation and enlightenment.

Having contemplated the above explanation, we should think:

> *Since I myself never wish to suffer and always want to be happy, I must abandon and purify my non-virtuous actions and sincerely perform virtuous actions.*

We should meditate on this determination every day, and put our determination into practice.

Atisha

The Path of a Person of Intermediate Scope

*I*n this context, a *person of intermediate scope* refers to someone who has a medium capacity for developing spiritual understanding and realizations.

WHAT WE SHOULD KNOW

In *Sutra of the Four Noble Truths*, Buddha says: "You should know sufferings." In saying this, Buddha is advising us that we should know about the unbearable sufferings that we will experience in our countless future lives, and therefore develop renunciation, the determination to liberate ourself permanently from these sufferings.

In general, everyone who has physical or mental pain, even animals, understands their own suffering; but when Buddha says, "You should know sufferings," he means that we should know the sufferings of our future lives. Through knowing these, we will develop a strong wish to liberate ourself from them. This practical advice is important for everybody, because if we have the wish to liberate ourself from the sufferings of future lives, we will definitely use our present human life for the freedom and happiness of our countless future lives. There is no greater meaning than this.

If we do not have this wish, we will waste our precious human life for the freedom and happiness of only this one short life. This would be foolish because our intention and actions would be no different from the intention and actions of animals who are only concerned with this life alone. The great Yogi Milarepa once said to a hunter called Gonpo Dorje:

> Your body is human but your mind is that of an animal.
> You, a human being, who possess an animal's mind, please listen to my song.

Normally we believe that solving the suffering and problems of our present life is most important, and we dedicate our whole life for this purpose. In reality, the duration of the suffering and problems of this life is very short; if we die tomorrow, they will end tomorrow. However, since the duration of the suffering and problems of future lives is endless, the freedom and happiness of our future lives is vastly more important than the freedom and happiness of this one short life. With the words "You should know sufferings," Buddha encourages us to use our present human life to prepare for the freedom and happiness of our countless future lives. Those who do this are truly wise.

In future lives, when we are born as an animal, such as a cow or a fish, we will become the food of other living beings, and we will have to experience many other kinds of animal suffering. Animals have no freedom, and are used by human beings for food, work, and enjoyment. They have no opportunity to improve themselves; even if they hear precious Dharma words it is as meaningless to them as hearing the wind blowing. When we are born as a hungry ghost we will not have even a tiny drop of water to drink;

our only water will be our tears. We will have to experience the unbearable sufferings of thirst and hunger for many hundreds of years. When we are born as a hell being in the hot hells our body will become inseparable from fire, and others will be able to distinguish between our body and fire only by hearing our suffering cries. We will have to experience the unbearable torment of our body being burned for millions of years. Like all other phenomena, the hell

Buddha is advising us that we should know the sufferings that we will experience in our future lives, and develop renunciation.

realms do not exist inherently but exist as mere appearances to mind, like dreams. When we are born as a desire realm god we experience great conflict and dissatisfaction. Even if we experience some superficial enjoyment, our desires grow even stronger, and we have even more mental suffering than human beings. When we are born as a demi-god we are always jealous of the gods' glory and because of this we have great mental suffering. Our jealousy is like a thorn piercing our mind, causing us to experience both mental and physical suffering for long periods of time. When we are born as a human being we will have to experience various kinds of human suffering such as the sufferings of birth, sickness, aging, and death.

BIRTH

When our consciousness first enters the union of our father's sperm and our mother's ovum, our body is a very hot, watery substance like white yogurt tinted red. In the first moments after conception we have no gross feelings, but as soon as these develop we begin to experience pain. Our body gradually becomes harder and harder, and as our limbs grow it feels as if our body is being stretched out on a rack. Inside our mother's womb it is hot and dark. Our home for nine months is this small, tightly compressed space full of unclean substances. It is like being squashed inside a small water tank full of filthy liquid with the lid tightly shut so that no air or light can come through.

While we are in our mother's womb we experience much pain and fear all on our own. We are extremely sensitive to everything our mother does. When she walks quickly it feels as if we are falling from a high mountain and we are terrified. If she has sexual intercourse it feels as if we are being crushed and suffocated between two huge weights and we panic. If our mother makes just a small jump it feels as if we are being thrown against the ground from a great height. If she drinks anything hot it feels like boiling water scalding our skin, and if she drinks anything cold it feels like an ice-cold shower in midwinter.

When we are emerging from our mother's womb it feels as if we are being forced through a narrow crevice between two hard rocks, and when we are newly born our body is so delicate that any kind of contact is painful. Even if someone holds us very tenderly, his or her hands feel like thorn bushes piercing our flesh, and the most delicate fabrics feel rough and abrasive. By comparison with the softness and smoothness of our mother's womb, every tactile sensation is harsh and painful. If someone picks us up it feels as if we are being swung over a huge precipice, and we feel frightened and insecure. We have forgotten everything we knew in our previous life—we bring only pain and confusion from our mother's womb. Whatever we hear is as meaningless as the sound of wind, and we cannot comprehend anything we perceive. In the first few weeks we are like someone who is blind, deaf, and dumb, and suffering from profound amnesia. When we are hungry we cannot say, "I need food," and when we are in pain we cannot say, "This is hurting me." The only signs we can make are hot tears and furious gestures. Our mother often has no idea what pains and discomforts we are experiencing. We are completely helpless and have to be taught everything—how to eat, how to sit, how to walk, how to talk.

Although we are most vulnerable in the first few weeks of our life, our pains do not cease as we grow up. We continue to experience various kinds of suffering throughout our life. Just as when we light a fire in a large house, the heat from the fire pervades the whole house and all the heat in the house comes from the fire, so when we are born in samsara, suffering pervades our whole life, and all the miseries we experience arise because we took a contaminated rebirth.

Our human rebirth, contaminated by the poisonous delusion of self-grasping, is the basis of our human suffering; without this basis, there are no human problems. The pains of birth gradually turn into the pains of sickness, aging, and death—they are one continuum.

SICKNESS

Our birth also gives rise to the suffering of sickness. Just as the wind and snow of winter take away the glory of green fields, trees, forests, and flowers, so sickness takes away the youthful splendor of our body, destroying its strength and the power of our senses. If we are usually fit and well, when we become sick we are suddenly unable to engage in all our normal physical activities. Even a champion boxer who is usually able to knock out all his opponents becomes completely helpless when sickness strikes. Sickness makes all our experiences of daily enjoyments disappear and causes us to experience unpleasant feelings day and night.

When we fall ill, we are like a bird that has been soaring in the sky and is suddenly shot down. When a bird is shot, it falls straight to the ground like a lump of lead, and all its glory and power are immediately destroyed.

When we fall ill, we are like a bird that has been soaring in the sky and is suddenly shot down.

In a similar way, when we become ill we are suddenly incapacitated. If we are seriously ill we may become completely dependent on others and even lose the ability to control our bodily functions. This transformation is hard to bear, especially for those who pride themselves on their independence and physical well-being.

When we are sick, we feel frustrated because we cannot do our usual work or complete everything we have to do. We easily become impatient with our illness and depressed about all the things we cannot do. We cannot enjoy the things that usually give us pleasure, such as sports, dancing, drinking, eating rich foods, or the company of our friends. All these limitations make us feel even more miserable; and to add to our unhappiness, we have to endure all the physical pains the illness brings.

When we are sick, not only do we have to experience all the unwanted pains of the illness itself, but we also have to experience all kinds of other undesirable things. For example, we have to accept whatever treatment is prescribed, whether it is a bad-tasting medicine, a series of injections, a major operation, or abstinence from something we like very much. If we need to have an operation, we have to go to the hospital and accept all the conditions there. We may have to eat food we do not like and stay in bed all day long with nothing to do, and we may feel anxious about the operation. Our doctor may not explain to us exactly what the problem is and whether or not he or she expects us to survive.

If we learn that our sickness is incurable, and we have no spiritual experience, we will suffer anxiety, fear, and regret. We may become depressed and give up hope, or we may become angry with our illness, feeling that it is an enemy that has maliciously deprived us of all joy.

AGING

Our birth also gives rise to the pains of aging. Aging steals our beauty, our health, our figure, our fine complexion, our vitality, and our comfort. Aging turns us into objects of contempt. It brings many unwanted pains and takes us swiftly to our death.

As we grow old we lose all the beauty of our youth and our strong, healthy body becomes weak and burdened with illness. Our figure, once firm and well-proportioned, becomes bent and disfigured, and our muscles and flesh shrink so that our limbs become like thin sticks and our bones poke out. Our hair loses its color and shine, and our complexion loses its luster. Our face becomes wrinkled and our features grow distorted. Milarepa said:

> How do old people get up? They get up as if they were heaving a stake out of the ground. How do old people walk around? Once they are on their feet they have to walk gingerly, like bird-catchers. How do old people sit down? They crash down like heavy luggage whose harness has snapped.

We can contemplate the following poem on the sufferings of growing old, written by the scholar Gungtang:

When we are old, our hair becomes white,
But not because we have washed it clean;
It is a sign we will soon encounter the Lord of Death.

We have wrinkles on our forehead,
But not because we have too much flesh;
It is a warning from the Lord of Death: "You are about to die."

Our teeth fall out,
But not to make room for new ones;
It is a sign we will soon lose the ability to eat human food.

Our faces are ugly and unpleasant,
But not because we are wearing masks;
It is a sign we have lost the mask of youth.

Our heads shake back and forth,
But not because we are in disagreement;
It is the Lord of Death striking our head with the stick he
    holds in his right hand.

We walk bent and gazing at the ground,
But not because we are searching for lost needles;
It is a sign we are searching for our lost beauty and
    memories.

We get up from the ground using all four limbs,
But not because we are imitating animals;
It is a sign our legs are too weak to support our bodies.

We sit down as if we had suddenly fallen,
But not because we are angry;
It is a sign our body has lost its strength.

Our body sways as we walk,
But not because we think we are important;
It is a sign our legs cannot carry our body.

Our hands shake,
But not because they are itching to steal;
It is a sign the Lord of Death's itchy fingers are stealing
    our possessions.

We eat very little,
But not because we are miserly;
It is a sign we cannot digest our food.

We wheeze frequently,
But not because we are whispering mantras to the sick;
It is a sign our breathing will soon disappear.

When we are young we can travel around the whole world, but
when we are old we can hardly make it to our own front yard. We
become too weak to engage in many worldly activities, and our
spiritual activities are often reduced. For example, we have little
physical strength to perform virtuous actions, and little mental
energy to memorize, contemplate, and meditate. We cannot attend teachings that are given in places that are hard to reach or
uncomfortable to inhabit. We cannot help others in ways that
require physical strength and good health. Deprivations such as
these often make old people very sad.

When we grow old, we become like someone who is blind and deaf. We cannot see clearly, and we need stronger and stronger glasses until we can no longer read. We cannot hear clearly, and so it becomes more and more difficult to listen to music or to the television, or to hear what others are saying. Our memory fades. All activities, worldly and spiritual, become more difficult. If we practice meditation it becomes harder for us to gain realizations because our memory and concentration are too weak. We cannot apply ourself to study. Thus, if we have not learned and trained in spiritual practices when we were younger, the only thing to do when we grow old is to develop regret and wait for the Lord of Death to come.

If we have not trained in spiritual practices, the only thing to do when we grow old is to develop regret.

When we are old we cannot derive the same pleasure from the things we used to enjoy, such as food, drink, and sex. We are too weak to play games and we are often too exhausted even for entertainment. As our lifespan runs out we cannot join young people in their activities. When they travel we have to stay behind. No one wants to take us with them when we are old, and no one wants to visit us. Even our own grandchildren do not want to stay with us for very long. Old people often think to themselves, "It would be wonderful if young people would stay with me. We could go out for walks and I could show them things." But young people do not want to be included in their plans. As their life comes to an end, old people experience the sorrow of abandonment and loneliness. They have many special sorrows.

DEATH

Our birth also gives rise to the sufferings of death. If during our life we have worked hard to acquire possessions, and if we have become very attached to them, we will experience great suffering at the time of death, thinking, "Now I have to leave all my precious possessions behind." Even now we find it difficult to lend one of our most treasured possessions to someone else, let alone to give it away. No wonder we become so miserable when we realize that in the hands of death we have to abandon everything.

When we die we are separated from even our closest friends. We have to leave our partner, even though we may have been together for years and never spent a day apart. If we are very attached to our friends we will experience great misery at the time of death, but all we will be able to do is hold their hands. We will not be able to stop the process of death, even if they plead with us not to die. Usually when we are very attached to someone we feel jealous if he or she leaves us on our own and spends time with someone else, but when we die we will have to leave our friends with others forever. We will have to leave everyone, including our family and all the people who have helped us in this life.

When we die, this body that we have cherished and cared for in so many ways will have to be left behind. It will become mindless like a stone, and will be buried in the ground or cremated. If we do not have the inner protection of spiritual experience, at the time of death we will experience fear and distress, as well as physical pain.

When our consciousness departs from our body at death, all the potentialities we have accumulated in our mind by performing virtuous and non-virtuous actions will go with it. Other than these we cannot take anything out of this world. All other things deceive us. Death ends all our activities—our conversation, our eating, our meeting with friends, our sleep. Everything comes to an end on the day of our death and we have to leave all things behind, even the rings on our fingers. In Tibet, beggars carry a stick to defend themselves against dogs. To understand the complete deprivation of death we should remember that at the time of death beggars have to leave even this old stick, the most meager of human possessions. All over the world we can see that names carved on stone are the only possessions of the dead.

OTHER TYPES OF SUFFERING

We also have to experience the sufferings of separation, having to encounter what we do not like, and not fulfilling our wishes—which include the sufferings of poverty, and of being harmed by humans and non-humans, and by water, fire, wind, and earth. Before the final separation at the time of death we often have to experience temporary separation from the people and things we like, which causes us mental pain. We may have to leave our country where all our friends and relatives live, or we may have to leave the job we like. We may lose our reputation. Many times in this life we have to experience the misery of departing from the people we like, or abandoning and losing the things we find pleasant and attractive. But when we die we have to part forever from all our companions and enjoyments—and from all the outer and inner conditions for our Dharma practice—of this life.

We often have to meet and live with people we do not like, or encounter situations we find unpleasant. Sometimes we may find ourself in a very dangerous situation such as in a fire or a flood, or where there is violence such as in a riot or a battle. Our lives are full of less extreme situations that we find annoying. Sometimes we are prevented from doing the things we want to do. On a sunny day we may set out for the beach but find ourself stuck in a traffic jam. We continually experience interference from our inner demon of delusions, which disturbs our mind and our spiritual practices. There are countless conditions that frustrate our plans and prevent us from doing what we want. It is as if we are naked and living in a thorn bush—whenever we try to move, we are wounded by circumstances. People and things are like thorns piercing our flesh and no situation ever feels entirely comfortable. The more desires and plans we have, the more frustrations we experience. The more we want certain situations, the more we find ourself stuck in situations we do not want. Every desire seems to invite its own obstacle. Undesired situations happen to us without our looking for them. In fact, the only things that come effortlessly are the things we do not want. No one wants to die, but death comes effortlessly. No one wants to be sick, but sickness comes effortlessly. Because we have taken rebirth without freedom or control, we have an impure body and inhabit an impure environment, and so undesirable things pour down on us. In samsara, this kind of experience is entirely natural.

We have countless desires, but no matter how much effort we make we never feel that we have satisfied them. Even when we get what we want, we do not get it in the way we want. We possess the object but we get no satisfaction from possessing it. For example, we may dream of becoming wealthy, but if we actually become wealthy our life is not the way we imagined it would be, and we do not feel that we have fulfilled our desire. This is because our desires do not decrease as our wealth increases. The more wealth we have, the more we desire. The wealth we seek cannot be found because we seek an amount that will satiate our desires, and no amount of wealth can do that. To make things worse, in obtaining the object of our desire we create new occasions for dissatisfaction. With every object we desire come other objects we do not want. For example, with wealth come taxes, insecurity, and complicated financial affairs. These unwished for side effects prevent us from ever feeling fully satisfied. Similarly, we may dream of a tropical vacation, and we may actually go on such a vacation, but the experience is never quite what we expect, and with our vacation come other things such as sunburn and great expense.

If we examine our desires we will see that they are excessive. We want all the best things in samsara—the best job, the best partner, the best reputation, the best house, the best car, the best vacation. Anything that is not the best leaves us with a feeling of disappointment—still searching for but not finding what we want. No worldly enjoyment, however, can give us the complete and perfect satisfaction we desire. Better things are always being produced. Everywhere, new advertisements announce that the very best thing has just arrived on the market, but a few days later another best thing arrives that is better than the best thing of a few days ago. There is no end of new things to captivate our desires.

Children in school can never satisfy their own or their parents' ambitions. Even if they become first in their class, they feel they cannot be content unless they do the same the following year. If they go on to be successful in their jobs, their ambitions will be as strong as ever. There is no point at which they can rest, feeling that they are completely satisfied with what they have done.

We may think that at least people who lead a simple life in the country must be content, but if we look at their situation we will find that even farmers search for but do not find what they want. Their lives are full of problems and anxieties, and they do not enjoy real peace and satisfaction. Their livelihoods depend on many uncertain factors beyond their control, such as the weather. Farmers have no more freedom from discontent than business people who live and work in the city. Businesspeople look well-dressed and efficient as they go to work each morning carrying their briefcases, but although they look so smooth on the outside, in their hearts they carry much dissatisfaction. They are still searching for but not finding what they want.

If we reflect on this situation we may decide that we can find what we are searching for by abandoning all our possessions. We can see, however, that even poor people are looking for but not finding what they seek, and many poor people have difficulty in finding even the most basic necessities of life; millions of people in the world experience the sufferings of extreme poverty.

We cannot avoid the suffering of dissatisfaction by frequently changing our situation. We may think that if we keep getting a new partner or a new job, or keep traveling around, we will eventually find what we want. But even if we traveled to every place on the globe, and had a new lover in every town, we would still be seeking another place and another lover. In samsara there is no real fulfillment of our desires.

Whenever we see anyone in a high or low position, male or female, they differ only in appearance, dress, behavior, and status. In essence they are all equal—they all experience problems in their lives. Whenever we have a problem, it is easy to think that it is caused by our particular circumstances, and that if we changed our circumstances our problem would disappear. We blame other people, our friends, our food, our government, our times, the weather, society, history, and so forth. However, external circumstances such as these are not the main causes of our problems. We need to recognize that all the physical suffering and mental

External circumstances are not the main causes of our problems.

pain we experience are the consequences of our taking a rebirth that is contaminated by the inner poison of delusions. Human beings have to experience various kinds of human suffering because they have taken a contaminated human rebirth; animals have to experience animal suffering because they have taken a contaminated animal rebirth; and hungry ghosts and hell beings have to experience their own sufferings because they have taken contaminated rebirth as hungry ghosts and hell beings. Even gods are not free from suffering because they too have taken a contaminated rebirth. Just as a person trapped inside a raging fire develops intense fear, so we should develop intense fear of the unbearable sufferings of the endless cycle of impure life. This fear is real renunciation and arises from our wisdom.

In conclusion, having contemplated the above explanation we should think:

There is no benefit in denying the sufferings of future lives; when they actually descend on me it will be too late to protect myself from them. Therefore I definitely need to prepare protection now, while I have this human life that gives me the opportunity to liberate myself permanently from the sufferings of my countless

*future lives. If I do not apply effort to accomplish this, but
allow my human life to become empty of meaning, there is no
greater deception and no greater foolishness. I must put effort
now into liberating myself permanently from the sufferings of
my countless future lives.*

We meditate on this determination continually until we develop the spontaneous wish to liberate ourself permanently from
the sufferings of countless future lives. This is the actual realization of renunciation. The moment we develop this realization we
enter the path to liberation. In this context, liberation refers to
the supreme permanent peace of mind known as *nirvana*, which
gives us pure and everlasting happiness.

WHAT WE SHOULD ABANDON

In *Sutra of the Four Noble Truths*, Buddha says: "You should
abandon origins." In saying this Buddha is advising us that if
we wish to liberate ourself permanently from the sufferings of
our countless future lives we should abandon origins. *Origins*
means our delusions, principally our delusion of self-grasping.
Self-grasping is called an *origin* because it is the source of all our
suffering and problems, and is also known as the "inner demon."
Delusions are wrong awarenesses whose function is to destroy
mental peace, the source of happiness; they have no function
other than to harm us. Delusions such as self-grasping abide at
our heart and continually harm us day and night without rest by
destroying our peace of mind. In samsara, the cycle of impure
life, no one has the opportunity to experience real happiness because their mental peace, the source of happiness, is continually

being destroyed by the inner demon of self-grasping.

Our self-grasping ignorance is a mind that mistakenly believes that our self, our body, and all the other things that we normally see actually exist. Because of this ignorance we develop attachment to the things we like and anger at the things we do not like. We then perform various kinds of non-virtuous action, and as a result of these actions we experience various kinds of suffering and problems in this life and in life after life.

Self-grasping ignorance is an inner poison that causes far greater harm than any outer poison. Because it is polluted by this inner poison, our mind sees everything in a mistaken way, and as a result we experience hallucination-like sufferings and problems. In reality, our self, our body, and all the other things that we normally see do not exist. Self-grasping can be compared to a poisonous tree, all other delusions to its branches, and all our suffering and problems to its fruit; it is the fundamental source of all our other delusions and of all our suffering and problems. Through this we can understand that if we abandon our self-grasping permanently, all our suffering and problems of this life and of countless future lives will cease permanently. The great Yogi Saraha said, "If your mind is released permanently from self-grasping, there is no doubt that you will be released permanently from suffering." Understanding this and having contemplated the above explanations, we should think:

I must apply great effort to recognizing, reducing, and finally abandoning my ignorance of self-grasping completely.

We should meditate on this determination continually, and put our determination into practice.

WHAT WE SHOULD PRACTICE

In *Sutra of the Four Noble Truths*, Buddha says: "You should practice the path." In this context, *path* does not mean an external path that leads from one place to another, but an inner path, a spiritual realization that leads us to the pure happiness of liberation and enlightenment.

The practice of the stages of the path to liberation can be condensed into the three trainings of higher moral discipline, higher concentration, and higher wisdom. These trainings are called *higher* because they are motivated by renunciation. They are therefore the actual path to liberation that we need to practice.

The nature of moral discipline is a virtuous determination to abandon inappropriate actions. When we practice moral discipline we abandon inappropriate actions, maintain pure behavior, and perform every action correctly with a virtuous motivation. Moral discipline is most important for everybody in order to prevent future problems for ourself and for others. It makes us pure because it makes our actions pure. We need to be clean and pure ourself—just having a clean body is not enough, since our body is not our self. Moral discipline is like a great earth that supports and nurtures the crops of spiritual realizations. Without practicing moral discipline it is very difficult to make progress in spiritual training. Training in higher moral discipline is learning to be deeply familiar with the practice of moral discipline, motivated by renunciation.

The second higher training is training in higher concentration. The nature of concentration is a single-pointed virtuous mind. For as long as we remain with this mind we will experience mental peace, and so we will be happy. When we practice concentration we prevent distractions and concentrate on virtuous objects. It is very important to train in concentration, because with distractions we cannot accomplish anything. Training in higher concentration is learning to be deeply familiar with the ability to stop distractions and concentrate on virtuous objects, with a motivation of renunciation. With regard to any Dharma practice, if our concentration is clear and strong it is very easy to make progress. Normally, distraction is the main obstacle to our Dharma practice. The practice of moral discipline prevents gross distractions, and concentration prevents subtle distractions; together they give rise to quick results in our Dharma practice.

Worldly intelligence is deceptive, but wisdom will never deceive us.

The third higher training is training in higher wisdom. The nature of wisdom is a virtuous intelligent mind that functions to understand meaningful objects such as the existence of past and future lives, karma, and emptiness. Understanding these objects brings great meaning to this life and countless future lives. Many people are very intelligent in destroying their enemies, caring for their families, finding what they want, and so forth, but this is not wisdom. Even animals have such intelligence. Worldly intelligence is deceptive, but wisdom will never deceive us. It is our inner Spiritual Guide who leads us to correct paths, and it is the divine eye through which we can see past and future lives and the special connection between our actions in past lives and our experiences in this life, known as *karma*. The subject of karma is very extensive and subtle, and we can understand it only through wisdom. Training in higher wisdom is learning to develop and increase our wisdom realizing emptiness through contemplating and meditating on emptiness, with a motivation of renunciation. This wisdom is extremely profound. Its object, emptiness, is not nothingness but is the real nature of all phenomena. A detailed explanation of emptiness is given in the chapter "Training in Ultimate Bodhichitta."

The three higher trainings are the actual method to attain permanent liberation from the suffering of this life and countless future lives. This can be understood through the following analogy. When we cut down a tree using a saw, the saw alone cannot cut the tree without the use of our hands, which in turn depend on our body. Training in higher moral discipline is like our body, training in higher concentration is like our hands, and training in higher wisdom is like the saw. By using these three together, we can cut down the poisonous tree of our self-grasping ignorance, and automatically all other delusions—its branches—and all our suffering and problems—its fruits—will cease completely. Then we will have attained the permanent cessation of the suffering of this life and future lives—the supreme permanent peace of mind known as *nirvana*, or liberation. We will have solved all our human problems and accomplished the real meaning of our life.

Contemplating the above explanation we should think:

Since the three higher trainings are the actual method to attain permanent liberation from the suffering of this life and countless future lives, I must put great effort into practicing them.

We should meditate on this determination continually, and put our determination into practice.

WHAT WE SHOULD ATTAIN

In *Sutra of the Four Noble Truths*, Buddha says: "You should attain cessations." In this context, *cessation* means the permanent cessation of suffering and its root, self-grasping ignorance. In saying this, Buddha is advising us not to be satisfied with a temporary liberation from particular sufferings, but that we should have the intention to accomplish the ultimate goal of human life, the supreme permanent peace of mind (nirvana), and the pure and everlasting happiness of enlightenment.

Every living being without exception has to experience the cycle of the sufferings of sickness, aging, death, and rebirth, in life after life, endlessly. Following Buddha's example, we should develop strong renunciation for this endless cycle. When he was living in the palace with his family, Buddha saw how his people were constantly experiencing these sufferings and he made the strong determination to attain enlightenment, great liberation, and to lead every living being to this state.

Buddha did not encourage us to abandon daily activities that provide necessary conditions for living, or that prevent poverty, environmental problems, particular diseases, and so forth. However, no matter how successful we are in these activities, we will never achieve permanent cessation of these problems. We will still have to experience them in our countless future lives, and even in this life, although we work very hard to prevent these problems, the sufferings of poverty, environmental pollution and disease are increasing throughout the world. Furthermore, because of the power of modern technology there are now many great dangers developing in the world that have never been experienced before.

Therefore, we should not be satisfied merely with temporary freedom from particular sufferings, but apply great effort to attaining permanent freedom while we have this opportunity.

We should remember the preciousness of our human life. Because of their previous deluded views denying the value of spiritual practice, those who have taken rebirth as animals, for example, have no opportunity to engage in spiritual practice, which alone gives rise to a meaningful life. Since it is impossible for them to listen to, understand, contemplate, and meditate on spiritual instructions, their present animal rebirth itself is an obstacle. As mentioned earlier, only human beings are free from such obstacles and have all the necessary conditions for engaging in spiritual paths, which alone lead to everlasting peace and happiness. This combination of freedom and the possession of necessary conditions is the special characteristic that makes our human life so precious.

In conclusion, we should think:

I should not be satisfied with merely a temporary cessation of particular sufferings, which even animals can experience. I must attain the permanent cessation of self-grasping ignorance—the root of suffering—through sincerely practicing the three higher trainings.

We should meditate on this determination every day, and put our determination into practice. In this way we guide ourself to the liberating path.

The Path of a Person of Great Scope

*I*n this context, a *person of great scope* refers to someone who has a great capacity for developing spiritual understanding and realizations.

Because this subject is extensive and profound, containing both Sutra and Tantra, a detailed explanation of it will be given in the following chapters.

Je Tsongkhapa

The Supreme Good Heart—Bodhichitta

We should maintain renunciation—the sincere wish to attain permanent liberation—day and night. It is the door to liberation—the supreme permanent peace of mind—and the basis of more advanced realizations. However, we should not be content with merely seeking our own liberation; we also need to consider the welfare of other living beings. There are countless beings drowning in samsara's ocean experiencing unbearable suffering. Each one of us is just one single person, but other living beings are countless in number. Therefore the happiness and freedom of others are much more important than our own. For this reason we must enter the Bodhisattva's path, which leads us to the state of full enlightenment.

The gateway through which we enter the Bodhisattva's path is bodhichitta. *Bodhi* means enlightenment and *chitta* means mind. Bodhichitta is a mind that spontaneously wishes to attain enlightenment to benefit each and every living being directly. The moment we develop this precious mind of bodhichitta, we become a Bodhisattva—a person who spontaneously wishes to attain enlightenment for the benefit of all living beings—and we become a Son or Daughter of the Conqueror Buddhas.

This supreme good heart of bodhichitta cannot be developed without training. Je Tsongkhapa said:

> Through watering the ground of affectionate love with
>   cherishing love,
> And then sowing the seeds of wishing love and
>   compassion,
> The medicinal tree of bodhichitta will grow.

This implies that there are five stages of training in bodhichitta: (1) training in affectionate love, (2) training in cherishing love, (3) training in wishing love, (4) training in universal compassion, and (5) training in actual bodhichitta.

TRAINING IN AFFECTIONATE LOVE

In this training we learn to develop and maintain a warm heart and a feeling of being close to all living beings without exception. This affectionate love makes our mind pure and balanced, and prepares the foundation for generating cherishing love for all living beings. Normally our mind is unbalanced; we feel either too close to someone out of attachment, or too distant from others out of anger. It is impossible to develop the supreme good heart of bodhichitta with such an unbalanced mind. This unbalanced mind is the source of all our daily problems. We may think that some people are our enemies because they are harming us, so how can we develop and maintain a warm heart and a feeling of being close to such people? This way of thinking is incorrect. The people who we believe are our enemies are in reality our mothers of former lives. Our mothers of former lives and our mother of this present life are all our mothers and are all equally kind to us.

It is incorrect to reason that our mothers of former lives are no longer our mothers just because a long time has passed since they actually cared for us. If our present mother died today, would she stop being our mother? No, we would still regard her as our mother and pray for her happiness. The same is true of all our previous mothers—they died, yet they remain our mothers. It is only because of the changes in our external appearance that we do not recognize each other.

In our daily life, we see many different living beings, both human and non-human. We regard some as friends, some as enemies, and most as strangers. These distinctions are made by our mistaken minds; they are not verified by valid minds. Rather than following such mistaken minds, we should recognize and believe that all living beings are our mothers. Whoever we meet, we should think, "This person is my mother." In this way, we will generate a warm heart and a feeling of being equally close to all living beings. Our belief that all living beings are our mothers is wisdom because it understands a meaningful object, which is that all living beings are our mothers. Through this understanding we will experience great meaning in this life and in countless future lives. We should never abandon this beneficial belief or view.

We should contemplate as follows:

Since it is impossible to find a beginning to my mental continuum, it follows that I have taken countless rebirths in the past. And if I have had countless rebirths, I must have had countless mothers. Where are all these mothers now? They are all the living beings alive today.

Having repeatedly contemplated this point we strongly believe that all living beings are our mothers, and we meditate on this belief.

THE KINDNESS OF LIVING BEINGS

Having become convinced that all living beings are our mothers, we contemplate the immense kindness we have received from each of them when they were our mother, as well as the kindness they have shown us at other times.

When we were conceived, if our mother had not wanted to keep us in her womb she could have had an abortion. If she had done this, we would not have this human life now. Through her kindness she allowed us to stay in her womb, and so we now enjoy a human life and experience all its advantages. When we were a baby, if we had not received her constant care and attention we would certainly have had an accident and could now be disabled or blind. Fortunately, our mother did not neglect us. Day and night, she gave us her loving care, regarding us as more important than herself. She saved our life many times each day. During the night she allowed her sleep to be interrupted, and during the day she went without her usual pleasures. She had to leave her job, and when her friends went out to enjoy themselves she had to stay behind. She spent all her money on us, giving us the best food and the best clothes she could afford. She taught us how to eat, how to walk, how to talk. Thinking of our future welfare, she did her best to ensure that we received a good education. Due to her kindness, we are now able to study whatever we choose. It is principally through the kindness of our mother that we now have the opportunity to practice Dharma and eventually to attain enlightenment.

Since there is no one who has not been our mother at some time in our previous lives, and since when we were their child they treated us with the same kindness as our present mother has treated us in this life, all living beings are very kind.

The kindness of living beings is not limited to the times when they have been our mother. All the time, our day-to-day needs are provided through the kindness of others. We brought nothing with us from our former life, yet as soon as we were born, we were given a home, food, clothes, and *We learn to maintain a warm heart and a feeling of being close to all living beings without exception.* everything we needed—all provided through the kindness of others. Everything we now enjoy has been provided through the kindness of other beings, past or present.

We are able to make use of many things with very little effort on our own part. If we consider facilities such as roads, cars, trains, airplanes, ships, houses, restaurants, hotels, libraries, hospitals, stores, money, and so on, it is clear that many people worked very hard to provide these things. Even though we make little or no contribution toward providing these facilities, they are all available for us to use. This shows the great kindness of others.

Both our general education and our spiritual training are provided by others. All our Dharma realizations, from our very first insights up to our eventual attainment of liberation and enlightenment, will be attained in dependence upon the kindness of others. As human beings we generally have the opportunity to attain the supreme happiness of enlightenment. This is because we have the opportunity to enter and follow the path to enlightenment, a spiritual path motivated by compassion for all living beings. The gateway through which we enter the path to enlightenment is therefore compassion for all living beings—universal compassion—and we develop this compassion only by relying on all living beings as the objects of our compassion. This shows that it is through the great kindness of all living beings acting as the objects of our compassion that we have the opportunity to enter the path to enlightenment and attain the supreme happiness of enlightenment. It is therefore clear that for us all living beings are supremely kind and precious.

From the depths of our heart we should think:

Each and every living being is supremely kind and precious to me. They provide me with the opportunity to attain the pure and everlasting happiness of enlightenment—the ultimate goal of human life.

Understanding and thinking in this way, we generate a warm heart and a feeling of being equally close to all living beings without exception. We transform our mind into this feeling, and we remain on it single-pointedly for as long as possible. Through continually contemplating and meditating in this way we will maintain a warm heart and a feeling of being close to each and every living being all the time, in every situation. Having understood the eight benefits of maintaining affectionate love that are listed below in the section "Wishing Love," we should apply continual effort in this practice.

TRAINING IN CHERISHING LOVE

This training has two stages: (1) equalizing self and others, and (2) exchanging self with others.

EQUALIZING SELF AND OTHERS

This practice is called *equalizing self and others* because we are learning to believe that the happiness and freedom of ourself and all other living beings are equally important. Learning to cherish others is the best solution to our daily problems, and it is the source of all our future happiness and good fortune.

There are two levels of cherishing others: (1) cherishing others as we cherish a close friend or relative, and (2) cherishing others as we cherish ourself. The second level is more profound. Through cherishing all living beings as we cherish ourself we will develop the profound universal compassion that functions as the quick path to enlightenment. This is one of the essential points of Kadam Lamrim.

To train in equalizing self and others we engage in the following contemplation, thinking:

I must believe that the happiness and freedom of myself and all other living beings are equally important because:

1. All living beings have shown me great kindness in both this and previous lives.

2. Just as I wish to be free from suffering and experience only happiness, so do all other beings. In this respect, I am no different from any other being; we are all equal.

3. I am only one, while others are countless, so how can I be concerned for myself alone while I neglect others? My happiness and suffering are insignificant when compared with the happiness and suffering of countless other living beings.

Having repeatedly contemplated these points, we strongly believe that the happiness and freedom of ourself and all other living beings are equally important. We then remain on this belief single-pointedly for as long as possible. We should continually practice this contemplation and meditation until we spontaneously believe that the happiness and freedom of ourself and all other living beings are equally important, which is the realization of equalizing self and others.

EXCHANGING SELF WITH OTHERS

This training has three stages: (1) contemplating the disadvantages of self-cherishing, (2) contemplating the advantages of cherishing others, and (3) the actual training in exchanging self with others.

CONTEMPLATING THE DISADVANTAGES OF SELF-CHERISHING

What is self-cherishing? When we think "I" and "mine" we perceive an inherently existent I, and we cherish it and believe that its happiness and freedom are the most important. This is self-cherishing. Caring for ourself is not self-cherishing. We need to care for ourself to maintain this human life so that we can continually apply effort to accomplishing its real meaning.

Self-cherishing and self-grasping are different aspects of one mind. Self-grasping grasps at an inherently existent "I," and self-cherishing believes that such an "I" is precious and that its happiness and freedom are supremely important. Self-cherishing is our normal view that believes "I am important" and "My happiness and freedom are important," and that neglects others' happiness and freedom. It is part of our ignorance because in reality there is no inherently existent I. Our self-cherishing mind nevertheless cherishes this I and believes that it is the most important. It is a foolish and deceptive mind that always interferes with our inner peace, and it is a great obstacle to our accomplishing the real meaning of our human life. We have had this self-cherishing mind in life after life since beginningless time, even while asleep and dreaming.

In *Guide to the Bodhisattva's Way of Life*, Shantideva says:

> . . . all the suffering there is in this world
> Arises from wishing ourself to be happy.

Sufferings are not given to us as a punishment. They all come from our self-cherishing mind, which wishes ourself to be happy while neglecting the happiness of others. There are two ways to understand this. First, the self-cherishing mind is the creator of all our suffering and problems; and second, self-cherishing is the basis for experiencing all our suffering and problems.

Sufferings are not given to us as a punishment.

We suffer because in our previous lives we performed actions that caused others to experience suffering, motivated by selfish intention—our self-cherishing. As a result of these actions, we now experience our present suffering and problems. Therefore, the real creator of all our suffering and problems is our self-cherishing mind.

Our present experience of particular suffering and problems has a special connection with particular actions we performed in our previous lives. This is very subtle. We cannot see this hidden connection with our eyes, but as already explained we can understand it through using our wisdom, and in particular through relying on Buddha's teachings on karma. In general, everyone knows that if they perform bad actions they will experience bad results and if they perform good actions they will experience good results.

The self-cherishing mind is also the basis for experiencing all our suffering and problems. For example, when people are unable to fulfill their wishes, many experience depression, discouragement, unhappiness, and mental pain, and some even want to kill themselves. This is because their self-cherishing believes that their own wishes are so important. It is therefore their self-cherishing that is mainly responsible for their problems. Without self-cherishing, there would be no basis for experiencing such suffering.

When we are seriously ill we find it difficult to bear our suffering, but illness harms us only because we cherish ourself. If another person is experiencing a similar illness, we have no problem. Why? Because we do not cherish him or her. However, if we cherished others as we cherish ourself, we would find their suffering difficult to bear. This is compassion. As Shantideva says:

The suffering I experience
Does not harm others,
But I find it hard to bear
Because I cherish myself.

Likewise, the suffering of others
Does not harm me,
But, if I cherish others,
I will find their suffering hard to bear.

In life after life, since beginningless time, we have tried to fulfill the wishes of our self-cherishing mind, believing its view to be true. We have put great effort into seeking happiness from external sources but have nothing to show for it now. Because self-cherishing has deceived us we have wasted countless previous lives. It has driven us to work for our own purpose, but we have gained nothing. This foolish mind has made all our previous lives empty—when we took this human rebirth we brought nothing with us but delusions. In every moment of every day, this self-cherishing mind continues to deceive us.

Having contemplated these points, we think:

Nothing causes me greater harm than the demon of my self-cherishing. It is the source of all my negativity, misfortune, problems, and suffering. Therefore I must abandon my self-cherishing.

We should meditate on this determination every day, and put our determination into practice.

CONTEMPLATING THE ADVANTAGES OF CHERISHING OTHERS

When we deeply think that others are important, and that their happiness and freedom are important, we are cherishing others. If we cherish others like this, we will always have good relationships and live in harmony with others, and our daily life will be peaceful and happy. We can begin this practice with our family, friends, and those around us, and then gradually we will develop and maintain cherishing love for all living beings without exception.

In *Guide to the Bodhisattva's Way of Life*, Shantideva says:

All the happiness there is in this world
Arises from wishing others to be happy.

If we think carefully about this, we will realize that all our present and future happiness depends on our cherishing others—on our wanting others to be happy. In our past lives, because we cherished others, we practiced virtuous actions such as refraining from killing or harming others and abandoning stealing from and cheating them. We gave them material help and protection, and practiced patience. As a result of these virtuous actions, we have now obtained this precious human life with the opportunity to experience human enjoyments.

The immediate effect of cherishing others will be that many of our daily problems, such as those that arise from anger, jealousy, and selfish behavior, will disappear, and our mind will become calm and peaceful. Since we will act in considerate ways, we will please others and not become involved in quarrels or disputes. If we cherish others we will be concerned with helping rather than harming them, so we will naturally avoid non-virtuous actions. Instead, we will practice virtuous actions, such as compassion, love, patience, and giving material help and protection, and thus create the cause to attain pure and everlasting happiness in the future.

In particular, if we cherish all other living beings as we cherish ourself we will find their suffering hard to bear. Our feeling that it is hard to bear the suffering of all other living beings is universal compassion, and this will lead us quickly to the pure and everlasting happiness of enlightenment. Just like all the previous Buddhas, we will be born an enlightened Buddha from the mother, universal compassion. This is why our cherishing all living beings will enable us to attain enlightenment very quickly.

Contemplating all these benefits, we think:

The precious mind that cherishes all living beings protects both myself and others from suffering, brings pure and everlasting happiness, and fulfills the wishes of both myself and others. Therefore I must always cherish all living beings without exception.

We should meditate on this determination every day, and out of meditation put our determination into practice. This means that we should actually cherish each and every living being, including animals.

THE ACTUAL TRAINING IN EXCHANGING SELF WITH OTHERS

Exchanging self with others means that we change the object of our cherishing from ourself to all other living beings. This is impossible without training. How do we train in exchanging self with others? With an understanding of the great disadvantages of cherishing ourself and the great advantages of cherishing all living beings, as explained above, and remembering that we have made the determination to abandon our self-cherishing and always cherish all living beings without exception, we think from the depths of our heart:

I must give up cherishing myself and instead cherish all other living beings without exception.

We then meditate on this determination. We should continually practice this meditation until we spontaneously believe that the happiness and freedom of each and every other living being are far more important than our own. This belief is the realization of exchanging self with others.

TRAINING IN WISHING LOVE

With the understanding and belief that the happiness and freedom of each and every living being are far more important than our own, we generate wishing love for all living beings, thinking:

It would be so wonderful if all living beings attained the pure and everlasting happiness of enlightenment! May they attain this happiness. I myself will work for this aim.

We remain single-pointedly on this precious mind of wishing love for all living beings for as long as possible. We repeat this meditation again and again until we spontaneously wish that each and every living being may experience the happiness of enlightenment. This spontaneous wish is the actual realization of wishing love.

Wishing love is also called *immeasurable love* because merely through meditating on wishing love we will receive immeasurable benefits in this life and in countless future lives. Based on Buddha's teachings, the great scholar Nagarjuna listed eight benefits of affectionate love and wishing love: (1) By meditating on affectionate love and wishing love for just one moment we accumulate greater merit than we would by giving food three times every day to all those who are hungry in the world.

When we give food to those who are hungry we are not giving real happiness. This is because the happiness that comes from eating food is not real happiness, but just a temporary reduction of the suffering of hunger. However, meditation on affectionate love and wishing love leads us and all living beings to the pure and everlasting happiness of enlightenment.

The remaining seven benefits of meditating on affectionate love and wishing love are that in the future: (2) we will receive great loving kindness from humans and non-humans, (3) we will be protected in various ways by humans and non-humans, (4) we will be mentally happy all the time, (5) we will be physically healthy all the time, (6) we will not be harmed by weapons, poison, and other harmful conditions, (7) we will obtain all necessary conditions without effort, and (8) we will be born in the superior heaven of a Buddha Land.

Having contemplated these benefits we should apply effort in meditating on wishing love many times every day.

TRAINING IN UNIVERSAL COMPASSION

Universal compassion is a mind that sincerely wishes to liberate all living beings from suffering permanently. If on the basis of cherishing all living beings, we contemplate the fact that they experience the cycle of physical suffering and mental pain in life after life without end, their inability to liberate themselves from suffering, their lack of freedom, and how by engaging in negative actions they create the causes of future suffering, we will develop deep compassion for them. We need to empathize with them and feel their pain as intensely as we feel our own.

No one wants to suffer, yet out of ignorance living beings create suffering by performing non-virtuous actions. We should therefore feel equal compassion for all living beings without exception; there is no single living being who is not a suitable object of our compassion.

All living beings suffer because they take contaminated re-births. Human beings have no choice but to experience immense human sufferings because they have taken human rebirth, which is contaminated by the inner poison of delusions. Similarly, animals have to experience animal suffering, and hungry ghosts and hell beings have to experience all the sufferings of their respective realms. If living beings experienced all this suffering for just one single life, it would not be so bad, but the cycle of suffering continues life after life, endlessly.

To develop renunciation, we previously contemplated how in our countless future lives we will have to experience the unbearable sufferings of animals, hungry ghosts, hells beings, humans, demi-gods, and gods. Now, at this point, to develop compassion for all living beings who are our mothers, we contemplate how in their countless future lives they will have to experience the unbearable sufferings of animals, hungry ghosts, hells beings, humans, demi-gods, and gods.

Having contemplated this we should think:

I cannot bear the suffering of these countless mother beings. Drowning in the vast and deep ocean of samsara, the cycle of contaminated rebirth, they have to experience unbearable physical suffering and mental pain in this life and in countless future lives. I must permanently liberate all these living beings from their suffering.

We should meditate continually on this determination, which is universal compassion, and apply great effort to fulfilling its goal.

TRAINING IN ACTUAL BODHICHITTA

The moment we develop bodhichitta we become a Bodhisattva, a person who spontaneously wishes to attain enlightenment for the benefit of all living beings. Initially we will be a Bodhisattva on the path of accumulation. Then, by following the path to enlightenment with the vehicle of bodhichitta, we can progress from being a Bodhisattva on the path of accumulation to being a Bodhisattva on the path of preparation, a Bodhisattva on the path of seeing, and then a Bodhisattva on the path of meditation. From there we will reach the Path of No More Learning, which is the actual state of enlightenment. As already mentioned, enlightenment is the inner light of wisdom that is permanently free from all mistaken appearance, and whose function is to bestow mental peace on each and every living being every day. When we attain a Buddha's enlightenment we will be able to benefit each and every living being directly through bestowing blessings and through our countless emanations.

This precious mind of bodhichitta leads us directly to the supreme happiness of enlightenment.

In Sutra teachings, Buddha says:

In this impure life of samsara
No one experiences real happiness;
The actions they perform
Will always be the causes of suffering.

The happiness that we normally experience through having good conditions, such as a good reputation, a good position, a good job, good relationships, seeing attractive forms, hearing good news or beautiful music, eating, drinking, and sex is not real happiness, but changing suffering—a reduction in our previous suffering. Out of ignorance, however, we believe that only these things bring happiness, and because of this we never wish to attain real happiness, the pure and everlasting happiness of liberation and enlightenment, even for our own benefit. We are always searching for happiness in this impure life of samsara, like the thief who searched for gold in Milarepa's empty cave and found nothing. The great Yogi Milarepa heard a thief rummaging around his cave one night and called out to him, "How do you expect to find anything valuable here at night, when I cannot find anything valuable here during the day?"

When through training, we develop the precious mind of enlightenment, bodhichitta, we spontaneously think:

It would be wonderful if I and all living beings attained real happiness, the pure and everlasting happiness of enlightenment! May we attain this happiness. I myself will work for this goal.

We need to have this precious mind of bodhichitta in our heart. It is our inner Spiritual Guide, who leads us directly to the state of supreme happiness of enlightenment; and it is the real wishfulfilling jewel through which we can fulfill our own and others' wishes. There is no greater beneficial intention than this precious mind.

Having contemplated the above explanation, we think from the depths of our heart:

I am one single person but other living beings are countless, and they are all my kind mothers. These countless mother beings have to experience unbearable physical suffering and mental pain in this life and in their countless future lives. Compared with the suffering of these countless living beings, my own suffering is insignificant. I must liberate all living beings from suffering permanently, and for this purpose I must attain a Buddha's enlightenment.

We meditate on this determination, which is bodhichitta, single-pointedly. We should practice this contemplation and meditation continually until we develop the spontaneous wish to attain enlightenment to benefit each and every living being directly, and then we should apply great effort to fulfilling our bodhichitta wish.

Buddha of Compassion

Training in the Path of Bodhichitta

There are three stages of training in the path of bodhichitta: (1) training in the six perfections, (2) training in taking in conjunction with the practice of the six perfections, and (3) training in giving in conjunction with the practice of the six perfections

TRAINING IN THE SIX PERFECTIONS

The six perfections are the actual path to enlightenment, and they are also the path of bodhichitta and the Bodhisattva's path. Through following this path with the vehicle of bodhichitta we will definitely reach the state of enlightenment. Our bodhichitta wish is to attain enlightenment to benefit each and every living being directly. To fulfill this wish, in front of our Spiritual Guide or an image of Buddha regarded as the living Buddha, we should promise to engage in the Bodhisattva's path or training while reciting the following ritual prayer three times. This promise is the Bodhisattva's vow.

> Just as all the previous Sugatas, the Buddhas,
> Generated the mind of enlightenment, bodhichitta,
> And accomplished all the stages
> Of the Bodhisattva's training,

So will I too, for the sake of all beings,
Generate the mind of enlightenment
And accomplish all the stages
Of the Bodhisattva's training.

When we take the Bodhisattva's vow we are taking the commitment to engage in the path to enlightenment, the Bodhisattva's training, which is the practice of the six perfections. Normally, when we start a job, we commit ourself to fulfilling our employer's wishes; otherwise we will quickly lose our job. In the same way, having generated bodhichitta—the determination to attain enlightenment to benefit each and every living being directly—we need to commit ourself to engaging in the practice of the six perfections. If we do not make this commitment by taking the Bodhisattva's vow, we will lose our opportunity to attain enlightenment. Through contemplating this we should encourage ourself to take the Bodhisattva's vow and sincerely practice the six perfections.

The six perfections are the practices of giving, moral discipline, patience, effort, concentration, and wisdom, motivated by bodhichitta. We should recognize that the six perfections are our daily practice.

In the practice of giving we should practice: (1) giving material help to those in poverty, including giving food to animals, (2) giving practical help to those sick or physically weak, (3) giving protection by always trying to save others' lives, including those of insects, (4) giving love, learning to cherish all living beings by always believing that their happiness and freedom are important, and (5) giving Dharma, helping others solve their problems of anger, attachment, and ignorance by giving Dharma teachings or meaningful advice.

In the practice of moral discipline we should abandon any inappropriate actions including those that cause others suffering. We should especially abandon breaking our commitments of the Bodhisattva's vow. This is the basic foundation on which we can make progress on the Bodhisattva's path. By doing this our actions of body, speech, and mind will be pure so that we become a pure being.

In the practice of patience we should never allow ourself to become angry or discouraged, by temporarily accepting any difficulties or harm from others. When we practice patience we are wearing the supreme inner armor that directly protects us from physical sufferings, mental pain, and other problems. Anger destroys our merit, or good fortune, so that we will continually experience *There is no greater evil than anger. There is no greater virtue than patience.* many obstacles, and due to lacking good fortune it will be difficult to fulfill our wishes, especially our spiritual goals. There is no greater evil than anger. With the practice of patience we can accomplish any spiritual goal; there is no greater virtue than patience.

In the practice of effort we should rely on irreversible effort to accumulate the great collections of merit and wisdom, which are the main causes of attaining Buddha's Form Body (Rupakaya), and Truth Body (Dharmakaya); and we should especially emphasize contemplation and meditation on emptiness, the way things really are. By doing this we can easily make progress on the path to enlightenment. With effort we can accomplish our goal, but with laziness we cannot achieve anything.

In the practice of concentration, at this stage we should emphasize accomplishing the concentration of tranquil abiding observing emptiness. An explanation is given below in the section "A Simple Training in Ultimate Bodhichitta." When through the power of this concentration, we experience a special wisdom called *superior seeing* that realizes the emptiness of all phenomena very clearly, we will have progressed from being a Bodhisattva on the path of accumulation to being a Bodhisattva on the path of preparation.

In the practice of wisdom, at this stage we need to emphasize increasing the power of our wisdom of superior seeing by continually meditating on the emptiness of all phenomena with bodhichitta motivation. Through this, when our superior seeing transforms into the path of seeing, which is the direct realization of the emptiness of all phenomena, we will have progressed from being a Bodhisattva on the path of preparation to being a Bodhisattva on the path of seeing. The moment we attain the path of seeing we are a Superior Bodhisattva and no longer experience samsara's sufferings. Even if someone cuts our body with a knife piece by piece we have no pain because we have the direct realization of the way things really are.

Having completed the path of seeing, to make further progress we need to engage continually in the meditation on the emptiness of all phenomena with bodhichitta motivation. This meditation is called the *path of meditation*. When we reach this stage we will have progressed from being a Bodhisattva on the path of seeing to being a Bodhisattva on the path of meditation.

Having completed the path of meditation, when our wisdom of the path of meditation transforms into an omniscient wisdom that is permanently free from all mistaken appearances, this omniscient wisdom is called the *Path of No More Learning*, which is actual enlightenment. When we reach this stage we will have progressed from being a Bodhisattva on the path of meditation to being an enlightened being, a Buddha. We will have completed the ultimate goal of living beings.

The Bodhisattva's initial training in accumulating merit or wisdom is the Bodhisattva's path of accumulation; the Bodhisattva's training in accumulating merit or wisdom that is a preparation for attaining the path of seeing is the Bodhisattva's path of preparation; the Bodhisattva's training that is the initial direct realization of emptiness is the Bodhisattva's path of seeing; after completing the path of seeing, the Bodhisattva's training that meditates continually on emptiness is the Bodhisattva's path of meditation; and Buddha's omniscient wisdom that is attained through completing all the trainings of Sutra and Tantra is the Path of No More Learning, the state of enlightenment.

TRAINING IN TAKING IN CONJUNCTION WITH THE PRACTICE OF THE SIX PERFECTIONS

There are four main benefits of the meditations on taking and giving: they are powerful methods (1) to purify the potentialities of non-virtuous actions that cause us to experience incurable diseases such as cancer, (2) to accumulate a great collection of merit, (3) to ripen our potentiality to be able to benefit all living beings, and (4) to purify our mind.

There was once a Lamrim practitioner called Kharak Gomchen who was seriously afflicted by leprosy. The treatments given by his doctors did not work, and each year his condition grew worse. Finally, his doctors told him that there was nothing they could do to cure his disease. Believing that he would soon die, Gomchen left his home and went to a cemetery to prepare for death. While staying in the cemetery, he concentrated day and night on practicing the meditations on taking and giving with strong compassion for all living beings. Through this practice he was completely cured and returned home healthy and with a happy mind. There are many other similar examples.

Right now we are unable to benefit all living beings but we have the potential for this ability, which is part of our Buddha nature. Through practicing the meditations on taking and giving with strong compassion for all living beings, the potential to be able to benefit all living beings will ripen, and when this happens we will become an enlightened being, a Buddha. When we purify our mind through the practices of taking and giving, every spiritual realization will grow easily in our mind. Through contemplating the four main benefits of meditating on taking and giving, we should encourage ourself to practice these meditations sincerely.

Taking in this context means taking others' sufferings on ourself through meditation. When we meditate on taking, our motivation should be compassion, thinking:

I must permanently liberate all living beings from their suffering and fears in this life and countless future lives.

In this way, by giving protection we are practicing the perfection of giving; by abandoning self-cherishing we are practicing the perfection of moral discipline; by willingly accepting any adverse conditions obstructing our practice of taking we are practicing the perfection of patience; by applying effort to practicing this meditation continually, free from laziness, we are practicing the perfection of effort; by concentrating single-pointedly on the meditation on taking, free from distraction, we are practicing the perfection of concentration; and by realizing that we ourself, all living beings, and their suffering all exist as mere names and do not inherently exist we are practicing the perfection of wisdom. This is how we should train in the meditation on taking in conjunction with practicing the six perfections. This

Right now we are unable to benefit all living beings but we have the potential for this ability.

is a very profound method of practicing the six perfections. We should apply this same method to all other meditations, such as the meditation on death, so that we can quickly make progress along the path to enlightenment.

There are two stages to the meditation on taking: (1) meditation on taking focusing on all living beings, and (2) meditation on taking focusing on particular living beings.

MEDITATION ON TAKING FOCUSING ON ALL LIVING BEINGS

In this first stage we focus on the assembly of all living beings without exception, and then think from the depths of our heart:

In their countless future lives these living beings will continually experience without choice the sufferings of humans, animals, hungry ghosts, hell beings, demi-gods, and gods. It would be wonderful if all these living beings were permanently freed from the suffering and fears in this life and countless future lives! May they achieve this. I myself will work for them to achieve this. I must do this.

Thinking in this way, we imagine that the sufferings of all living beings gather together in the aspect of black smoke. This dissolves into our ignorance of self-grasping and self-cherishing at our heart. We then strongly believe that all living beings are permanently freed from suffering, and that our ignorance of self-grasping and self-cherishing is completely destroyed. We meditate on this belief single-pointedly for as long as possible.

With compassion for all living beings we should continually practice this meditation until we experience signs that indicate our mind has been purified. These signs can include: the healing of any sickness we may have; the reducing of our delusions; our having a more peaceful and happy mind; the increasing of our faith, correct intention, and correct view; and especially the strengthening of our experience of universal compassion.

MEDITATION ON TAKING FOCUSING
ON PARTICULAR LIVING BEINGS

In this meditation we can focus, for example, on the assembly of living beings who experience the suffering of sickness. We then think:

These living beings experience the suffering of sickness in this life and in their countless future lives without end. It would be wonderful if these living beings were permanently freed from sickness! May they achieve this. I myself will work for them to achieve this. I must do this.

Thinking in this way, we imagine that the suffering of sickness of all living beings gathers together in the aspect of black smoke. This dissolves into our ignorance of self-grasping and self-cherishing at our heart. We then strongly believe that all these living beings are permanently freed from sickness, and that our ignorance of self-grasping and self-cherishing is completely destroyed. We meditate on this belief single-pointedly for as long as possible.

In the same way, we can practice the meditation on taking while focusing on a particular individual or group of living beings who are experiencing other sufferings such as poverty, fighting, and famine.

In particular, we should apply effort to developing deep familiarity with the meditation on taking focusing on all living beings. This meditation makes our mind pure, which in turn makes our actions pure so that we become a pure being. If we die with strong compassion for all living beings we will definitely be born in the Pure Land of a Buddha. This is because our compassion that manifests when we are dying will directly cause our potential for taking rebirth in the Pure Land of a Buddha to ripen. This is the good result of a good heart. The result of maintaining the good heart of sincerely wishing to permanently liberate all living beings from suffering is that we ourself will experience permanent liberation from suffering by taking rebirth in the Pure Land of a Buddha.

For example, when Geshe Chekhawa was dying he developed the sincere wish to be reborn in hell in order to help hell beings directly, but he received clear visions that he would be reborn in Sukhavati, the Pure Land of Buddha Amitabha. He told his assistant, "Unfortunately my wish will not be fulfilled." The assistant asked him, "What is your wish?" and Geshe Chekhawa replied, "My wish is to take rebirth in hell so that I can help hell beings directly, but I have seen clear signs that I will be born in the Pure Land of Buddha

Amitabha." Although Geshe Chekhawa wanted to take rebirth in hell, his compassion for all living beings prevented him from taking a lower rebirth; he had no choice but to go to a Buddha's Pure Land where he experienced permanent liberation from suffering. However, although Geshe Chekhawa took rebirth in a Pure Land, he was able to help hell beings through his emanations.

We may think our belief that living beings have attained permanent liberation from suffering through our meditation is incorrect, because living beings have not actually attained this. Although it is true that living beings have not actually attained permanent liberation, our belief is still correct because it arises from our compassion and wisdom. Meditating on this belief will cause our potentiality of being able to liberate all living beings permanently from suffering to ripen quickly, so that we will attain enlightenment quickly. Therefore we should never abandon such a beneficial belief, which is the nature of wisdom. Meditation on taking is the quick path to enlightenment, and has a similar function to Tantric practice. It is said that Tantric realizations can be achieved simply by relying on correct belief and imagination. This practice is very simple; all we need to do is to become deeply familiar with meditation on correct belief and imagination as presented in Tantra, by applying continual effort.

TRAINING IN GIVING IN CONJUNCTION WITH THE PRACTICE OF THE SIX PERFECTIONS

Giving in this context means giving our own happiness to others through meditation. In general, in the cycle of impure life, samsara, there is no real happiness at all. As mentioned previously, the happiness that we normally experience through eating, drinking, sex, and so forth is not real happiness, but merely a reduction of a previous problem or dissatisfaction. For example, if the happiness we experience from sex is real happiness, then it would follow that sex itself would be a real cause of happiness. If this were true, then the more we had sex, the more our happiness would increase, but actually, the opposite would happen; instead of happiness increasing, our suffering would increase. In *Four Hundred Verses*, the Buddhist Master Aryadeva says:

> The experience of suffering will never be changed by the same cause,
> But we can see the experience of happiness will be changed by the same cause.

This means that, for example, the suffering caused by fire will never be changed into happiness by that fire, but we can see that the happiness caused, for example, by eating will change into suffering just through eating.

How do we meditate on giving? In *Guide to the Bodhisattva's Way of Life*, Shantideva says:

> . . . to accomplish the welfare of all living beings
> I will transform my body into an enlightened wishfulfilling jewel.

We should regard our continuously residing body, our very subtle body, as the real wishfulfilling jewel; this is our Buddha nature through which the wishes of ourself and all other living beings will be fulfilled. We then think:

All living beings wish to be happy all the time, but they do not know how to do this. They never experience real happiness, because out of ignorance they destroy their own happiness, by developing delusions such as anger and performing non-virtuous actions. It would be so wonderful if all these living beings experienced the pure and everlasting happiness of enlightenment! May they experience this happiness. I will now give my own future happiness of enlightenment to each and every living being.

Thinking in this way we imagine that from our continuously residing body at our heart we emanate infinite rays of light, which are in nature our future happiness of enlightenment. These reach all living beings of the six realms, and we strongly believe that each and every living being experiences the pure and everlasting happiness of enlightenment. We meditate on this belief single-pointedly for as long as possible. We should continually practice this meditation until we spontaneously believe that all living beings have actually received our future happiness of enlightenment now. Through this practice we are like a Bodhisattva who practices shepherd-like bodhichitta. Just as a shepherd wishes to provide protection and necessary conditions for his flock before he himself relaxes, a Bodhisattva who practices shepherd-like bodhichitta wishes to prepare protection and ultimate happiness for all beings before accomplishing it for himself.

This meditation has four main benefits: (1) it increases our wishing love for all living beings, (2) it ripens our potential ability to benefit all living beings, (3) it accumulates a great collection of merit, or good fortune, and (4) it causes our ordinary appearances and conceptions to cease.

Our future happiness of enlightenment is the result of our generating compassion for all living beings. The meditation on giving brings this future result into the path, and is therefore a quick path to enlightenment that has a similar function to Tantric practice. We should apply great effort to practice this meditation so that we can quickly make progress on the path to enlightenment.

When we are meditating on giving our motivation should be wishing love. By giving love in this way we are practicing the perfection of giving; by abandoning self-cherishing we are practicing the perfection of moral discipline; by willingly accepting any adverse conditions obstructing our practice of giving we are practicing the perfection of patience; by applying effort to practicing this meditation continually, free from laziness, we are practicing the perfection of effort; by concentrating single-pointedly on the meditation on giving, free from distraction, we are practicing the perfection of concentration; and by realizing that we ourself, all living beings, and their happiness all exist as mere names and do not inherently exist we are practicing the perfection of wisdom. This is how we should train in the meditation on giving in conjunction with practicing the six perfections.

By meditating on wishing love we receive immeasurable benefits in this life and in countless future lives.

Training in giving is a special meditation on wishing love that sincerely wishes all living beings to attain real happiness—the pure and everlasting happiness of liberation and enlightenment. As mentioned above, meditation on wishing love is also called *immeasurable love*, because just by meditating on wishing love we receive immeasurable benefits in this life and in countless future lives.

Arya Tara

Training in Ultimate Bodhichitta

When we meditate on emptiness to develop or increase ultimate bodhichitta, we are training in ultimate bodhichitta. Actual ultimate bodhichitta is a wisdom that directly realizes emptiness motivated by bodhichitta. It is called *ultimate bodhichitta* because its object is ultimate truth, emptiness, and it is one of the main paths to enlightenment. The bodhichitta that has been explained so far is conventional bodhichitta, and this is the nature of compassion, while ultimate bodhichitta is the nature of wisdom. These two bodhichittas are like the two wings of a bird with which we can fly to the enlightened world.

If we do not know the meaning of emptiness there is no basis for training in ultimate bodhichitta, because emptiness is the object of ultimate bodhichitta. Je Tsongkhapa said:

The knowledge of emptiness is superior to any other
      knowledge,
The Teacher who teaches emptiness unmistakenly is
      superior to any other teacher,
And the realization of emptiness is the very essence of
      Buddhadharma.

WHAT IS EMPTINESS?

Emptiness is the way things really are. It is the way things exist as opposed to the way they appear. We naturally believe that the things we see around us, such as tables, chairs, and houses are truly existent, because we believe that they exist in exactly the way that they appear. However, the way things appear to our senses is deceptive and completely contradictory to the way they actually exist. Things appear to exist from their own side, without depending on our mind. This book that appears to our mind, for example, seems to have its own independent, objective existence. It seems to be "outside" while our mind seems to be "inside." We feel that the book can exist without our mind; we do not feel that our mind is involved in any way in bringing the book into existence. This way of existing independent of our mind is variously called *true existence, inherent existence, existence from its own side,* and *existence from the side of the object.*

Although things appear directly to our senses to be truly, or inherently, existent, in reality all phenomena lack, or are empty of, true existence. This book, our body, our friends, we ourself, and the entire universe are in reality just appearances to mind, like things seen in a dream. If we dream of an elephant, the elephant appears vividly in all its detail—we can see it, hear it, smell it, and touch it—but when we wake up we realize that it was just an appearance to mind. We do not wonder, "Where is the elephant now?" because we understand that it was simply a projection of our mind and had no existence outside our mind. When the dream awareness that apprehended the elephant ceased, the elephant did not go anywhere—it simply disappeared, because it was just an appearance to the mind and did not exist separately from the mind. Buddha said that the same is true for all phenomena; they are mere appearances to mind, totally dependent on the minds that perceive them.

The world we experience when we are awake and the world we experience when we are dreaming are both mere appearances to mind that arise from our mistaken conceptions. If we want to say that the dream world is false, we also have to say that the waking world is false; and if we want to say that the waking world is true, we also have to say that the dream world is true. The only difference between them is that the dream world is an appearance to our

> *The knowledge of emptiness is superior to any other knowledge. Emptiness is the way things really are.*

subtle dreaming mind while the waking world is an appearance to our gross waking mind. The dream world exists only for as long as the dream awareness to which it appears exists, and the waking world exists only for as long as the waking awareness to which it appears exists. Buddha said, "You should know that all phenomena are like dreams." When we die, our gross waking minds dissolve into our very subtle mind and the world we experienced when we were alive simply disappears. The world as others perceive it will continue, but our personal world will disappear as completely and irrevocably as the world of last night's dream.

Buddha also said that all phenomena are like illusions. There are many different types of illusion, such as mirages, rainbows, or drug-induced hallucinations. In ancient times, there used to be magicians who would cast a spell over their audience, causing them to see objects, such as a piece of wood, as something else, such as a tiger. Those deceived by the spell would see what appeared to be a real tiger and develop fear, but those who arrived after the spell had been cast would simply see a piece of wood. What all illusions have in common is that the way they appear does not coincide with the way they exist. Buddha likened all phenomena to illusions, because through the force of the imprints of self-grasping ignorance accumulated since beginningless time, whatever appears to our mind naturally appears to be truly existent and we instinctively assent to this appearance, but in reality everything is totally empty of true existence. Like a mirage that appears to be water but is not actually water, things appear in a deceptive way. Not understanding their real nature we are fooled by appearances, and grasp at books and tables, bodies and worlds, as truly existent. The result of grasping at phenomena like this is that we develop self-cherishing, attachment, hatred, jealousy, and other delusions, our mind becomes agitated and unbalanced, and our peace of mind is destroyed. We are like travelers in a desert who exhaust themselves running after mirages, or like someone walking down a road at night mistaking the shadows of the trees for criminals or wild animals waiting to attack.

THE EMPTINESS OF OUR BODY

To understand how phenomena are empty of true, or inherent, existence we should consider our own body. Once we have understood how our body lacks true existence we can easily apply the same reasoning to other objects.

In *Guide to the Bodhisattva's Way of Life*, Bodhisattva Shanti-deva says:

Therefore, there is no body,
But, because of ignorance, we see a body within the
    hands and so forth,
Just like a mind mistakenly apprehending a person
When observing the shape of a pile of stones at dusk.

On one level we know our body very well—we know whether it is healthy or unhealthy, beautiful or ugly, and so forth. However, we never examine it more deeply, asking ourself, "What precisely is my body? Where is my body? What is its real nature?" If we did examine our body in this way we would not be able to find it—instead of finding our body the result of this examination would be that our body disappears. The meaning of the first part of Shantideva's verse, "Therefore, there is no body," is that if we search for our "real" body, there is no body; our body exists only if we do not search for a real body behind its mere appearance.

There are two ways of searching for an object. An example of the first way, which we can call a "conventional search," is searching for our car in a parking lot. The conclusion of this type of search is that we find the car, in the sense that we see the thing that everyone agrees is our car. However, having located our car in the parking lot, suppose we are still not satisfied with the mere appearance of the car and we want to determine exactly what the car is. We might then engage in what we can call an "ultimate search" for the car, in which we look within the object itself to find something that is the object. To do this we ask ourself, "Are any of the individual parts of the car, the car? Are the wheels the car? Is the engine the car? Is the chassis the car?" and so forth. When conducting an ultimate search for our car we are not satisfied with just pointing to the hood, wheels, and so forth, and then saying "car"; we want to know what the car really is. Instead of just using the word "car" as ordinary people do, we want to know what the word really refers to. We want to mentally separate the car from all that is not car, so that we can say, "This is what the car really is." We want to find a car, but in truth there is no car; we can find nothing. In *Condensed Perfection of Wisdom Sutra*, Buddha says, "If you search for your body with wisdom you cannot find it." This also applies to our car, our house, and all other phenomena.

In *Guide to the Bodhisattva's Way of Life*, Shantideva says:

When examined in this way,
Who is living and who is it who will die?
What is the future and what is the past?
Who are our friends and who are our relatives?

I beseech you who are just like me,
Please know that all things are empty, like space.

The essential meaning of these words is that when we search for things with wisdom, there is no person who is living or dying, there is no past or future, and there is no present, including our friends and relatives. We should know that all phenomena are empty, like space, which means we should know that all phenomena are not other than emptiness.

To understand Shantideva's claim that in reality there is no body, we need to conduct an ultimate search for our body. If we

Wed. Cash 5 Jkpt. $300,000; Wed.
Powerball Jkpt. $620 Mil.; Fri. Mega
Mil. Jkpt. $40 Mil.; Wed. Match 6
Jkpt. $4,200,000

POWERBALL jackpot tonight is $620
MILLION! Please play responsibly.

Term: 353370   aa7c0d3d
7232-000033759270-40-61   Oct 24, 2018 17:09

$12.00 - 1 Draw
Wed 24-Oct-2018
PowerPlay No

POWERBALL

A. 32 59 60 61 65   Powerball: 01 QP
B. 15 27 33 42 68   Powerball: 21 QP
C. 06 10 18 55 60   Powerball: 18 QP
D. 02 12 14 40 43   Powerball: 24 QP
E. 17 20 28 45 69   Powerball: 23 QP
F. 02 30 36 40 56   Powerball: 23 QP

NAME _____ PHONE _____

ADDRESS _____

CITY _____ STATE _____ ZIP _____

SIGNATURE _____

E-MAIL _____

Heat-sensitive paper – avoid prolonged exposure to heat or light.

Ticket valid only for drawing date(s) shown. Fast Play prizes expire one year from purchase date. Draw Game prizes expire one year from draw date. Void if torn, incomplete, illegible or altered. Not responsible for lost or stolen tickets. Winning claims subject to official rules & regulations of the Pennsylvania Lottery, 1200 Fulling Mill Road, Middletown, PA 17057.

PROBLEM GAMBLING HELP: 1-800-GAMBLER (1-800-426-2537)
PA Lottery Toll-Free: 1-800-692-7481

POD	RETAILER NUMBER	DATE PAID	GOLD 9
			02/04/17

71267713

PENNSYLVANIA LOTTERY - Benefits Older Pennsylvanians. Every Day.
DRAWING RESULTS: palottery.com or **1-877-282-4639**

NAME _____ PHONE _____

ADDRESS _____

CITY _____ STATE _____ ZIP _____

SIGNATURE _____

E-MAIL _____

Heat-sensitive paper – avoid prolonged exposure to heat or light.

Ticket valid only for drawing date(s) shown. Fast Play prizes expire one year from purchase date. Draw Game prizes expire one year from draw date. Void if torn, incomplete, illegible or altered. Not responsible for lost or stolen tickets. Winning claims subject to official rules & regulations of the Pennsylvania Lottery, 1200 Fulling Mill Road, Middletown, PA 17057.

PROBLEM GAMBLING HELP: 1-800-GAMBLER (1-800-426-2537)
PA Lottery Toll-Free: 1-800-692-7481

POD	RETAILER NUMBER	DATE PAID	GOLD 9
			02/04/17

71267714

PENNSYLVANIA LOTTERY - Benefits Older Pennsylvanians. Every Day.
DRAWING RESULTS: palottery.com or **1-877-282-4639**

NAME _____ PHONE _____

ADDRESS _____

CITY _____ STATE _____ ZIP _____

SIGNATURE _____

E-MAIL _____

are ordinary beings, all objects, including our body, appear to exist inherently. As mentioned above, objects seem to be independent of our mind and independent of other phenomena. The universe appears to consist of discrete objects that have an existence from their own side. These objects appear to exist in themselves as stars, planets, mountains, people, and so forth, "waiting" to be experienced by conscious beings. Normally it does not occur to us that we are involved in any way in the existence of these phenomena. For example, we feel that our body exists from its own side and does not depend on our mind, or anyone else's, to bring it into existence. However, if our body did exist in the way that we instinctively grasp it—as an external object rather than just a projection of mind—we should be able to point to our body without pointing to any phenomenon that is not our body. We should be able to find it among its parts or outside its parts. Since there is no third possibility, if our body cannot be found either among its parts or outside its parts we must conclude that our body that we normally see does not exist.

It is not difficult to understand that the individual parts of our body are not our body—it is absurd to say that our back, our legs, or our head are our body. If one of the parts, for example our back, is our body, then the other parts are equally our body, and it would follow that we have many bodies. Furthermore, our back, legs, and so forth cannot be our body because they are parts of our body. The body is the part-possessor, and the back, legs, and so forth are the possessed parts; and possessor and possessed cannot be one and the same.

Some people believe that although none of the individual parts of the body is the body, the collection of all the parts assembled together is the body. According to them, it is possible to find our body when we search for it analytically because the collection of all the parts of our body is our body. However, this assertion can be refuted with many valid reasons. The force of these reasons may not be immediately obvious to us, but if we contemplate them carefully with a calm and positive mind we will come to appreciate their validity.

Since none of the individual parts of our body is our body, how can the collection of all the parts be our body? For example, *Know that all things are empty, like space.* a collection of dogs cannot be a human being, because none of the individual dogs is human. Since each individual member is "non-human," how can this collection of non-humans magically transform into a human? Similarly, since the collection of the parts of our body is a collection of things that are not our body, it cannot be our body. Just as the collection of dogs remains simply dogs, so the collection of all the parts of our body remains simply parts of our body—it does not magically transform into the part-possessor, our body.

We may find this point difficult to understand, but if we think about it for a long time with a calm and positive mind, and discuss it with more experienced practitioners, it will gradually become clearer. We can also consult authentic books on the subject, such as *Heart of Wisdom* and *Ocean of Nectar*.

There is another way we can know that the collection of the parts of our body is not our body. If we can point to the collection of the parts of our body and say that this is, in itself, our body, then the collection of the parts of our body must exist independently of all phenomena that are not our body. Therefore it would follow that the collection of the parts of our body exists independently of the parts themselves. This is clearly absurd—if it were true, we could remove all the parts of our body and the collection of the parts would remain. We can therefore conclude that the collection of the parts of our body is not our body.

Since the body cannot be found within its parts, either as an individual part or as the collection, the only possibility that remains is that it exists separately from its parts. If this is the case, it should be possible mentally or physically to remove all the parts of our body and still be left with the body. However, if we remove our arms, our legs, our head, our trunk, and all the other parts of our body, no body is left. This proves that there is no body separate from its parts. It is because of ignorance that whenever we point to our body we are pointing only to a part of our body, which is not our body.

We have now searched in every possible place and have been unable to find our body either among its parts or anywhere else. We can find nothing that corresponds to the vividly appearing body that we normally grasp at. We are forced to agree with Shantideva that when we search for our body, there is no body to be found. This clearly proves that our body that we normally see does not exist. It is almost as if our body does not exist at all. In fact, the only sense in which we can say that our body does exist is if we are satisfied with the mere name "body" and do not expect to find a real body behind the name. If we try to find, or point to, a real body to which the name "body" refers, we will not find anything at all. Instead of finding a truly existent body, we will perceive the mere absence of our body that we normally see. This mere absence of our body that we normally see is the way our body actually exists. We will realize that the body we normally perceive, grasp at, and cherish does not exist at all. This non-existence of the body we normally grasp at is the emptiness of our body, the true nature of our body.

The term *true nature* is very meaningful. Not being satisfied with the mere appearance and name "body" we examined our body to discover its true nature. The result of this examination was a definite non-finding of our body. Where we expected to find a truly existent body, we discovered the utter non-existence of that truly existent body. This non-existence, or emptiness, is the true nature of our body. Aside from the mere absence of a truly existent body, there is no other true nature of our body—every other attribute of the body is just part of its deceptive nature. Since this is the case, why do we spend so much time focusing on the deceptive nature of our body? Right now we ignore the true nature of our body and other phenomena, and concentrate only on their deceptive nature. Yet the result of concentrating on deceptive objects all the time is that our mind becomes disturbed and we remain in the miserable life of samsara. If we wish to experience pure happiness, we must familiarize our mind with the truth. Instead of wasting our energy focusing only on meaningless, deceptive objects, we should focus on the true nature of things.

Although it is impossible to find our body when we search for it analytically, when we do not engage in analysis our body appears very clearly. Why is this? Shantideva says that because of ignorance we see our body within the hands and other parts of our body. In reality, our body does not exist within its parts. Just as at dusk we might see a pile of stones as a man even though there is no man within the stones, so in the same way our ignorant mind sees a body within the collection of arms, legs, and so forth, even though no body exists there. The body we see within the collection of arms and legs is simply a hallucination of our ignorant mind. Not recognizing it as such, however, we grasp at it very strongly, cherish it, and exhaust ourself trying to protect it from any discomfort.

The way to familiarize our mind with the true nature of the body is to use the above reasoning to search for our body, and then when we have searched in every possible place and not found it, to concentrate on the space-like emptiness that is the mere absence of the body that we normally see. This space-like emptiness is the true nature of our body. Although it resembles empty space, it is a meaningful emptiness. Its meaning is the utter non-existence of the body that we normally see, the body that we grasp at so strongly and have cherished all our life.

Through becoming familiar with the ultimate nature of the body, our physical tension will diminish and our health will improve.

Through becoming familiar with the experience of the space-like ultimate nature of the body, our grasping at our body will be reduced. As a result we will experience far less suffering, anxiety, and frustration in relation to our body. Our physical tension will diminish and our health will improve, and even when we do become sick our physical discomfort will not disturb our mind. Those who have a direct experience of emptiness do not feel any pain even if they are beaten or shot. Knowing that the real nature of their body is like space, for them being beaten is like space being beaten and being shot is like space being shot. In addition, good and bad external conditions no longer have the power to disturb their mind, because they realize these to be like a magician's illusion, with no existence separate from the mind.

Instead of being pulled here and there by changing conditions like a puppet on a string, their minds remain free and tranquil in the knowledge of the equal and unchanging ultimate nature of all things. In this way, a person who directly realizes emptiness, the true nature of phenomena, experiences peace and happiness day and night, life after life.

We need to distinguish between the conventionally existent body that does exist and the inherently existent body that does not exist; but we must be careful not to be misled by the words into thinking that the conventionally existent body is anything more than a mere appearance to mind. It may be less confusing to simply say that for a mind that directly sees the truth, or emptiness, there is no body. A body exists only for an ordinary mind to which a body appears.

Shantideva advises us that unless we wish to understand emptiness we should not examine conventional truths such as our body, possessions, places, and friends, but instead be satisfied with their mere names, as worldly people are. Once a worldly person knows an object's name and purpose, he is satisfied that he knows the object and does not investigate further. We must do the same, unless we want to meditate on emptiness. However, we should remember that if we did examine objects more closely we would not find them, because they would simply disappear, just like a mirage disappears if we try to look for it.

The same reasoning that we have used to prove the lack of true existence of our body can be applied to all other phenomena. This book, for example, seems to exist from its own side, somewhere within its parts. But when we examine the book more precisely we discover that none of the individual pages is the book and the collection of the pages is not the book either, yet without them there is no book. Instead of finding a truly existent book we are left beholding an emptiness that is the non-existence of the book we previously held to exist. Because of our ignorance the book appears to exist separately from our mind, as if our mind were inside and the book outside, but through analyzing the book we discover that this appearance is completely false. There is no book outside the mind. There is no book "out there," within the pages. The only way the book exists is as a mere appearance to mind, a mere projection of the mind.

This book appears to exist separately from our mind, as if our mind were inside and the book outside.

All phenomena exist by way of convention; nothing is inherently existent. This applies to mind, to Buddha, and even to emptiness itself. Everything is merely imputed by mind. All phenomena have parts—physical phenomena have physical parts, and non-physical phenomena have various parts, or attributes, that can be distinguished by thought. Using the same type of reasoning as above, we can realize that any phenomenon is not one of its parts, not the collection of its parts, and not separate from its parts. In this way we can realize the emptiness of all phenomena, the mere absence of all phenomena that we normally see or perceive.

It is especially helpful to meditate on the emptiness of objects that arouse strong delusions in us like attachment or anger. By analyzing correctly we will realize that the object we desire, or the object we dislike, does not exist from its own side. Its beauty or ugliness, and even its very existence, are imputed by mind. By thinking like this we will discover that there is no basis for attachment or anger.

THE EMPTINESS OF OUR MIND

In *Training the Mind in Seven Points*, after outlining how to engage in analytical meditation on the emptiness of inherent existence of outer phenomena such as our body, Geshe Chekhawa continues by saying that we should then analyze our own mind to understand how it lacks inherent existence.

Our mind is not an independent entity, but an ever-changing continuum that depends on many factors, such as its previous moments, its objects, and the inner energy winds that our minds are mounted on. Like everything else, our mind is imputed on a collection of many factors and therefore lacks inherent existence. A primary mind, or consciousness, for example, has five parts or *mental factors*: feeling, discrimination, intention, contact, and attention. Neither the individual mental factors nor the collection of these mental factors is the primary mind itself, because they are mental factors and therefore parts of the primary mind. However, there is no primary mind that is separate from these mental factors. A primary mind is merely imputed on the mental factors that are its basis of imputation, and therefore it does not exist from its own side.

Having identified the nature of our primary mind, which is an empty like space that perceives or understands objects, we then search for it within its parts—feeling, discrimination, intention, contact, and attention—until finally we realize its unfindability. This unfindability is its ultimate nature, or emptiness. We then think:

All phenomena that appear to my mind are the nature of my mind. My mind is the nature of emptiness.

In this way we feel that everything dissolves into emptiness. We perceive only the emptiness of all phenomena and we meditate on this emptiness. This way of meditating on emptiness is more profound than the meditation on the emptiness of our body. Gradually our experience of emptiness will become clearer and clearer until finally we gain an undefiled wisdom that directly realizes the emptiness of all phenomena.

THE EMPTINESS OF OUR I

The object we grasp at most strongly is our self or I. Due to the imprints of self-grasping ignorance accumulated over time without beginning, our I appears to us as inherently existent, and our self-grasping mind automatically grasps at it in this way. Although we grasp at an inherently existent I all the time, even during sleep, it is not easy to identify how it appears to our mind. To identify it clearly, we must begin by allowing it to manifest strongly by contemplating situations in which we have an exaggerated sense of I, such as when we are embarrassed, ashamed, afraid, or indignant. We recall or imagine such a situation and then, without any comment or analysis, try to gain a clear mental image of how the I naturally appears at such times. We have to be patient at this stage because it may take many sessions before we gain a clear image. Eventually we will see that the I appears to be completely solid and real, existing from its own side without depending on the body or the mind. This vividly appearing I is the inherently existent I that we cherish so strongly. It is the I that we defend when we are criticized and that we are so proud of when we are praised.

Once we have an image of how the I appears in these extreme circumstances, we should try to identify how it appears normally, in less extreme situations. For example, we can observe the I that is now reading this book and try to discover how it appears to our mind. Eventually we will see that although in this case there is not such an inflated sense of I, nevertheless the I still appears to be inherently existent, existing from its own side without depending on the body or the mind. Once we have an image of the inherently existent I, we focus on it for a while with single-pointed concentration. Then in meditation we proceed to the next stage, which is to contemplate valid reasons to prove that the inherently existent I we are grasping at does not actually exist. The inherently existent I and our self that we normally see are the same; we should know that neither exists, both are objects negated by emptiness.

If the I exists in the way that it appears, it must exist in one of four ways: as the body, as the mind, as the collection of the body and mind, or as something separate from the body and mind; there is no other possibility. We contemplate this carefully until we become convinced that this is the case and then we proceed to examine each of the four possibilities:

1. If our I is our body, there is no sense in saying "my body," because the possessor and the possessed are identical.

   If our I is our body, there is no future rebirth because the I ceases when the body dies.

   If our I and our body are identical, then since we are capable of developing faith, dreaming, solving mathematical puzzles, and so on, it follows that flesh, blood, and bones can do the same.

   Since none of this is true, it follows that our I is not our body.

2. If our I is our mind, there is no sense in saying "my mind," because the possessor and the possessed are identical; but usually when we focus on our mind we say "my mind." This clearly indicates that our I is not our mind.

   If our I is our mind, then since we have many types of mind, such as the six consciousnesses, conceptual minds, and non-conceptual minds, it follows that we have just as many I's. Since this is absurd, our I cannot be our mind.

3. Since our body is not our I and our mind is not our I, the collection of our body and mind cannot be our I. The collection of our body and mind is a collection of things that are not our I, so how can the collection itself be our I? For example, in a herd of cows none of the animals is a sheep, therefore the herd itself is not sheep. In the same way, in the collection of our body and mind, neither our body nor our mind is our I, therefore the collection itself is not our I.

4. If our I is not our body, not our mind, and not the collection of our body and mind, the only possibility that remains is that it is something separate from our body and mind. If this is the case, we must be able to apprehend our I without either our body or our mind appearing, but if we imagine that our body and our mind were to completely disappear nothing would remain that could be called our I. Therefore it follows that our I is not separate from our body and mind.

We should imagine that our body gradually dissolves into thin air, and then our mind dissolves, our thoughts scatter with the wind, our feelings, wishes, and awareness melt into nothingness. Is there anything left that is our I? There is nothing. Clearly our I is not something separate from our body and mind.

We have now examined all four possibilities and have failed to find our I or self. Since we have already decided that there is no fifth possibility, we must conclude that our I that we normally grasp at and cherish does not exist at all. Where there previously appeared an inherently existent I, there now appears an absence of that I. This absence of an inherently existent I is emptiness, ultimate truth.

We contemplate in this way until there appears to us a generic, or mental, image of the absence of our self that we normally see. This image is our object of placement meditation. We try to become completely familiar with it by meditating on it continually and single-pointedly for as long as possible.

Because we have grasped at our inherently existent I since beginningless time, and have cherished it more dearly than anything else, the experience of failing to find our self in meditation can be quite shocking at first. Some people develop fear, thinking, "I have become completely non-existent." Others feel great joy, as if the source of all their problems were vanishing. Both reactions are good signs and indicate correct meditation. After a while these initial reactions will subside and our mind will settle into a more balanced state. Then we will be able to meditate on the emptiness of our self in a calm, controlled manner.

We should allow our mind to become absorbed in space-like emptiness for as long as possible. It is important to remember that our object is emptiness, the mere absence of our self that we normally see, not mere nothingness. Occasionally we should check our meditation with alertness. If our mind has wandered to another object, or if we have lost the meaning of emptiness and are focusing on mere nothingness, we should return to the contemplations to bring the emptiness of our self clearly to mind once again.

We may wonder, "If my self that I normally see does not exist, then who is meditating? Who will get up from meditation, speak to others, and reply when my name is called?" Although our self that we normally see does not exist, this does not mean that our self does not exist at all. We exist as a mere imputation. As long as we are satisfied with the mere imputation of our "self," there is no problem. We can think, "I exist," "I am going to town," and so on. The problem arises only when we look for our self other than the mere conceptual imputation "I," our "self." Our mind grasps at an I that ultimately exists, in-

Although our self that we normally see does not exist, this does not mean that our self does not exist at all.

dependently of conceptual imputation, as if there were a "real" I existing behind the label. If such an I existed, we would be able to find it, but we have seen that our I cannot be found on investigation. The conclusion of our search was a definite non-finding of our self. This unfindability of our self is the emptiness of our self, the ultimate nature of our self. Our self that exists as mere imputation is the conventional nature of our self.

When we first realize emptiness we do so conceptually, by means of a generic image. By continuing to meditate on emptiness over and over again, the generic image gradually becomes more and more transparent until it disappears entirely and we see emptiness directly. This direct realization of emptiness will be our first completely non-mistaken awareness, or undefiled mind. Until we realize emptiness directly, all our minds are mistaken awarenesses, because due to the imprints of self-grasping or true-grasping ignorance, their objects appear as inherently existent.

Most people veer toward the extreme of existence, thinking that if something exists it must exist inherently, thus exaggerating the way things exist without being satisfied with them as mere name. Others may veer toward the extreme of non-existence, thinking that if phenomena do not exist inherently they do not exist at all, thus exaggerating their lack of inherent existence. We need to realize that although phenomena lack any trace of existence from their own side, they do exist conventionally as mere appearances to a valid mind.

The conceptual minds grasping at our I and other phenomena as being truly existent are wrong awarenesses and should therefore be abandoned, but I am not saying that all conceptual thoughts are wrong awarenesses and should therefore be abandoned. There are many correct conceptual minds that are useful in our day-to-day lives, such as the conceptual mind remembering what we did yesterday or the conceptual mind understanding what we will do tomorrow. There are also many conceptual minds that need to be cultivated on the spiritual path. For example, conventional bodhichitta in the mental continuum of a Bodhisattva is a conceptual mind because it apprehends its object, great enlightenment, by means of a generic image. In addition, before we can realize emptiness directly with a non-conceptual mind, we need to realize it by means of an inferential cognizer, which is a conceptual mind. Through contemplating the reasons that refute inherent existence, there appears to our mind a generic image of the absence, or emptiness, of inherent existence. This is the only way that emptiness of inherent existence can initially appear to our mind. We then meditate on this image with stronger and stronger concentration until we finally perceive emptiness directly.

Where do all our good and bad experiences come from?

There are some people who say that the way to meditate on emptiness is simply to empty our mind of all conceptual thoughts, arguing that just as white clouds obscure the sun as much as black clouds, so positive conceptual thoughts obscure our mind as much as negative conceptual thoughts. This view is completely mistaken, because if we make no effort to gain a conceptual understanding of emptiness, but try instead to suppress all conceptual thoughts, actual emptiness will never appear to our mind. We may achieve a vivid experience of a space-like vacuity, but this is just the absence of conceptual thought—it is not emptiness, the true nature of phenomena. Meditation on this vacuity may temporarily calm our mind, but it will never destroy our delusions or liberate us from samsara and its sufferings.

THE EMPTINESS OF THE EIGHT EXTREMES

If all the necessary atmospheric causes and conditions come together, clouds will appear. If these are absent, clouds cannot form. The clouds are completely dependent on causes and conditions for their development; without these they have no power to develop.

The same is true for mountains, planets, bodies, minds, and all other produced phenomena. Because they depend on factors outside themselves for their existence, they are empty of inherent, or independent, existence and are mere imputations of the mind.

Contemplating the teachings on karma, actions and their effects, can help us understand this. Where do all our good and bad experiences come from? According to Buddhism they are the result of the positive and negative karma we created in the past. As a result of positive karma, attractive and agreeable people appear in our life, pleasant material conditions arise, and we live in a beautiful environment. But as a result of negative karma, unpleasant people and things appear. This world is the effect of the collective karma created by the beings who inhabit it. Because karma originates in the mind—specifically in our mental intentions—we can see that all worlds arise from the mind. This is similar to the way appearances arise in a dream. Everything we perceive when we are dreaming is the result of the ripening of karmic potentials in our mind and has no existence outside our mind. When our mind is calm and pure, positive karmic imprints ripen and pleasant dream appearances arise. But when our mind is agitated and impure, negative karmic imprints ripen and unpleasant, nightmarish appearances arise. In a similar way, all the appearances of our waking world are simply the ripening of positive, negative, or neutral karmic imprints in our mind.

Once we understand how things arise from their inner and outer causes and conditions and have no independent existence, then just seeing or thinking about the production of phenomena will remind us of their emptiness. Instead of reinforcing our sense of the solidity and objectivity of things, we will begin to see things as manifestations of their emptiness, with no more concrete existence than a rainbow arising out of an empty sky.

Just as the production of things depends on causes and conditions, so too does the disintegration of things. Therefore, neither production nor disintegration can be truly existent. For example, if our new car were destroyed we would feel unhappy because we grasp at both the car and the disintegration of the car as truly existent. But if we understood that our car is merely an appearance to our mind, like a car in a dream, its destruction would not disturb us. This is true for all objects of our attachment: if we realize that both objects and their cessations lack true existence, there is no basis for becoming upset if we are separated from them.

All functioning things—our environments, enjoyments, body, mind, and our self—change from moment to moment. They are impermanent in the sense that they do not last for a second moment. The book you are reading in this moment is not the same book you were reading a moment ago, and it could only come into existence because the book of a moment ago ceased to exist. When we understand subtle impermanence—that our body, our mind, our self, and so forth do not abide for a second moment—it is not difficult to understand that they are empty of inherent existence.

Even though we may agree that impermanent phenomena are empty of inherent existence, we might think that because permanent phenomena are unchanging and do not arise from causes and conditions, they must exist inherently. However, even permanent phenomena such as emptiness and unproduced space—the mere absence of physical obstruction—are dependent-related phenomena because they depend on their parts, their bases, and the minds that impute them; and therefore they are not inherently existent.

Although emptiness is ultimate reality, it is not independent or inherently existent because it too depends on its parts, its bases, and the minds that impute it. Just as a gold coin does not exist separately from its gold, so the emptiness of our body does not exist separately from our body, because it is simply our body's lack of inherent existence.

Whenever we go anywhere we develop the thought, "I am going," and grasp at an inherently existent act of going. In a similar way, when someone comes to visit us we think, "They are coming," and we grasp at an inherently existent act of coming. Both these conceptions are self-grasping and wrong awarenesses. When someone goes away we feel that a truly existent person has truly left, and when they come back we feel that a truly existent person has truly returned. However, the coming and going of people is like the appearance and disappearance of a rainbow in the sky. When the causes and conditions for a rainbow to appear are assembled, a rainbow appears; and when the causes and conditions for the continued appearance of the rainbow disperse, the rainbow disappears. But the rainbow does not come from anywhere, nor does it go anywhere.

When we observe one object, such as our I, we feel strongly that it is a single, indivisible entity, and that its singularity is inherently existent. In reality, however, our I has many parts, such as the parts that look, listen, walk, and think, or the parts that are, for example, a teacher, a mother, a daughter, and a wife. Our I is imputed on the collection of all these parts. As with each individual phenomenon it is a singularity, but its singularity is merely imputed, like an army that is merely imputed on a collection of soldiers or a forest that is imputed on a collection of trees.

When we see more than one object, we regard the multiplicity of these objects to be inherently existent. However, just as singularity is merely imputed, likewise plurality is just an imputation by mind and does not exist from the side of the object. For example, instead of looking at a collection of soldiers or trees from the point of view of the individual soldiers or trees, we could look at them as an army or a forest, that is, as a singular collection or whole, in which case we would be looking at a singularity rather than a plurality.

In summary, singularity does not exist from its own side because it is just imputed on a plurality—its parts. In the same way, plurality does not exist from its own side because it is just imputed on a singularity—the collection of its parts. Therefore singularity and plurality are mere imputations by conceptual mind and they lack true existence. If we realize this clearly, there is no basis for developing attachment and anger toward objects, either singular or plural. We tend to project the faults or qualities of the few onto the many, and then develop hatred or attachment on the basis of, for example, race, religion, or country. Contemplating the emptiness of singularity and plurality can be helpful in reducing such hatred and attachment.

Although production, disintegration, and so forth do exist, they do not exist inherently. It is our conceptual minds of self-grasping ignorance that grasp them as inherently existent. These conceptions grasp at the eight extremes: inherently existent production, inherently existent disintegration, inherently existent impermanence, inherently existent permanence, inherently existent going, inherently existent coming, inherently existent singularity, and inherently existent plurality. Although these extremes do not exist, due to our ignorance we are always grasping them. The conceptions of these extremes lie at the root of all other delusions, and because delusions give rise to our performing contaminated actions that keep us trapped in the prison of samsara, these conceptions are the root of samsara, the cycle of impure life.

Inherently existent production is the same as the production that we normally see, and we should know that in reality neither of these exists. This is the same for the remaining seven extremes. For example, inherently existent disintegration and destruction and the disintegration and destruction that we normally see are the same, and we should know that neither of these exists. Our minds that grasp at these eight extremes are different aspects of our self-grasping ignorance. Because it is our self-grasping ignorance that causes us to experience endless suffering and problems, when this ignorance ceases permanently through meditation on the emptiness of all phenomena, all our suffering of this life and countless future lives will cease permanently and we will accomplish the real meaning of human life.

The subject of the eight extremes is profound and requires detailed explanation and lengthy study. Buddha explains them in detail in the *Perfection of Wisdom Sutras*. And in *Fundamental Wisdom*, a commentary to the *Perfection of Wisdom Sutras*, Nagarjuna also uses many profound and powerful reasons to prove that the eight extremes do not exist by showing how all phenomena are empty of inherent existence. Through analyzing conventional truths he establishes their ultimate nature, and shows why it is necessary to understand both the conventional and ultimate natures of an object in order to understand that object fully.

CONVENTIONAL AND ULTIMATE TRUTHS

Whatever exists is either a conventional truth or an ultimate truth, and since ultimate truth refers just to emptiness, everything except emptiness is a conventional truth. For example, things such as houses, cars and tables are all conventional truths.

All conventional truths are false objects because the way they appear and the way they exist do not correspond. If someone seems friendly and kind but his real intention is to gain our confidence in order to rob us, we would say that he is false or deceptive because there is a discrepancy between the way he appears and his real nature. Similarly, objects such as forms and sounds are false or deceptive because they appear to exist inherently but in reality are completely devoid of inherent existence. Because the way they appear does not coincide with the way they exist, conventional truths are known as *deceptive phenomena*. A cup, for instance, appears to exist independently of its parts, its causes, and the mind that apprehends it, but in reality it totally depends on these things. Because the way the cup appears to our mind and the way it exists do not correspond, the cup is a false object.

Although conventional truths are false objects, nevertheless they actually exist because a mind directly perceiving a conventional truth is a valid mind, a completely reliable mind. For example, an eye consciousness directly perceiving a cup on the table is a valid mind because it will not deceive us—if we reach out to pick up the cup we will find it where our eye consciousness sees it. In this respect, an eye consciousness perceiving a cup on the table is different from an eye consciousness mistaking a cup reflected in a mirror for a real cup, or an eye consciousness seeing a mirage as water. Even though a cup is a false object, for practical purposes the eye consciousness that directly perceives it is a valid, reliable mind. However, although it is a valid mind it is nevertheless a mistaken awareness because the cup appears to that mind to be truly existent. It is valid and non-deceptive with respect to the conventional characteristics of the cup—its position, size, color, and so forth—but mistaken with respect to its appearance.

To summarize, conventional objects are false, because although they appear to exist from their own side, in reality they are mere appearances to mind, like things seen in a dream. Within the context of a dream, however, dream objects have a relative validity, and this distinguishes them from things that do not exist at all. Suppose in a dream we steal a diamond and someone then asks us whether we were the one who stole it. Even though the dream is merely a creation of our mind, if we answer "yes" we are telling the truth while if we answer "no" we are telling a lie. In the same way, even though in reality the whole universe is just an appearance to mind, within the context of the experience of ordinary beings we can distinguish between relative truths and relative falsities.

Conventional truths can be divided into gross conventional truths and subtle conventional truths. We can understand how all phenomena have these two levels of conventional truth by considering the example of a car. The car itself, the car depending on its causes, and the car depending on its parts are all gross conventional truths of the car. They are called "gross" because they are relatively easy to understand. The car depending on its basis of imputation is quite subtle and is not easy to understand, but it is still a gross conventional truth. The basis of imputation of the car is the parts of the car. To apprehend car, the parts of the car must appear to our mind; without the parts appearing, there is no way to develop the thought "car." For this reason, the parts are the basis of imputation of the car. We say, "I see a car," but strictly speaking all we ever see is parts of the car. However, when we develop the thought "car" by seeing its parts, we see the car. There is no car other than its parts, there is no body other than its parts, and so on. The car existing merely as an im-

Emptiness is not a separate reality existing behind conventional appearances, but is the real nature of those appearances.

putation by thought is the subtle conventional truth of the car. We have understood this when we realize that the car is nothing more than a mere imputation by a valid mind. We cannot understand subtle conventional truths unless we have understood emptiness. When we thoroughly realize subtle conventional truth we have realized both conventional truth and ultimate truth.

Strictly speaking, truth, ultimate truth, and emptiness are synonymous because conventional truths are not real truths but false objects. They are true only for the minds of those who have not realized emptiness. Only emptiness is true because only emptiness exists in the way that it appears. When the mind of any living being directly perceives conventional truths, such as forms, they appear to exist from their own side. When the mind of a Superior being directly perceives emptiness, however, nothing appears other than emptiness; this mind is totally mixed with the mere absence of inherently existent phenomena. The way emptiness appears to the mind of a non-conceptual direct perceiver corresponds exactly to the way emptiness exists.

It should be noted that although emptiness is ultimate truth it is not inherently existent. Emptiness is not a separate reality existing behind conventional appearances, but is the real nature of those appearances. We cannot talk about emptiness in isolation, because emptiness is always the mere lack of inherent existence of something. For example, the emptiness of our body is the lack of inherent existence of our body, and without our body as its basis this emptiness cannot exist. Because emptiness necessarily depends on a basis, it lacks inherent existence.

In *Guide to the Bodhisattva's Way of Life*, Shantideva defines ultimate truth as a phenomenon that is true for the uncontaminated mind of a Superior being. An uncontaminated mind is a mind that realizes emptiness directly. This mind is the only unmistaken awareness and is possessed exclusively by Superior beings. Because uncontaminated minds are completely unmistaken, anything directly perceived by them to be true is necessarily an ultimate truth. In contrast, anything that is directly perceived to be true by the mind of an ordinary being is necessarily not an ultimate truth, because all minds of ordinary beings are mistaken, and mistaken minds can never directly perceive the truth.

Due to the imprints of conceptual thoughts that grasp at the eight extremes, everything that appears to the minds of ordinary beings appears to be inherently existent. Only the wisdom of meditative equipoise that directly realizes emptiness is undefiled by the imprints, or stains, of these conceptual thoughts. This is the only wisdom that has no mistaken appearance.

When a Superior Bodhisattva meditates on emptiness, his or her mind mixes with emptiness completely, with no appearance of inherent existence. He develops a completely pure, uncontaminated wisdom that is ultimate bodhichitta. When he arises from meditative equipoise, however, due to the imprints of true-grasping, conventional phenomena again appear to his mind as inherently existent, and his uncontaminated wisdom becomes temporarily non-manifest. Only a Buddha can manifest uncontaminated wisdom at the same time as directly perceiving conventional truths. An uncommon quality of a Buddha is that a single moment of a Buddha's mind realizes both conventional truth and ultimate truth directly and simultaneously. There are many levels of ultimate bodhichitta. For example, the ultimate bodhichitta attained through Tantric practice is more profound than that developed through Sutra practice alone, and the supreme ultimate bodhichitta is that of a Buddha.

If through valid reasoning we realize the emptiness of the first extreme, the extreme of production, we will easily be able to realize the emptiness of the remaining seven extremes. Once we have realized the emptiness of the eight extremes we have realized the emptiness of all phenomena. Having gained this realization, we continue to contemplate and meditate on the emptiness of produced phenomena and so forth, and as our meditations deepen we will feel all phenomena dissolving into emptiness. We will then be able to maintain a single-pointed concentration on the emptiness of all phenomena.

To meditate on the emptiness of produced phenomena we can think:

My self who was born, through causes and conditions, as a human being is unfindable when I search for it with wisdom within my body and my mind, or separate from my body and mind. This proves that my self that I normally see does not exist at all.

Having contemplated in this way, we feel our self that we normally see disappears and we perceive a space-like emptiness that is the mere absence of our self that we normally see. We feel that our mind enters into this space-like emptiness and remains there single-pointedly. This meditation is called *space-like meditative equipoise on emptiness*.

Just as eagles soar through the vast expanse of the sky without meeting any obstructions, needing only minimal effort to maintain their flight, so advanced meditators concentrating on emptiness can meditate on emptiness for a long time with little effort. Their minds soar through space-like emptiness, undistracted by any other phenomenon. When we meditate on emptiness we should try to emulate these meditators. Once we have found our object of meditation, the mere absence of our self that we normally see, we should refrain from further analysis and simply rest our mind in the experience of this emptiness. From time to time we should check to make sure that we have not lost either the clear appearance of emptiness or the recognition of its meaning, but we should not check too forcefully because this will disturb our concentration. Our meditation should not be like the flight of a small bird, which never stops flapping its wings and is always changing direction, but like the flight of an eagle, which soars gently with only occasional adjustments to its wings. Through meditating in this way we will feel our mind dissolving into and becoming one with emptiness.

If we are successful in doing this, then during our meditation we are free from manifest self-grasping. If on the other hand, we spend all our time checking and analyzing, never allowing our mind to relax into the space of emptiness, we will never gain this experience and our meditation will not function to reduce our self-grasping.

In general we need to improve our understanding of emptiness through extensive study, approaching it from many angles and using many different lines of reasoning. It is also important to become thoroughly familiar with one complete meditation on emptiness through continuous contemplation, understanding exactly how to use the reasoning to lead to an experience of emptiness. We can then concentrate on emptiness single-pointedly and try to mix our mind with it, like water mixing with water.

THE UNION OF THE TWO TRUTHS

The union of the two truths means that conventional truths, such as our body, and ultimate truths, such as the emptiness of our body, are the same nature. When something such as our body appears to us, both the body and the inherently existent body appear simultaneously. This is dualistic appearance, which is subtle mistaken appearance. Only Buddhas are free from such mistaken appearances. The main purpose of understanding and meditating on the union of the two truths is to prevent dualistic appearances—appearances of inherent existence to the mind that is meditating on emptiness—and thereby enable our mind to dissolve into emptiness. Once we can do this, our meditation on emptiness will be very powerful in eliminating our delusions. If we correctly identify and negate the inherently existent body, the body that we normally see, and meditate on the mere absence of such a body with strong concentration, we will feel our normal body dissolving into emptiness. We will understand that the real nature of our body is emptiness and that our body is merely a manifestation of emptiness.

Emptiness is like the sky and our body is like the blue of the sky. Just as the blue is a manifestation of the sky itself and cannot be separated from it, so our blue-like body is simply a manifestation of the sky of its emptiness and cannot be separated from it. If we realize this, when we focus on the emptiness of our body we feel that our body itself dissolves into its ultimate nature. In this way, we can easily overcome the conventional appearance of the body in our meditations, and our mind naturally mixes with emptiness.

In the *Heart Sutra*, Bodhisattva Avalokiteshvara says, "Form is not other than emptiness." This means that conventional phenomena, such as our body, do not exist separately from their emptiness. When we meditate on the emptiness of our body with this understanding, we know that the emptiness appearing to our mind is the very nature of our body, and that apart from this emptiness there is no body. Meditating in this way will greatly weaken our self-grasping mind. If we really believed that our body and its emptiness were the same nature, our self-grasping would definitely become weaker.

Although we can divide emptinesses from the point of view of their bases, and speak of the emptiness of the body, the emptiness of the I, and so forth, in truth all emptinesses are the same nature. If we look at ten bottles, we can distinguish ten different spaces inside the bottles, but in reality these spaces are the same nature; and if we break the bottles the spaces become indistinguishable. In the same way, although we can speak of the emptiness of the body, the mind, the I, and so forth, in reality they are the same nature and indistinguishable. The only way they can be distinguished is by their conventional bases.

There are two principal benefits of understanding that all emptinesses are the same nature: in the meditation session our mind will mix with emptiness more easily, and in the meditation break we will be able to see all appearances as equal manifestations of their emptiness.

For as long as we feel that there is a gap between our mind and emptiness—that our mind is "here" and emptiness is "there"—our mind will not mix with emptiness. Knowing that all emptinesses are the same nature helps close this gap. In ordinary life we experience many different objects—good, bad, attractive, unattractive—and our feelings toward them differ. Because we feel that the differences exist from the side of the objects, our mind is unbalanced and we develop attachment to attractive objects, aversion to unattractive objects, and indifference to neutral objects. It is very difficult to mix such an uneven mind with emptiness. To mix our mind with empti-

In emptiness, everything becomes very peaceful and comfortable, balanced and harmonious, joyful and wonderful.

ness we need to know that, although phenomena appear in many different aspects, in essence they are all empty. The differences we see are just appearances to mistaken minds; from the point of view of ultimate truth all phenomena are equal in emptiness. For a qualified meditator single-pointedly absorbed in emptiness, there is no difference between production and disintegration, impermanence and permanence, going and coming, singularity and plurality—everything is equal in emptiness and all problems of attachment, anger, and self-grasping ignorance are solved. In this experience, everything becomes very peaceful and comfortable, balanced and harmonious, joyful and wonderful. There is no heat, no cold, no lower, no higher, no here, no there, no self, no other, no samsara—everything is equal in the peace of emptiness. This realization is called the *yoga of equalizing samsara and nirvana*, and is explained in detail in both the Sutras and Tantras.

Since all emptinesses are the same nature, the ultimate nature of a mind that is meditating on emptiness is the same nature as the ultimate nature of its object. When we first meditate on emptiness our mind and emptiness appear to be two separate phenomena, but when we understand that all emptinesses are the same nature we will know that this feeling of separation is simply the experience of a mistaken mind. In reality our mind and emptiness are ultimately of one taste. If we apply this knowledge in our meditations, it will help prevent the appearance of the conventional nature of our mind and allow our mind to dissolve into emptiness.

Having mixed our mind with emptiness, when we arise from meditation we will experience all phenomena equally as manifestations of their emptiness. Instead of feeling that the attractive, unattractive and neutral objects we see are inherently different, we will know that in essence they are the same nature. Just as both the gentlest and most violent waves in an ocean are equally water, likewise both attractive forms and repulsive forms are equally manifestations of emptiness. Realizing this, our mind will become balanced and peaceful. We will recognize all conventional appearances as the magical play of the mind, and we will not grasp strongly at their apparent differences.

When Milarepa once taught emptiness to a woman, he compared emptiness to the sky and conventional truths to clouds and told her to meditate on the sky. She followed his instructions with great success, but she had one problem—when she meditated on the sky of emptiness everything disappeared, and she could not understand how phenomena could exist conventionally. She said to Milarepa, "I find it easy to meditate on the sky but difficult to establish the clouds. Please teach me how to meditate on the clouds." Milarepa replied, "If your meditation on the sky is going well, the clouds will not be a problem. Clouds simply appear in the sky—they arise from the sky and dissolve back into the sky. As your experience of the sky improves, you will naturally come to understand the clouds."

In Tibetan, the word for both sky and space is *namkha*, although space is different from sky. There are two types of space, produced space and unproduced space. Produced space is the visible space we can see inside a room or in the sky. This space may become dark at night and light during the day, and because it undergoes change in this way it is an impermanent phenomenon. The characteristic property of produced space is that it does not obstruct objects—if there is space in a room we can place objects there without obstruction. Similarly, birds are able to fly through the space of the sky because it lacks obstruction, but they cannot fly through a mountain! Therefore it is clear that produced space lacks, or is empty of, obstructive contact. This mere lack, or emptiness, of obstructive contact is unproduced space.

Because unproduced space is the mere absence of obstructive contact, it does not undergo momentary change and is therefore a permanent phenomenon. While produced space is visible and quite easy to understand, unproduced space is a mere absence of obstructive contact and is much more subtle. However, once we understand unproduced space we will find it easier to understand emptiness.

The only difference between emptiness and unproduced space is their object of negation. The object of negation of unproduced space is obstructive contact while the object of negation of emptiness is inherent existence. Because unproduced space is the best analogy for understanding emptiness, it is used in the Sutras and in many scriptures. Unproduced space is a non-affirming negative phenomenon—a phenomenon that is realized by a mind that merely eliminates its negated object without realizing another positive phenomenon. Produced space is an affirmative, or positive, phenomenon—a phenomenon that is realized without the mind explicitly eliminating a negated object. More details on these two types of phenomenon can be found in *Heart of Wisdom* and *Ocean of Nectar*.

THE PRACTICE OF EMPTINESS IN OUR DAILY ACTIVITIES

In our daily activities, we should believe that all appearances are illusory. Although things appear to us as inherently existent we should remember that these appearances are deceptive and that in reality the things that we normally see do not exist. As mentioned earlier, in *King of Concentration Sutra*, Buddha says:

A magician creates various things
Such as horses, elephants and so forth.
His creations do not actually exist;
You should know all things in the same way.

The last two lines of this verse mean that just as we know that the horses and elephants created by the magician do not exist, in the same way we should know that all the things that we normally see do not actually exist. This chapter "Training in Ultimate Bodhichitta" has extensively explained how all the things that we normally see do not exist.

When a magician creates an illusory horse, a horse appears very clearly to his mind but he knows that it is just an illusion. In fact, the very appearance of the horse reminds him that there is no horse in front of him. In the same way, when we are very familiar with emptiness, the very fact that things appear to be inherently existent will remind us that they are not inherently existent. We should therefore recognize that whatever appears to us in our daily life is like an illusion and lacks inherent existence. In this way our wisdom will increase day by day, and our self-grasping ignorance and other delusions will naturally diminish.

Between meditation sessions we should be like an actor. When an actor plays the part of a king, he dresses, speaks, and acts like a king, but he knows all the time that he is not a real king. In the same way we should live and function in the conventional world but always remember that we ourself, our environment, and the people around us that we normally see do not exist at all.

If we think like this we will be able to live in the conventional world without grasping at it. We will treat it lightly and have the flexibility of mind to respond to every situation in a constructive way. Knowing that whatever appears to our mind is mere appearance, when attractive objects appear we will not grasp at them and develop attachment, and when unattractive objects appear we will not grasp at them and develop aversion or anger.

In *Training the Mind in Seven Points*, Geshe Chekhawa says, "Think that all phenomena are like dreams." Some of the things we see in our dreams are beautiful and some are ugly, but they are all mere appearances to our dreaming mind. They do not exist from their own side, and are empty of inherent existence. It is the same with the objects we perceive when we are awake—they too are mere appearances to mind and lack inherent existence.

All phenomena lack inherent existence. When we look at a rainbow it appears to occupy a particular location in space, and it seems that if we searched we would be able to find where the rainbow touches the ground. However, we know that no matter how hard we search we will never be able to find the end of the rainbow, because as soon as we arrive at the place where we saw the rainbow touch the ground, the rainbow will have disappeared. If we do not search for it, the rainbow appears clearly; but when we look for it, it is not there. All phenomena are like this. If we do not analyze them they appear clearly, but when we search for them analytically, trying to isolate them from everything else, they are not there.

We should be like an actor. We will have the flexibility of mind to respond to every situation in a constructive way.

If something did exist inherently, and we investigated it by separating it from all other phenomena, we would be able to find it. However, all phenomena are like rainbows—if we search for them we will never find them. At first we might find this idea very uncomfortable and difficult to accept, but this is quite natural. With greater familiarity we will find this reasoning more acceptable, and eventually we will realize that it is true.

It is important to understand that emptiness does not mean nothingness. Although things do not exist from their own side, independent of the mind, they do exist in the sense that they are understood by a valid mind. The world we experience when we are awake is similar to the world we experience when we are dreaming. We cannot say that dream things do not exist, but if we believe that they exist as more than mere appearances to the mind, existing "out there," then we are mistaken, as we will discover when we wake up.

As mentioned before, there is no greater method for experiencing peace of mind and happiness than to understand and meditate on emptiness. Since it is our self-grasping that keeps us bound to the prison of samsara and is the source of all our suffering, meditation on emptiness is the universal solution to all our problems. It is the medicine that cures all mental and physical diseases, and the nectar that bestows the everlasting happiness of nirvana and enlightenment.

A SIMPLE TRAINING IN ULTIMATE BODHICHITTA

We begin by thinking:

I must attain enlightenment to benefit each and every living being directly every day. For this purpose I will attain a direct realization of the way things really are.

With this bodhichitta motivation, we contemplate:

Normally I see my body within its parts—the hands, back, and so forth—but neither the individual parts nor the collection of the parts are my body because they are the parts of my body and not the body itself. However, there is no "my body" other than its parts. Through searching with wisdom for my body in this way, I realize that my body is unfindable. This is a valid reason to prove that my body that I normally see does not exist at all.

Through contemplating this point we try to perceive the mere absence of the body that we normally see. This mere absence of the body that we normally see is the emptiness of our body, and we meditate on this emptiness single-pointedly for as long as possible.

We should continually practice this contemplation and meditation, and then move to the next stage, meditation on the emptiness of our self. We should contemplate and think:

Normally I see my self within my body and mind, but neither my body, nor my mind, nor the collection of my body and mind are my self, because these are my possessions and my self is the possessor; and possessor and possessions cannot be the same. However, there is no "my self" other than my body and mind. Through searching with wisdom for my self in this way, I realize that my self is unfindable. This is a valid reason to prove that my self that I normally see does not exist at all.

Through contemplating this point we try to perceive the mere absence of our self that we normally see. This mere absence of our self that we normally see is the emptiness of our self, and we meditate on this emptiness single-pointedly for as long as possible.

We should continually practice this contemplation and meditation, and then move to the next stage, meditation on the emptiness of all phenomena. We should contemplate and think:

Just like my body and my self, all other phenomena are unfindable when I search for them with wisdom. This is a valid reason to prove that all phenomena that I normally see or perceive do not exist at all.

Through contemplating this point we try to perceive the mere absence of all phenomena that we normally see or perceive. This mere absence of all phenomena that we normally see or perceive is the emptiness of all phenomena. We meditate continually on this emptiness of all phenomena with bodhichitta motivation until we are able to maintain our concentration clearly for one minute every time we meditate on it. Our concentration that has this ability is called the *concentration of placing the mind.*

In the second stage, with the concentration of placing the mind, we meditate continually on the emptiness of all phenomena until we are able to maintain our concentration clearly for five minutes every time we meditate on it. Our concentration that has this ability is called the *concentration of continual placement.* In the third stage, with the concentration of continual placement, we meditate continually on the emptiness of all phenomena until we are able to immediately remember our object of meditation—the mere absence of all phenomena that we normally see or perceive—whenever we lose it during meditation. Our concentration that has this ability is called the *concentration of replacement.* In the fourth stage, with the concentration of replacement, we meditate continually on the emptiness of all phenomena until we are able to maintain our concentration clearly during the entire meditation session without forgetting the object of meditation. Our concentration that has this ability is called the *concentration of close placement.* At this stage we have very stable and clear concentration focused on the emptiness of all phenomena.

Then, with the concentration of close placement, we meditate continually on the emptiness of all phenomena until finally we

We need to rely on our Spiritual Guide until we attain enlightenment.

attain the concentration of tranquil abiding focused on emptiness, which causes us to experience special physical and mental
suppleness and bliss. With this concentration of tranquil abiding
we will develop a special wisdom that realizes the emptiness of
all phenomena very clearly. This wisdom is called *superior seeing*.
Through continually meditating on the concentration of tranquil
abiding associated with superior seeing, our wisdom of superior
seeing will transform into the wisdom that directly realizes the
emptiness of all phenomena. This direct realization of emptiness
is the actual ultimate bodhichitta. The moment we attain the wisdom of ultimate bodhichitta we become a Superior Bodhisattva.
As mentioned before, conventional bodhichitta is the nature of
compassion and ultimate bodhichitta is the nature of wisdom.
These two bodhichittas are like the two wings of a bird with which
we can fly and very quickly reach the enlightened world.

In *Advice from Atisha's Heart*, Atisha says:

Friends, until you attain enlightenment, the Spiritual
Teacher is indispensible, therefore rely upon the holy
Spiritual Guide.

We need to rely on our Spiritual Guide until we attain enlightenment. The reason for this is very simple. The ultimate goal
of human life is to attain enlightenment, and this depends on
continually receiving the special blessings of Buddha through our
Spiritual Guide. Buddha attained enlightenment with the sole
intention of leading all living beings along the stages of the path
to enlightenment through his emanations. Who is his emanation
who is leading us along the stages of the path to enlightenment?
It is clearly our present Spiritual Teacher who is sincerely and

correctly leading us along the paths of renunciation, bodhichitta, and the correct view of emptiness by giving these teachings and showing a practical example of someone who is sincerely practicing them. With this understanding we should strongly believe that our Spiritual Guide is an emanation of Buddha, and develop and maintain deep faith in him or her.

Atisha also says:

> Until you realize ultimate truth, listening is indispensible, therefore listen to the instructions of the Spiritual Guide.

Even if we mistakenly saw two moons in the sky, this mistaken appearance would remind us that there are not actually two moons, but only one. In a similar way, if seeing inherently existent things reminds us there are no inherently existent things, this indicates that our understanding of emptiness, ultimate truth, is correct. Until our understanding of emptiness is perfect, and to prevent ourself from falling into one of the two extremes—the extreme of existence and the extreme of non-existence —we should listen to, read, and contemplate the instructions of our Spiritual Guide. A more detailed explanation of relying on our Spiritual Guide can be found in *Joyful Path of Good Fortune*.

All the contemplations and meditations presented in Part One of this book, from "The Preciousness of our Human Life" to "A Simple Training in Ultimate Bodhichitta," should be practiced in conjunction with the preliminary practices for meditation presented in Appendix II: *Prayers for Meditation*. These preliminary practices will enable us to purify our mind, accumulate merit, and receive the blessings of the enlightened beings, and in this way ensure that our meditation practice is successful.

Examination of our Lamrim Practice

Through practicing the stages of the paths of persons of initial scope, intermediate scope, and great scope we may have developed some experience of renunciation, bodhichitta, and the correct view of emptiness, which are known as the *three principal paths*. We should now examine ourself to see whether or not our experiences of renunciation, bodhichitta, and the correct view of emptiness are qualified. Through judging our mind, if we realize that our attachment to the things of this life still remains, this is the sign that our renunciation is unqualified; if our self-cherishing that believes our own happiness and freedom are important, while neglecting others' happiness and freedom, still remains, this is the sign that our bodhichitta is unqualified; and if our self-grasping that grasps at ourself, our body, and all other things that we normally see still remains, this is the sign that our understanding of emptiness is unqualified.

We therefore need to apply great effort to become deeply familiar with the trainings in renunciation, bodhichitta, and the correct view of emptiness. We need to practice these trainings continually until our attachment, self-cherishing, and self-grasping reduce and we are able to control these delusions. When we have accomplished this, we have "passed our examination" and we have "graduated" to being a great Yogi or Yogini.

PART TWO

Tantra

Wisdom Dharma Protector

The Preciousness of Tantra

*I*n his Sutra teachings, Buddha gives us great encouragement to accomplish the ultimate goal of human life. This goal will be accomplished quickly through the practice of Tantra. Tantra, also known as *Secret Mantra* or *Vajrayana*, is a special method to purify our world, our self, our enjoyments, and our activities; and if we put this method into practice we will attain enlightenment very quickly. As explained in Part One, our world does not exist from its own side—like a dream world, it is a mere appearance to our mind. In dreams we can see and touch our dream world, but when we wake up we realize that it was simply a projection of our mind and had no existence outside our mind. In the same way, the world we see when we are awake is simply a projection of our mind and has no existence outside our mind. Milarepa said:

> You should know that all appearances are the nature of mind, and mind is the nature of emptiness.

Because our world, our self, our enjoyments, and our activities are the nature of our mind, when our mind is impure they are impure, and when our mind becomes pure through purification practice they become pure. There are many different levels of purifying our mind. The subtle mistaken appearance of our mind cannot be purified through the practice of Sutra alone; we need to engage in the practice of Highest Yoga Tantra. When we completely purify our mind through Tantric practice, our world, our self, our enjoyments, and our activities also become completely pure—this is the state of enlightenment. Attaining enlightenment is therefore very simple; all we need to do is apply effort to purifying our mind.

We know that when our mind is impure, because we are feeling angry with our friend, we see him as bad; but when our mind is pure, because we are feeling affectionate love for the same friend, we see him as good. Therefore, it is because our own mind changes from pure to impure, or from impure to pure, that for us our friend changes from good to bad or from bad to good. This indicates that everything that is good, bad, or neutral for us is a projection of our mind and has no existence outside our mind. Through practicing Tantra we will completely purify our mind and thus experience the complete purity of our world, our self, our enjoyments, and our activities—the *four complete purities*.

Although Tantra is very popular, not many people understand its real meaning. Some people deny Buddha's Tantric teachings, while others misuse them for worldly attainments; and many people are confused about the union of Sutra and Tantra practice, mistakenly believing that Sutra and Tantra are contradictory. In *Condensed Heruka Root Tantra*, Buddha says:

> You should never abandon Highest Yoga Tantra,
> But realize that it has inconceivable meaning
> And is the very essence of Buddhadharma.

When we understand the real meaning of Tantra there will be no basis for misusing it, and we will see that there are no contradictions at all between Sutra and Tantra. Practicing Sutra teachings is the basic foundation for practicing Tantric teachings, and the practice of Tantra is the quick method to fulfill the ultimate goal of Sutra teachings. For example, in his Sutra teachings Buddha encourages us to abandon attachment, and in Tantra he encourages us to transform our attachment into the spiritual path. Some people may think this a con-

Through practicing Tantra we will completely purify our mind, our world, our self, our enjoyments, and our activities.

tradiction, but it is not, because Buddha's Tantric instructions on how to transform attachment into the spiritual path are the quick method for abandoning attachment! In this way, they are the method to fulfill the aims of Sutra teachings.

We should take care not to misunderstand the meaning of transforming attachment into the spiritual path. Attachment itself cannot be transformed directly into the spiritual path; it is a delusion, an inner poison, and an object to be abandoned in both Sutra and Tantra. Transforming attachment into the path means that we transform the causes of attachment—our experiences of worldly pleasure—into the spiritual path. There are many methods for doing this that are explained in Tantric teachings.

The universal compassion accomplished through the practice of Sutra teachings, and the wisdom of Mahamudra Tantra accomplished through the practice of Tantric teachings, are like the two wings of a bird. Just as both wings are equally important for a bird to fly, so both Sutra and Tantra are equally important for practitioners seeking enlightenment.

Tantra is defined as an inner realization that functions to prevent ordinary appearances and conceptions and to accomplish the four complete purities. Although Buddha's Tantric scriptures are sometimes called "Tantra" because they reveal Tantric practices, actual Tantra is necessarily an inner realization that protects living beings from ordinary appearances and conceptions, which are the root of samsara's sufferings. Ordinary appearance is our perception of all the things that we normally see, such as our self and body. This appearance is subtle mistaken appearance. It is mistaken because our self, our body, and all other things that we normally see do not exist, even though we always mistakenly see them; and it is subtle because for us it is difficult to understand that this appearance is mistaken. Our subtle mistaken appearance is the root of self-grasping, which is the root of all other delusions and suffering. We can abandon this subtle mistaken appearance completely only through the practice of Highest Yoga Tantra. When we do this we will have accomplished the four complete purities mentioned above.

In general, our experience of worldly pleasure or enjoyments gives rise to attachment, which is the source of all suffering. However, through practicing Tantra we can transform our experience of worldly pleasure into a profound spiritual path that leads us very quickly to the supreme happiness of enlightenment. The instructions of Tantra are therefore superior to all other instructions.

For living beings, the experience of worldly pleasures is the main cause of increasing their attachment, and therefore the main cause of increasing their problems. To stop attachment arising from the experience of worldly pleasures, Buddha taught Tantra as a method to transform worldly pleasures into the path to enlightenment. In accordance with the different levels of transforming worldly pleasures into the path, Buddha taught four levels or classes of Tantra:

Action Tantra, Performance Tantra, Yoga Tantra and Highest Yoga Tantra. The first three are called the *lower Tantras*. In Highest Yoga Tantra, Buddha taught the most profound instructions for transforming sexual bliss into the quick path to enlightenment. Since the effectiveness of this practice depends on gathering and dissolving the inner winds into the central channel through the power of meditation, these instructions were not explained by Buddha in the lower Tantras. In the lower Tantras, Buddha taught instructions on how to transform worldly pleasures—other than sexual bliss—into the path to enlightenment through imagination, which is a simpler practice of Tantra.

The gateway through which we enter Tantra is receiving a Tantric empowerment. An empowerment bestows special blessings upon us that heal our mental continuum and awaken our Buddha nature. When we receive a Tantric empowerment we are sowing the special seeds of the four bodies of a Buddha on our mental continuum. These four bodies are the Nature Truth Body, the Wisdom Truth Body, the Enjoyment Body, and the Emanation Body. Ordinary beings do not possess more than one body, while Buddhas possess four bodies simultaneously. A Buddha's Emanation Body is his or her gross body, which can be seen by ordinary beings. The Enjoyment Body is his subtle body, which can be seen only by practitioners who have gained higher realizations. And the Nature and Wisdom Truth Bodies are his very subtle bodies that only Buddhas themselves can see.

In Tantra, the principal objects to be abandoned are ordinary conceptions and ordinary appearances. The terms *ordinary conceptions* and *ordinary appearances* are best explained by the following example. Suppose there is a Heruka practitioner called

John. Normally he appears to himself as John that he normally sees, and his environment, enjoyments, body, and mind appear as those of John that he normally sees. These appearances are ordinary appearances. The mind that assents to these ordinary appearances by holding them to be true is ordinary conception. The appearances we have of an inherently existent "I," "mine," and other phenomena are also ordinary appearances; self-grasping and all other delusions are ordinary conceptions. Ordinary conceptions are obstructions to liberation, and ordinary appearances are obstructions to enlightenment. In general, all living beings, except Bodhisattvas who have attained the vajra-like concentration of the path of meditation, have ordinary appearances.

Now if John were to meditate on the generation stage of Heruka, strongly regarding himself as Heruka and believing his surroundings, experiences, body, and mind to be those of Heruka, at that time he would have the divine pride that prevents ordinary conceptions. If he were also to attain clear appearance of himself as Heruka, with the environment, enjoyments, body, and mind of Heruka, at that time he would have the clear appearance that prevents him from developing ordinary appearances.

At the beginning, ordinary conceptions are more harmful than ordinary appearances. This is illustrated by the following analogy. Suppose a magician conjures up an illusion of a tiger in front of an audience. The tiger appears to both the audience and the magician, but while the audience believes that the tiger actually exists, and consequently becomes afraid, the magician does not assent to the appearance of the tiger and so remains calm. The problem for the audience is not so much that a tiger appears to them, as their conception that the tiger actually exists. It is this conception, rather than the mere appearance of the tiger, that causes them to experience fear. If like the magician, they had no conception that the tiger existed, then even though they still had an appearance of a tiger they would not be afraid. In the same way, even though things appear to us as ordinary, if we do not conceptually grasp them as ordinary this will not be so harmful. Similarly, it is less damaging to our spiritual development that our Spiritual Guide appears to us as ordinary and yet we hold him or her to be in essence a Buddha, than it is for our Spiritual Guide to appear to us as ordinary and for us to believe that he or she is ordinary. The conviction that our Spiritual Guide is a Buddha, even though he or she may appear to us as an ordinary person, helps our spiritual practice progress rapidly.

To reduce ordinary appearances and conceptions Buddha taught the Tantra of generation stage; and to abandon these two obstructions completely Buddha taught the Tantra of completion stage, especially Mahamudra Tantra. By completing our training in these Tantras we will become a Tantric enlightened being, such as Heruka, with the four complete purities.

Twelve-armed Heruka

The Tantra of Generation Stage

The following chapters present the instructions on the practices of Heruka and Vajrayogini, which are the very essence of Highest Yoga Tantra. The practice of Highest Yoga Tantra can be divided into two stages: generation stage and completion stage. In generation stage, through the power of correct imagination arising from wisdom, Tantric practitioners generate themselves as Tantric enlightened Deities such as Heruka, and their environment, body, enjoyments, and activities as those of Heruka. This imagined new world of Heruka is their object of meditation and they meditate on this new generation with single-pointed concentration. Through continually training in this meditation, Heruka practitioners will gain deep realizations of themselves as Heruka, and their environment, body, enjoyments, and activities as those of Heruka. This inner realization is generation stage Tantra.

Generation stage Tantra is defined as an inner realization of a creative yoga that is attained through training in divine pride and clear appearance of being an enlightened Deity. It is called a *creative yoga* because the object of meditation is created by imagination and wisdom. The main function of generation stage Tantra is to purify ordinary death, intermediate state, and rebirth, and to accomplish a Buddha's Truth Body, Enjoyment

Body, and Emanation Body. It is the quick method to ripen our Buddha nature.

Heruka is an enlightened Deity of Highest Yoga Tantra who is the manifestation of the compassion of all Buddhas. In generation stage Heruka practice, practitioners emphasize training in divine pride and clear appearance of being Heruka. Before training in divine pride, practitioners need to learn to perceive their body and mind as Heruka's body and mind. Having accomplished this, they then use their imagined Heruka's body and mind as the basis of imputation for their "I" or "self" and develop the thought, "I am Buddha Heruka." They then meditate on this divine pride with single-pointed concentration. Through training in this meditation they will gain a deep realization of divine pride, which spontaneously believes that they are Heruka. At this time they have changed the basis of imputation for their I.

From beginningless time, in life after life, the basis of imputation for our self or I has been only a contaminated body and mind. Because our self or I is imputed on a contaminated body and mind, whenever we develop the thought "I" we simultaneously develop self-grasping ignorance, a mind grasping at an inherently existent "I" and "mine," which is the root of all our suffering. However, for qualified Heruka practitioners, their deep realization of divine pride prevents self-grasping ignorance from arising so there is no basis for their experiencing suffering; they will enjoy their pure environment, enjoyments, body, and mind of Heruka.

We may ask, if these practitioners are not yet actually Buddha Heruka, how can they believe that they are? And how is it possible for them to gain the realization of divine pride if their view that believes themselves to be Heruka is a mistaken view? Although these practitioners are not actually Buddha Heruka, they can still believe that they are because they have changed their basis of imputation from their contaminated aggregates to the uncontaminated aggregates of Heruka. Their view that believes they are Buddha Heruka is not a mistaken view because it is non-deceptive and arises from the wisdom realizing that the inherently existent "I" and "mine" do not exist. Their realization of divine pride that spontaneously believes themselves to be Heruka therefore has the power to prevent self-grasping ignorance, the root of samsara, from arising.

As explained earlier, things do not exist from their own side. There are no inherently existent "I," "mine," or other phenomena; all phenomena exist as mere imputations. Things are imputed on their basis of imputation by thought. What does *basis of imputation* mean? For example, the parts of a car are the basis of imputation for the car. The parts of a car are not the car, but there is no car other than its parts. Car is imputed on its parts by thought. How does this happen? Through perceiving any of the parts of the car we naturally develop the thought, "This is the car." Similarly, our body and mind are not our self but are the basis of imputation for our self. Our self is imputed on our body or mind by thought. Through perceiving our body or mind we naturally develop the thought "I" or "mine." Without a basis of imputation things cannot exist; everything depends on its basis of imputation.

Why is it necessary to change the basis of imputation for our self? As mentioned above, since beginningless time, in life after life until now, the basis of imputation for our self has only been the contaminated aggregates of body and mind. Because the basis of imputation for our self is contaminated by the poison of self-grasping ignorance, we experience the endless cycle of suffering.

To free ourself from suffering permanently we therefore need to change our basis of imputation from contaminated aggregates to uncontaminated aggregates.

How can we change our basis of imputation? In general, we have changed our basis of imputation countless times. In our previous lives we took countless rebirths, and each time the basis of imputation for our self was different. When we took a human rebirth our basis of imputation was a human body and mind, and when we took an animal rebirth our basis of imputation was an animal's body and mind. Even in this life, when we were a baby our basis of imputation was a baby's body and mind, when we were a teenager our basis of imputation was a teenager's body and mind, and when we grow old our basis of imputation will be an old person's body and mind. All these countless bases of imputation are contaminated aggregates. We have never changed our basis of imputation from contaminated to uncontaminated aggregates. Only through relying on Buddha's Tantric teachings can we accomplish this.

We change our basis of imputation from contaminated to uncontaminated aggregates by training in the clear appearance and divine pride of being Heruka. As Buddha explained in his Tantric teachings, first we learn to purify our body and mind by meditating on the emptiness of the body, mind, and all other phenomena. Perceiving only emptiness, we then generate ourself as an enlightened Deity such as Heruka. We then learn to perceive clearly our body and mind as Heruka's body and mind, our world as Heruka's Pure Land, and all those around us as enlightened Heroes and Heroines. This is called *training in clear appearance*. Perceiving our body and mind as the uncontaminated aggregates of

Heruka's body and mind, we develop the thought, "I am Buddha Heruka." We then meditate on this divine pride continually with single-pointed concentration, until we gain a deep realization of divine pride that spontaneously believes we are Buddha Heruka. At this time we have changed our basis of imputation from contaminated to uncontaminated aggregates.

Tantric realizations can be achieved simply through relying on correct belief and imagination.

If we are normally called John, for example, we should never believe that John is Buddha Heruka, but we should feel that John disappeared into emptiness before we generated as Buddha Heruka. We then believe that our I, which is imputed on Heruka's body and mind, is Buddha Heruka. This belief is not a mistaken view, because it arises from wisdom, while mistaken views necessarily arise from ignorance. The realization of divine pride arises from wisdom and is a powerful method for accumulating great merit and wisdom.

Even if we have the realization that spontaneously believes that we are Buddha Heruka we should never indicate or declare this to others, because such behavior is inappropriate in normal society. People will still see us as John and not Heruka, and we also know that John is not Heruka. The realizations of divine pride and clear appearance are inner experiences that have the power to control our delusions, and from which pure actions will naturally develop. There is therefore no basis for us to show inappropriate behavior; we must continue to engage in our daily activities and communicate with others as normal.

As mentioned before, Tantric realizations can be achieved simply through relying on correct belief and imagination. This practice is very simple: all we need to do is to become deeply familiar with meditation on correct belief and imagination as presented in Tantra, by applying continual effort. Understanding this we should be confident in our ability to accomplish generation stage realizations of Highest Yoga Tantra. Also, because our world and our self that we normally see do not exist, we have the precious opportunity to generate our new world and our self that are completely pure—this is generation stage. If our world and our self that we normally see existed it would be impossible to generate our world and our self as completely pure. When the strong perception of our world and our self that we normally see ceases through training in generation stage, we will naturally experience our world and our self as completely pure. It is most important that our motivation for training in generation stage is the compassionate mind of bodhichitta.

The Tantra of Completion Stage

Generation stage is like drawing the basic outline of a picture and completion stage is like completing the picture. While the principal objects of generation stage meditation—the mandala and Deities—are generated by correct imagination, the principal objects of completion stage meditation—the channels, drops, and winds—already exist within our body so there is no need to generate them through the power of imagination. For this reason completion stage is not a creative yoga.

Completion stage Tantra is defined as an inner realization of learning developed in dependence upon the inner winds entering, abiding, and dissolving within the central channel through the force of meditations. The objects of these meditations are the central channel, the indestructible drop, and the indestructible wind and mind.

THE CENTRAL CHANNEL

The central channel is located exactly midway between the left and right halves of the body, but is closer to the back than the front. Immediately in front of the spine is the life channel, which is quite thick, and in front of this is the central channel. It begins at the point between the eyebrows, from where it ascends in an arch to the crown of the head, and then descends in a straight line to the tip of the sex organ.

The central channel is pale blue on the outside and has four attributes: (1) it is very straight, like the trunk of a plantain tree; (2) inside it is an oily red color, like pure blood; (3) it is very clear and transparent, like a candle flame; and (4) it is very soft and flexible, like a lotus petal.

On either side of the central channel, with no intervening space, are the right and left channels. The right channel is red in color and the left is white. The right channel begins at the tip of the right nostril and the left channel at the tip of the left nostril. From there, they both ascend in an arch to the crown of the head, on either side of the central channel. From the crown of the head down to the navel, these three main channels are straight and adjacent to one another. As the left channel continues down below the level of the navel, it curves a little to the right, separating slightly from the central channel and rejoining it at the tip of the sex organ. There it functions to hold and release sperm, blood, and urine. As the right channel continues down below the level of the navel, it curves a little to the left and terminates at the tip of the anus, where it functions to hold and release feces and so forth.

The right and left channels coil around the central channel at various places, thereby forming the so-called *channel knots*. The four places where these knots occur are, in ascending order: the navel channel wheel, or navel chakra, the heart channel wheel, the throat channel wheel, and the crown channel wheel. At each of these places, except at the heart, there is a twofold knot formed by a single coil of the right channel and a single coil of the left. As the right and left channels ascend to these places, they coil around the central channel by crossing in front and then looping around it. They then continue upward to the level of the next knot. At the heart level, the same thing happens, except that here there is a sixfold knot formed by three overlapping loops of each of the flanking channels. The channels are the paths through which the inner winds and drops flow. To begin with, it is sufficient simply to become familiar with

Generation stage is like drawing the outline of a picture and completion stage is like completing the picture.

the description and visualization of the three channels. A more detailed explanation of channels can be found in Appendix III.

THE INDESTRUCTIBLE DROP

There are two types of drop in the body: white drops and red drops. The former are the pure essence of white seminal fluid or sperm, and the latter are the pure essence of blood. Both have gross and subtle forms. It is easy to recognize gross drops, but it is more difficult to recognize subtle drops.

The principal seat of the white drop (also known as *white bodhichitta*) is the crown channel wheel, and it is from here that the white seminal fluid originates. The principal seat of the red drop (also known as *red bodhichitta*) is the navel channel wheel, and it is from here that the blood originates. The red drop at the navel is also the foundation of the warmth of the body and the basis for attaining inner fire, or tummo, realizations. When the drops melt and flow through the channels, they give rise to an experience of bliss.

As just explained, at the heart channel wheel there is a sixfold knot formed by the right and left channels coiling around the central channel and constricting it. This is the most difficult knot to loosen, but when it is loosened through meditation we will develop great power—the realization of clear light. Because the central channel at the heart is constricted by this sixfold knot, it is blocked like a tube of bamboo. Inside the central channel, at the very center of this sixfold knot, is a small vacuole, and inside this is a drop called the *indestructible drop*. It is the size of a small pea, with the upper half white in color and the lower half red. The substance of the white half is the very clear essence of sperm, and the substance of the red half is the very clear essence of blood. This drop, which is very pure and subtle, is the very essence of all drops. All the ordinary red and white drops throughout the body originally come from this drop.

The indestructible drop is like a small pea that has been cut in half, slightly hollowed out, and then rejoined. It is called the *indestructible drop* because its two halves never separate until death. When we die, all the inner winds dissolve into the indestructible drop, and this causes the drop to open. As the two halves separate, our consciousness immediately leaves our body and goes to the next life.

THE INDESTRUCTIBLE WIND AND MIND

The nature of the indestructible wind is a very subtle *inner wind*. Inner winds are energy winds that flow through the channels of the body, and they are much more subtle than outer winds. They are associated with, and act as mounts for, various minds. Without these winds our mind cannot move from one object to another. It is said that inner winds are like someone who is blind but has legs, because they cannot perceive anything but can move from one place to another. Minds are like someone who has eyes but no legs, because minds can see but cannot move without their mount, the inner winds. Because minds are always mounted on their associated inner winds, they can both see and move.

Inner winds that flow through the left and right channels are impure and harmful because they act as mounts for the minds of self-grasping, self-cherishing, and other delusions. We need to make great effort to bring and dissolve these inner winds into the central channel so that we can prevent these delusions from arising.

For ordinary beings, inner winds enter, abide, and dissolve within the central channel only during the death process and deep sleep. At these times the indestructible wind and mind manifest, but ordinary beings cannot recognize them because their memory or mindfulness is unable to function then. Completion stage Tantric practitioners can cause their inner winds to enter, abide, and dissolve within the central channel at any time through the power of their meditation on the channels, drops, and winds. They can therefore accomplish the realizations of the five stages of completion stage Tantra: (1) the initial realization of spontaneous great bliss (isolated body and speech of completion stage), (2) ultimate example clear light, (3) illusory body, (4) meaning clear light, and (5) the union of meaning clear light and the pure illusory body. From the fifth stage, practitioners will attain actual enlightenment within a few months.

There are five root and five branch winds. The root winds are: (1) the life-supporting wind, (2) the downward-voiding wind, (3) the upward-moving wind, (4) the equally-abiding wind, and (5) the pervading wind. The five branch winds are: (1) the moving wind, (2) the intensely-moving wind, (3) the perfectly-moving wind, (4) the strongly-moving wind, and (5) the definitely-moving wind. A detailed explanation of inner winds can be found in Appendix IV.

The indestructible wind is the very subtle wind that is associated with, and acts as the mount for, the very subtle mind. It is called the *continuously residing body* because we have had this body continuously in life after life. Although our mind of self-cherishing believes that our present body is our own body and cherishes it, in reality our present body is a part of others' bodies because it is part of our parents' bodies. Our self imputed on our present body and mind will cease at the end of the death process, while our self imputed on our continuously residing body and mind will never cease, but goes from one life to the next. It is this person or I that will finally become an enlightened being. Through this we can understand that, according to Highest Yoga Tantra, in the mental continuum of each and every living being there is a deathless person or I who possesses a deathless body. However, without relying on the profound instructions of Highest Yoga Tantra we cannot recognize our own deathless body and deathless I, our actual self. A Yogi once said:

First, due to fear of death, I ran toward Dharma.
Then I trained in the state of deathlessness.
Finally I realized there is no death and I relaxed!

Inside the indestructible drop resides the indestructible wind and mind, the union of our very subtle wind and very subtle mind. The very subtle wind is our own body, or continuously residing body. The very subtle mind, or indestructible mind, is our own mind, or continuously residing mind, and is mounted on the very subtle wind. Because the union of our very subtle wind and very subtle mind never ceases, it is called the *indestructible wind and mind.* Our indestructible wind and mind have never separated since beginningless time, and they will never separate in the future. The potential to communicate possessed by the combination of our very subtle body and mind is our very subtle speech, which is our own speech, or continuously residing speech. This will become a Buddha's speech in the future. In short, inside the indestructible drop is our own body, speech, and mind, which in the future will become the enlightened body, speech, and mind of a Buddha. These three, our very subtle body, speech, and mind, are our real Buddha nature.

According to Highest Yoga Tantra, in the mental continuum of each and every living being there is a deathless person.

Having gained some experience of generation stage Tantra, which is like drawing the basic outline of a picture, we need to engage in the meditations on completion stage Tantra in order to complete the picture. These are the meditations on the central channel, indestructible drop, and indestructible wind and mind, known as the *yogas of the channel, drop, and wind.*

HOW TO MEDITATE ON THE CENTRAL CHANNEL

First, we should learn to perceive what our central channel looks like, contemplating as follows:

My central channel is located exactly midway between the left and right halves of my body, but is closer to the back than the front. Immediately in front of the spine, there is the life channel, which is quite thick, and in front of this is the central channel. It begins at the point between my eyebrows, from where it ascends in an arch to the crown of my head, and then descends in a straight line to the tip of my sex organ. It is pale blue in color on the outside, and it is an oily red color on the inside. It is clear and transparent, and very soft and flexible.

At the very beginning we can, if we wish, visualize the central channel as being fairly wide, and then gradually visualize it as being thinner and thinner until finally we are able to visualize it as being the width of a drinking straw. We contemplate like this repeatedly until we perceive a generic image of our central channel. Then, while believing that our mind is inside the central channel at our heart, we focus single-pointedly on the central channel at the level of our heart and meditate on this. We should train continually in this way until we gain deep experience of this meditation.

HOW TO MEDITATE ON THE INDESTRUCTIBLE DROP

To perceive our indestructible drop, we contemplate as follows:

Inside my central channel at the level of my heart there is a small vacuole. Inside this is my indestructible drop. It is the size of a small pea, with the upper half white in color and the lower half red. It is like a pea that has been cut in half, slightly hollowed out, and then rejoined. It is the very essence of all drops and is very pure and subtle. Even though it is the substance of

blood and sperm, it has a very clear nature, like a tiny ball of
crystal that radiates five-colored rays of light.

We contemplate like this repeatedly until we perceive a clear generic image of our indestructible drop at our heart inside our central channel. With the feeling that our mind is inside our indestructible drop at our heart, we meditate on this drop single-pointedly without distraction.

This meditation is a powerful method for causing our inner winds to enter, abide, and dissolve within the central channel. Master Ghantapa said:

> We should meditate single-pointedly
> On the indestructible drop that always abides at our heart.
> Those who are familiar with this meditation
> Will definitely develop exalted wisdom.

Here *exalted wisdom* means the wisdom of the clear light of bliss experienced when the knots at the heart channel wheel are loosened. Of all the knots in the central channel, these are the most difficult to loosen; but if from the beginning of our completion stage practice we concentrate on our heart channel wheel, this will help us to loosen these knots. This meditation, therefore, is a powerful method for gaining qualified completion stage realizations.

HOW TO MEDITATE ON THE INDESTRUCTIBLE WIND AND MIND

To gain deeper experience of the wisdom of the clear light of bliss, we engage in meditation on the indestructible wind and mind. First we find the object of this meditation, that is, the clear perception of our indestructible wind and mind, by contemplating as follows:

> *Inside my indestructible drop is the union of my indestructible wind and mind in the aspect of a tiny nada, which symbolizes Heruka's mind of clear light. It is reddish-white in color and radiates five-colored rays of light. My indestructible drop, located inside my central channel at my heart, is like a cave, and the union of my indestructible wind and mind is like someone living inside this cave.*

An illustration of the nada appears in Appendix VIII. We contemplate repeatedly in this way until we perceive the nada, which is the nature of the union of our indestructible wind and mind. With the strong recognition that the nada is the union of our very subtle wind and mind, and feeling that our mind has entered into this nada, we meditate single-pointedly on the nada without forgetting it.

Through gaining deep experience of the meditations on the central channel, the indestructible drop, and the union of the indestructible wind and mind, our inner winds will enter, abide, and dissolve within the central channel, and we will experience special signs. We can tell whether or not the winds have entered the central channel by checking our breathing. Normally there are imbalances in our breath—more air is exhaled through one nostril than through the other, and the air begins to leave one nostril before the other. However, when the winds have entered the central channel as a result of the meditations explained above, the pressure and the timing of the breath will be the same for both nostrils during inhalation and exhalation. Therefore, the first sign to be noticed is that we will be breathing evenly through both nostrils. Another noticeable imbalance in the normal breath is that the inhalation is stronger than the exhalation, or vice versa. The second sign that the winds have entered the central channel is that the pressure of the inhalation will be exactly equal to that of the exhalation.

There are also two signs indicating that the winds are abiding in the central channel: (1) our breathing becomes weaker and weaker, eventually ceasing completely, and (2) all abdominal movement normally associated with the breath stops. In the normal course of events, if our breathing stopped we would be filled with panic and think that we were close to death, but if we are able to stop breathing through the force of meditation, far from panicking our mind will become even more confident, comfortable, and flexible.

When the winds are abiding within the central channel, we no longer have to rely on gross air to survive. Normally our breathing stops only at the time of death. During sleep our breathing becomes much more subtle, but it never stops completely. During completion stage meditation, however, our breath can come to a complete halt without our becoming unconscious. After the winds have been abiding in the central channel for five or ten minutes, it is possible that they will escape again into the right and left channels. If this happens, we will resume breathing. Air flowing through the nostrils is an indication that the winds are not abiding within the central channel.

What are the signs that the winds have dissolved within the central channel? There are seven winds that must dissolve, and each has a specific sign indicating that its dissolution has been completed. The seven winds are (1) the earth element wind, (2) the water element wind, (3) the fire element wind, (4) the wind element wind, (5) the wind mounted by the mind of white appearance, (6) the wind mounted by the mind of red increase, and (7) the wind mounted by the mind of black near-attainment. The first four of these winds are gross and the last three are subtle. These seven winds dissolve gradually in sequence, and with each dissolution there is a particular appearance.

The earth element wind supports and increases everything that is associated with the earth element in our body, such as our bones, cartilage, and fingernails. When this wind dissolves within the central channel, we perceive an appearance known as the *mirage-like appearance*. This is like the appearance of shimmering water that is sometimes seen on the floor of a desert. There are three levels on which this mirage-like appearance is perceived, depending on the degree to which the earth element wind has dissolved within the central channel. If the dissolution is only slight the appearance will be vague, the least clear, and very difficult to recognize; if the dissolution is almost complete the appearance will be clearer and more vivid; and if the wind dissolves completely the appearance will be unmistakably clear and vivid, and impossible not to perceive. When the earth element wind has dissolved and the mirage-like appearance has been perceived, the next wind will dissolve and a different appearance will manifest. The more completely the first wind dissolves, the more vivid our perception of this next appearance will be.

The second wind to dissolve is the water element wind, which supports and increases the liquid elements of the body such as the blood. The appearance associated with this dissolution is called the *smoke-like appearance*. Some texts say that this appearance is like smoke billowing from a chimney, but this is not the actual appearance. There is an appearance like billowing smoke, but this occurs just prior to the actual dissolution of the water element wind. It is not until this initial appearance has subsided that the actual smoke-like appearance is perceived. This is like thin wisps of wafting blue smoke drifting in the air in a slowly swirling haze. As before, there are three levels on which this appearance is perceived, depending on the degree to which the water element wind has dissolved.

Next comes the dissolution of the fire element wind. This wind supports and increases the fire element in the body and is responsible for bodily heat and so forth. The sign that this wind has dissolved is the *sparkling-fireflies-like appearance*. This appearance is sometimes described in terms of an open crackling fire seen at night, with the mass of ascending sparks swirling above the fire resembling the sparkling-fireflies-like appearance. Once again, there are three levels on which this appearance is perceived, depending on the degree of dissolution.

Following this, the wind element wind dissolves. This is the wind mounted by gross conceptual thought. It powers gross dualistic appearances and the gross conceptual thoughts that result from holding these appearances to be true. The sign that the fourth of the gross winds has started to dissolve is the *candle-flame-like appearance*. This is like the steady, erect flame of a candle in a room without a draft. Once again there are three levels on which this appearance is perceived.

When the earth element wind has dissolved within the central channel and the power of the earth element is thereby diminished, it may seem as though the water element has increased, because as the power of the former element diminishes, the latter is perceived more clearly. For this reason, the dissolution of the earth element wind into the central channel is often described as *the earth element dissolving into the water element*. For similar reasons, the subsequent dissolutions are referred to as *the water element dissolving into the fire element*, *the fire element dissolving into the wind element*, and *the wind element dissolving into consciousness*.

After the candle-flame-like appearance, all gross conceptual minds have ceased functioning because the winds on which they are mounted have dissolved and disappeared. When the meditator has completed the dissolution of the fourth wind, the first subtle mind—the mind of white appearance—arises. With this mind, the meditator perceives an appearance of whiteness, like the bright light of the moon pervading an empty sky on a clear autumn night. As before, there are three levels of clarity to this appearance depending on the ability of the meditator.

At this point the mind is completely free from gross conceptions, such as the eighty indicative conceptions listed in *Clear Light of Bliss*, and the only perception is that of white, empty space. Ordinary beings also perceive this appearance, for example, at the time of death, but they are unable to recognize it or to prolong it because at this stage the ordinary gross level of mindfulness has stopped functioning. However, even though there is no gross mindfulness at this stage, those who have trained properly according to the practices of completion stage Tantra are able to use the subtle mindfulness they have developed during meditation to recognize and prolong the white appearance, something that ordinary beings are unable to do.

When the subtle wind mounted by the mind of white appearance dissolves, the mind of red increase arises. This mind and its mounted wind are more subtle than the mind and wind of white appearance. The sign that occurs when this mind arises is an appearance like red sunlight pervading an empty sky. Once again, there are three levels of clarity to this appearance.

When the subtle wind mounted by the mind of red increase dissolves, the mind of black near-attainment arises. This mind and its mounted wind are even more subtle than the mind and wind of red increase. The mind of black near-attainment has two levels: the upper part and the lower part. The upper part of the mind of black near-attainment still possesses subtle mindfulness, but the lower part has no mindfulness at all. It is experienced as an overwhelming unconsciousness, like that of a very deep faint. At this point, we would appear to others to be dead.

The sign that occurs when the mind of black near-attainment arises is an appearance like a very black, empty sky. This appearance comes with the upper part of the mind of black near-attainment, immediately after the cessation of the mind of red increase. As the experience of black near-attainment progresses and we approach complete unconsciousness, our subtle mindfulness ceases. The more strongly the wind dissolves into the central channel, the more deeply unconscious we become during the mind of black near-attainment; and the more deeply unconscious we become at this time, the more vividly we will perceive the subsequent appearance of clear light. This is similar to the experience of someone who stays in a dark room for a long time; the longer he stays there, the brighter the outside world will appear when he eventually emerges. Thus, the degree of brightness experienced depends on the depth and duration of the previous darkness.

When the subtle wind mounted by the mind of black near-attainment dissolves, the mind of clear light arises. This mind and its mounted wind are the most subtle of all. The sign that occurs when this mind arises is an appearance like an autumn sky at dawn—perfectly clear and empty.

When the mind of clear light arises, a very subtle mindfulness is restored, according to the meditator's level of development. The very subtle wind, and the very subtle mind that is mounted on it, reside in the indestructible drop in the center of the heart channel wheel. Normally the very subtle mind does not function, but at the time of the clear light it manifests and becomes active. If we have trained in the techniques of completion stage Tantra, and have become proficient in them, we will be able to perceive and maintain the appearance of clear light. Eventually, by learning to use the very subtle mindfulness developed at this stage, we will be able to focus our very subtle mind on emptiness, and in this way use the mind of clear light as the means for attaining a Buddha's Truth Body.

Our mind cannot become more subtle than the mind of clear light. During the first four appearances (mirage-like, smoke-like, sparkling-fireflies-like, and candle-flame-like) the gross winds dissolve; and during the next three (white appearance, red increase, and black near-attainment) the subtle winds dissolve. Then, with the appearance of the clear light, the very subtle mind and its mounted wind manifest and become active. These cannot dissolve because they are indestructible. After death, they simply pass to the next life.

Of the three subtle winds mounted by the three subtle minds, the least subtle is that mounted by the mind of white appearance. This mind is called *white appearance* because all that is perceived is an appearance of white, empty space. It is also called *empty* because the mind of white appearance perceives this white space as empty. At this stage the appearance of white and the appearance of empty are of equal strength.

When the wind mounted by the mind of white appearance dissolves, the second of the three subtle minds—the mind of red increase—arises. The mounted wind of this mind is more subtle than that mounted by the mind of white appearance. This mind is called *red increase* because the appearance of red space is increasing. It is also called *very empty* because the appearance of empty is stronger than that of the previous mind. At this stage the appearance of empty is stronger than the appearance of red.

When the wind of the mind of red increase dissolves, the third subtle mind—the mind of black near-attainment—arises. This mind is called *near-attainment* because the experience of clear light is now close at hand. It is also called *great empty* because the appearance of empty is even greater than that of the previous mind.

When the third subtle wind, that mounted by the mind of black near-attainment, dissolves, the mind of clear light arises. This mind is called *clear light* because its nature is very lucid and clear, and because it perceives an appearance like the light of an autumn dawn. It is also called *all-empty* because it is empty of all gross and subtle winds and perceives only an empty appearance. The object of the mind of clear light is very similar in appearance to the object perceived by a Superior being in meditative equipoise on emptiness. Collectively, the four minds—the mind of white appearance, the mind of red increase, the mind of black near-attainment, and the mind of clear light—are referred to as the *four empties*.

If a completion stage meditator is highly accomplished, he or she will have a very vivid experience of clear light and will be able to maintain that experience for a long time. Just how vivid our experience of clear light is depends on how vivid the previous seven appearances were, and this in turn depends on how strongly the winds dissolve within the central channel. If the winds dissolve very strongly, the meditator will have a vivid experience of all the appearances and will be able to prolong the experience of each one. The longer we are able to remain with the experience of each appearance, the longer we will be able to remain with the clear light itself.

If a person dies a violent death, he or she progresses through these appearances very rapidly, but if the death is slow or natural the appearances from mirage-like to clear light will be experienced more gradually and for longer. If we have developed the realization of ultimate example clear light, we will be able to have exactly the same experience of these appearances while in deep concentration that we would have if we were actually dying. In addition, if we have trained well in the meditations explained above, we will be able to meditate on emptiness throughout all four empties, except during the time spent in the swoon, or faint, of the mind of black near-attainment.

To be able to perceive the four empties clearly, exactly as in the death process, we must be able to dissolve all the winds into the indestructible drop in the center of the heart channel wheel. If they dissolve into another channel wheel of the central channel, such as the navel channel wheel, we will experience similar appearances, but they will be artificial—not the true appearances that occur when the winds dissolve into the indestructible drop, as they do at the time of death.

Although an accomplished meditator can abide within the clear light for a long time, he or she must eventually move on. When we arise from the clear light, the first thing we experience is the mind of black near-attainment of reverse order. Then we experience in sequence the mind of red increase,

The mind of clear light is the foundation of all other minds.

the mind of white appearance, the eighty gross conceptual minds, the minds of the candle-flame-like appearance and so forth, as the minds evolve in an order that is the reverse of that in which they previously dissolved.

Thus the mind of clear light is the foundation of all other minds. When the gross and subtle minds and their mounted winds dissolve into the indestructible drop at the heart, we remain with only the clear light, and then it is from this clear light that all the other minds evolve, each one grosser than the previous one.

These sequences of serial and reverse order are experienced by ordinary beings during sleep and the initial stages of waking up, during death and the initial stages of their next rebirth, and by qualified completion stage practitioners during meditation. Because enlightened beings have attained permanent cessation of the seven winds listed above, they experience only the very subtle mind of clear light—even their compassion and bodhichitta are part of their mind of clear light.

Ghantapa

The Completion Stage of Mahamudra

The term *Mahamudra* is Sanskrit. *Maha* means "great" and refers to great bliss, and *mudra* here means "non-deceptive" and refers to emptiness. Mahamudra is the union of great bliss and emptiness. Mahamudra Tantra is defined as a mind of fully qualified clear light that experiences great bliss and realizes emptiness directly. Because emptiness is explained in detail in Buddha's Sutra teachings and is a part of Mahamudra, some texts say that it is Sutra Mahamudra; but actual Mahamudra is necessarily a realization of Highest Yoga Tantra.

The instructions on Mahamudra Tantra given by the Wisdom Buddha Je Tsongkhapa Losang Dragpa are superior to those given by other scholars. As the scholar Gungtang says in *Prayer for the Flourishing of the Doctrine of Je Tsongkhapa*:

> The emptiness that is explained in Buddha's Sutra
>   teachings,
> And the great bliss that is explained in Buddha's Tantric
>   teachings—
> The union of these two is the very essence of Buddha's
>   eighty-four thousand teachings.

May the doctrine of Conqueror Losang Dragpa flourish
for evermore.

The nature of Mahamudra is a fully qualified clear light. As
mentioned previously there are many different levels of the experience of clear light depending on the degree of dissolution of the
inner winds into the central channel. The realization of great bliss
developed in dependence upon the inner winds entering, abiding,
and dissolving within the central channel, prior to attaining the
fully qualified clear light, is the first of the five stages of completion stage. It is called *isolated body and speech of completion stage*,
which means that at this stage the practitioner is free, or isolated,
from gross ordinary appearances and conceptions of body and
speech.

A fully qualified clear light mind experiencing great bliss that
realizes emptiness with a generic image is called *ultimate example
clear light*. This realization is called "ultimate" because it is a fully
qualified clear light. It is called "example" because by using this
realization as an example, practitioners understand that they can
accomplish a fully qualified clear light mind experiencing great
bliss that realizes emptiness directly, which is called *meaning clear
light*. The realization of ultimate example clear light is the second
of the five stages of completion stage. It is also called *isolated mind*
because at this stage practitioners are free, or isolated, from gross
ordinary appearances and conceptions of mind.

When practitioners arise from the concentration of ultimate
example clear light, their indestructible wind—their continuously
residing body—transforms into the illusory body. This is a divine
body, which in nature is wisdom light having the aspect of the

divine body of an enlightened Deity such as Heruka. The color of the illusory body is white. The realization of this illusory body is the third of the five stages of completion stage, and is called *illusory body of the third stage.*

Practitioners who have attained the illusory body of the third stage meditate on emptiness again and again with their clear light mind of bliss until they directly realize the emptiness of all phenomena. When they accomplish this they attain *meaning clear light,* a fully qualified clear light mind experiencing great bliss that realizes the emptiness of all phenomena directly. This realization of meaning clear light is the fourth of the five stages of completion stage, and is called *meaning clear light of the fourth stage. Meaning clear light* and *Mahamudra Tantra* are synonymous.

When practitioners arise from the concentration of meaning clear light they attain the pure illusory body and completely abandon ordinary conceptions and all other delusions. When these practitioners manifest meaning clear light again, they will attain the union of meaning clear light and pure illusory body. The realization of this union is the fifth of the five stages of completion stage, and is called *union of the fifth stage.* From this fifth stage practitioners will attain actual enlightenment—the Path of No More Learning, or Buddhahood.

Mahamudra Tantra is a mind that experiences great bliss and realizes emptiness directly.

As mentioned above, Mahamudra is the union of great bliss and emptiness. This means that Mahamudra Tantra is a single mind that is both bliss and wisdom—it experiences great bliss and realizes emptiness directly. Mahamudra Tantra is a collection of merit that is the main cause of a Buddha's Form Body, and a collection of wisdom that is the main cause of a Buddha's Truth Body, or Dharmakaya. When training in the meditations of Mahamudra Tantra we are transforming our continuously residing body and mind into a Buddha's Form Body and Truth Body. Mahamudra Tantra, therefore, gives inconceivable meaning to our life.

GREAT BLISS

The bliss explained by Buddha in completion stage Tantra is unequalled among all other types of bliss and is therefore called *great bliss*.

In general, there are many different types of bliss. For example, ordinary beings sometimes experience some artificial bliss when they engage in sexual activity, and qualified meditators experience a special bliss of suppleness during deep meditation due to their pure concentration, especially when they attain tranquil abiding and accomplish the concentration of the absorption of cessation. In addition when Dharma practitioners, through training in higher moral discipline, higher concentration, and higher wisdom, attain permanent inner peace by abandoning self-grasping, they experience a profound bliss of inner peace day and night in life after life. These types of bliss are mentioned in Buddha's Sutra teachings. The bliss of completion stage, however, is quite different from all of these, and is vastly superior. The bliss of completion stage—great bliss—is a bliss that possesses two special characteristics: (1) its nature is a bliss arisen from the melting of the drops inside the central channel, and (2) its function is to prevent subtle mistaken appearance. No other form of bliss possesses these two characteristics.

A bliss possessing these two characteristics can be experienced only by those who are engaged in Highest Yoga Tantra practice, and by Buddhas. Even many high Bodhisattvas abiding in Pure Lands have no opportunity to experience it, because although they have very high realizations, their bodies lack the necessary physical conditions for generating bliss possessing the two characteristics. What are these conditions? They are the three elements of flesh, skin, and blood that come from the mother; and the three elements of bone, marrow, and sperm that come from the father. These six elements are essential for accomplishing this bliss, which is the quick path to Buddhahood. It was because humans possessed these conditions that Buddha explained Tantric teachings to us in the first place. Therefore, from this point of view, we are more fortunate than many high Bodhisattvas abiding in Pure Lands who are experiencing great enjoyments. It is said that these Bodhisattvas pray to be born in the human world so that they can meet a qualified Vajra Master and practice the quick path to enlightenment. In *Song of the Spring Queen*, Je Tsongkhapa says that without experiencing this bliss there is no possibility of attaining liberation in this life. It goes without saying, therefore, that without this bliss there is no possibility of attaining full enlightenment in this life.

If we develop and maintain this bliss through the practice of completion stage meditation, we can transform our attachment into a special method for completing the quick path to enlightenment. Before we attain this bliss, our attachment causes us to be reborn in samsara, but once we have this bliss our attachment causes us to be released from samsara. In addition, once we attain this bliss we will be able to stop our samsaric rebirths very quickly. The cause of samsara is our mind of self-grasping. According to the teachings of Highest Yoga Tantra, self-grasping depends on its mounted wind, which flows through the right and left channels. For human beings, without this wind self-grasping cannot develop. By gaining the bliss of completion stage, we can gradually reduce the inner winds of the right and left channels until they finally cease completely. When they cease, our self-grasping ceases, and we experience liberation from samsara.

From this we can see that in Sutra alone there is no liberation, not to mention full enlightenment. The Highest Yoga Tantra teachings are Buddha's ultimate intention, and the Sutra teachings are like the basic foundation. Although there are many explanations of how to attain liberation or nirvana in the Sutra teachings, if we check precisely it is very difficult to understand from Sutra teachings how nirvana can be attained. *Nirvana* means "the state beyond sorrow"—the permanent cessation of self-grasping and its mounted wind—and its nature is emptiness. If we have never heard Highest Yoga Tantra teachings and someone asks us precisely how we attain such a nirvana, we cannot give a perfect answer. As Je Tsongkhapa said, the final answer can be found only in teachings on Highest Yoga Tantra.

The bliss that arises from the melting of drops inside channels other than the central channel has no special qualities. When ordinary beings engage in sexual intercourse, for example, this causes their downward-voiding wind to move upward, and this in turn causes their ordinary inner heat, or tummo, to increase in their right and left channels, principally in the left. As a result the red drops of the woman and the white drops of the man melt and flow through the left channel. This flowing of the drops causes them to experience some bliss, but it is very short-lived and the drops are soon released. Having had this brief experience of bliss, they are not left with any good results, except maybe a baby!

By contrast, when a qualified Tantric practitioner practices the completion stage meditations that are explained above, he or she will cause his inner winds to gather, abide, and dissolve within the central channel. This will cause the downward-voiding wind located just below the navel to move upward. Normally this wind functions to release the drops, but because it is now rising within the central channel, the inner heat lo-cated at the navel will increase inside the central channel, thereby causing the drops to melt and flow also inside the central channel.

In Sutra alone there is no liberation. The answer can be found only in teachings on Highest Yoga Tantra.

For the practitioner of a male Deity, the white drop begins to flow down from the crown, and when it reaches the throat, the practitioner experiences a very special bliss possessing the two characteristics, or qualities. As the drop flows down to the heart, the bliss becomes stronger and more qualified; as it flows down to the navel, the bliss becomes even stronger and more qualified; and finally, as it flows down to the tip of the sex organ, the practitioner experiences spontaneous great bliss—the great bliss of completion stage. Because the downward-voiding wind is reversed, the drop is not released at this point but flows up again through the central channel, causing the practitioner to experience even greater bliss. For such a practitioner, the drops are never released and so they flow up and down the central channel for a very long time, giving rise to unceasing bliss. The practitioner can cause such bliss to manifest at any time simply by penetrating the central channel with concentration.

The stronger this bliss becomes, the more subtle our mind becomes. Gradually our mind becomes very peaceful, all conceptual distractions disappear, and we experience very special suppleness. This mind is infinitely superior to the experience of tranquil abiding explained in Sutra teachings. In addition, as our mind becomes more subtle our subtle mistaken appearance is reduced, and eventually our mind becomes the very subtle mind of the clear light of bliss. This is a very high realization. When the clear light of bliss concentrates on emptiness it mixes with emptiness very easily because subtle mistaken appearance is greatly reduced. Finally it realizes emptiness directly, and while previously it felt as if our bliss and emptiness were two things, now they have become one nature. This mind is the union of great bliss and emptiness, or meaning clear light.

The initial realization of the union of great bliss and emptiness is the path of seeing of Highest Yoga Tantra. However, even though it is only the path of seeing, it has the power to eliminate both the intellectually-formed delusions and innate delusions together. When the practitioner rises from this concentration of the union of bliss and emptiness, he or she has abandoned all the delusions and has attained liberation. At the same time, he or she has attained the pure illusory body. From that moment, the practitioner's body is a vajra body, which means a deathless body, and he or she will never again experience aging, sickness, or contaminated rebirth.

As mentioned above, previously when the practitioner was ordinary, he or she was using a body taken from others—from his or her parents. We normally say, "My body, my body," as if our present gross body is our real body, but this is not our actual body because originally it was part of our parents' bodies. When a Tantric practitioner attains a vajra body, however, he has manifested his own body, the continuously residing body. When he perceives this vajra body he develops the thoughts "I" and "mine." Such a practitioner has now become a deathless person.

We have had our very subtle body, very subtle speech, and very subtle mind since beginningless time. These are the continuously residing body, the continuously residing speech, and the continuously residing mind, and they are our actual Buddha nature. The Buddha nature explained in Sutra is not actual Buddha nature because it is a gross object that will cease; actual Buddha nature is explained only in Highest Yoga Tantra. Normally, for ordinary beings, the only times their very subtle body, speech, and mind become manifest are during deep sleep and death. However, even though they are not normally manifest, our very subtle body is the seed of a Buddha's body, our very subtle speech is the seed of a Buddha's speech, and our very subtle mind is the seed of a Buddha's mind.

As already mentioned, the very subtle body is the very subtle wind on which the very subtle mind is mounted. This very subtle body and very subtle mind are always together. Since they are the same nature, and are never separated, they are called the *indestructible wind* and the *indestructible mind*. The union of the indestructible wind and mind is normally located inside the indestructible drop, inside the central channel at the heart.

Our very subtle mind manifests only when all our inner winds dissolve within our central channel. When this happens we gradually experience the eight signs described previously, as we pass through the different levels of dissolution. Finally, with the last level of dissolution, the very subtle mind of clear light becomes manifest. At the same time, the very subtle body also becomes manifest.

During death, the inner winds dissolve naturally and fully within the central channel and the very subtle mind and very subtle body naturally become manifest, but we cannot recognize them. However, by practicing the completion stage meditations explained above, we can cause our very subtle mind and body to become manifest during meditation. Until we attain the realization of illusory body, our very subtle body will not maintain a definite shape or color. When we attain the union of bliss and emptiness, our very subtle mind transforms into meaning clear light, and when we rise from that meditation, our very subtle body transforms into the vajra body, or pure illusory body, which does have definite shape, color, and so forth.

For example, if we are a Heruka practitioner, whenever we do self-generation as Heruka with a blue-colored body, four faces, twelve arms, and so on, we are building the basic foundation for the illusory body. In the future, when our very subtle body transforms into the illusory body it will look like real Heruka. Previously it was merely an imagined body, but at this time it will become real. This is a very good reason for now practicing generation stage very sincerely.

When we attain the pure illusory body, we will no longer think of our gross body as our body. The basis for imputing our I will have completely changed, and we will now impute I in dependence upon our subtle body. When we have reached this attainment, we will have become deathless because our body and mind will never separate. Death is the permanent separation of body and mind, but the body and mind of those who have attained the illusory body never separate because they are indestructible. Finally, our pure illusory body will transform into Buddha's Form Body and our union of bliss and emptiness will transform into Buddha's Truth Body, and we will experience the union of Buddha's Form Body and Truth Body, the Union of No More Learning.

In the section on the benefits of bodhichitta in *Guide to the Bodhisattva's Way of Life*, Shantideva says:

Just like the supreme elixir that transmutes into gold,
Bodhichitta can transform this impure body we have
 taken
Into the priceless jewel of a Buddha's form;
Therefore, firmly maintain bodhichitta.

Here "elixir" refers to a special substance that can transform iron into gold, like that used by great Masters such as Nagarjuna. This verse says that bodhichitta is a special method that, like a supreme elixir, has the power to transform our impure body into a Buddha's Form Body. How can it do this? According to Sutra, a practitioner cannot attain enlightenment in one life but must practice for many lives until finally he or she is born into Akanishta Pure Land with a pure body. It is only with this pure body that he or she can attain Buddhahood. There is no method in either Sutra or Tantra for transforming our present impure body into a Buddha's body. This impure body must eventually die; it must be left behind. Even the holy Buddha Shakyamuni himself left behind the gross body that came from his parents when he passed away. Thus, if we ask how bodhichitta can transform this impure body into a Buddha's body, there is no correct answer within Sutra teachings. This is because, according to Sutra teachings, the gross body is the real body; the Sutras never mention the continuously residing body, the vajra body, or the deathless body.

By following the Tantric view, however, we can answer this question as follows. The body referred to by Shantideva is not the gross body, but our own body, our continuously residing body, which is the very subtle wind on which our very subtle mind is mounted. This is currently an impure body because it is obscured by delusions and other obstructions, like a blue sky covered by clouds.

Bodhichitta has the power to transform our impure body into a Buddha's Form Body.

These defilements are not the nature of our subtle body, but are temporary defilements. The method for transforming this impure body into a Buddha's Form Body is not conventional bodhichitta, but the ultimate bodhichitta of Highest Yoga Tantra, the union of great bliss and emptiness. This ultimate bodhichitta can directly transform our impure continuously residing body first into the pure illusory body and finally into the Form Body of a Buddha. Since Shantideva himself was a sincere Tantric practitioner, we can be certain that this was his intended meaning.

As mentioned previously, to generate the bliss that possesses two special qualities we need to gather and dissolve our inner winds within our central channel. There are two ways to do this: by penetrating our own body or by penetrating another's body.

We begin by penetrating our own body. Here the term "our own body" refers to our channels, drops, and winds, and "penetrate" to concentrating on our central channel, drops, and winds, as already explained. Meditation on the central channel is called the *yoga of the central channel*, meditation on the drops is called the *yoga of the drop*, and meditation on the winds is called the *yoga of wind*.

Penetrating another's body means relying on an action mudra, or consort, and engaging in sexual intercourse. However, just penetrating another's body will not bring our inner winds into our central channel if we do not already have deep experience of and familiarity with the yoga of the central channel, the yoga of the drop, and the yoga of wind. This means that we must have gained the experience of dissolving some of our inner winds within the central channel at the heart channel wheel, and through this practice, be able to perceive clearly the eight signs of dissolution from the mirage-like appearance to the clear light. Only when we have such experience is it the right time to rely on an action mudra. This order of practice is very important.

There are only ten doors through which the winds can enter the central channel. They are located along the central channel as follows: (1) the upper tip of the central channel—the point between the eyebrows, (2) the lower tip—the tip of the sex organ, (3) the center of the crown channel wheel—located in the apex of the cranium, (4) the center of the throat channel wheel—located near the back of the throat, (5) the center of the heart channel wheel—located between the two breasts, (6) the center of the navel channel wheel, (7) the center of the secret place channel wheel—four finger-widths below the navel, (8) the center of the jewel channel wheel—located in the center of the sex organ, near its tip, (9) the wheel of wind—the center of the forehead channel wheel, and (10) the wheel of fire—the center of the channel wheel located midway between the throat and the heart channel wheels. Just as we can enter a house through any of the doors leading in from the outside, so the winds can enter the central channel through any of these ten doors.

The central channel is in reality one single channel, but it is divided into different sections: the central channel of the crown channel wheel, the central channel of the throat channel wheel, the central channel of the heart channel wheel, the central channel of the navel channel wheel, and so forth. Because there are these different locations, when a practitioner wants to bring his or her winds into the central channel, he or she must choose one of these points to concentrate on.

In *Clear Light of Bliss*, I explain how to bring the inner winds into the central channel through the sixth of the ten doors, the center of the navel channel wheel. We do this by visualizing our inner heat, known as tummo, inside our central channel at the navel in the aspect of a short-AH and meditating on this. This common practice, known as *tummo meditation*, accords with the tradition of the Six Yogas of Naropa. It was originally explained in *Hevajra Root Tantra* by Buddha Vajradhara, and since then has been used by many practitioners such as Milarepa and his disciples, and later by practitioners in Je Tsongkhapa's tradition. However, the instructions of the Ganden Oral Lineage present an uncommon Mahamudra Tantra practice. This is a very special practice of Mahamudra that Je Tsongkhapa received directly from Manjushri, who had received it directly from Buddha. The lineage of this instruction, the Ganden Oral Lineage, which is a close lineage, was then passed on to Togden Jampel Gyatso, Baso Chokyi Gyaltsen, Mahasiddha Dharmavajra, and so on. A full list of the lineage Gurus of this special instruction is given in *Clear Light of Bliss*. These Spiritual Guides are the close lineage Gurus.

In this Mahamudra Tantra practice, we choose the center of the heart channel wheel from among the ten doors to bring the winds into the central channel. This practice is indicated in the following verse from the sadhana *Offering to the Spiritual Guide*, which is the uncommon preliminary practice of Mahamudra Tantra according to Je Tsongkhapa's tradition:

> I seek your blessings, O Protector, that you may place
>   your feet
> On the center of the eight-petalled lotus at my heart,
> So that I may manifest within this life
> The paths of illusory body, clear light, and union.

These words actually reveal that penetrating the central channel of the heart channel wheel, the indestructible drop, and the indestructible wind—the three yogas explained above—are meditations on isolated body. These lead to the meditations on isolated speech and isolated mind, which in turn lead to the meditations on illusory body, meaning clear light, and union.

Because penetrating and concentrating on the indestructible drop at the heart is a powerful method for attaining the realizations of completion stage, Buddha Vajradhara praises this method in *Ambhidana Tantra*, where he says:

> Those who meditate on the drop
> That always abides at the heart,
> Single-pointedly and without change,
> Will definitely attain realizations.

Guru Sumati Buddha Heruka

The Practice of Heruka Body Mandala

THE LINEAGE OF THESE INSTRUCTIONS

As mentioned above, Heruka—also known as Chakrasambara—is an enlightened Deity of Highest Yoga Tantra who is the manifestation of the compassion of all Buddhas.

To lead living beings to the supreme happiness of enlightenment, all the Buddhas' compassion appears in the form of Heruka who has a blue-colored body, four faces, and twelve arms, and embraces the consort Vajravarahi. Every part of Heruka's body is the nature of wisdom light. Although each aspect of Heruka's body has great meaning, as explained in the commentary to Heruka body mandala practice called *Essence of Vajrayana*, at first we should be satisfied with the mere name Heruka. There is no need to search closely for Heruka's body, because like a rainbow the closer we search for it the more it will disappear. The name Heruka has three parts, *He*, *ru*, and *ka*. *He* refers to the emptiness of all phenomena, *ru* refers to great bliss, and *ka* refers to the union of great bliss and emptiness. This indicates that through relying on Heruka with faith we will attain the realization of the union of great bliss and emptiness, which is the actual quick path to enlightenment.

Heruka imputed on Buddha's Enjoyment Body is *Enjoyment Body Heruka*, and Heruka imputed on Buddha's Emanation Body is *Emanation Body Heruka*; together they are called *interpretative Heruka*. Emanation Body Heruka can be seen even by ordinary beings who have a special pure mind. When, through training, we are able to believe spontaneously that our Spiritual Guide is an emanation of Heruka, we will see Emanation Body Heruka. Heruka imputed on Buddha's Truth Body, or Dharmakaya, is called *definitive Heruka*, and always lacks form, shape, and color. Because its basis of imputation, Buddha's Truth Body, is extremely subtle, definitive Heruka can be seen only by Buddhas and not by other beings. It is also called *wisdom being Buddha Heruka*. Definitive Heruka pervades the entire universe; there is no single place where definitive Heruka is absent.

Buddha expounded extensive, middling, and condensed Heruka root Tantras. The *Condensed Root Tantra* and many of its commentaries written by Indian Buddhist Tantric scholars, including the great Yogis Ghantapa and Naropa, were translated from Sanskrit into Tibetan. Later, many Tibetan Tantric scholars, including the great translator Marpa, the founder of the Kagyu tradition, and Je Tsongkhapa, the founder of the Gelug tradition, wrote commentaries to the practice of Heruka Tantra. In this present age, the great Lama Je Phabongkhapa wrote special commentaries to the practices of Heruka body mandala and Vajrayogini. He also wrote many profound ritual prayers, or sadhanas, and gave extensive teachings on these. It is through the great kindness of Je Phabongkhapa and his heart disciple, Kyabje Trijang Rinpoche, that even in these times of extreme spiritual degeneration the profound practices of Heruka body mandala and Vajrayogini are flourishing both in the East and the West.

Je Phabongkhapa had direct visions of Heruka. At one time Heruka told him, "For seven generations, the practitioners of your instructions of Heruka and Vajrayogini will have the special good fortune to accomplish the realizations of these practices easily." Whenever I contemplate this I think, "We are so fortunate."

It is said that as the general level of spirituality decreases, it becomes increasingly difficult for practitioners to receive the blessings of other Deities, such as Guhyasamaja and Yamantaka; but the opposite is the case with Heruka and Vajrayogini—the more times degenerate, the more easily practitioners can receive their blessings. This is because the people of this world have a special karmic connection with Heruka and Vajrayogini, and the emanations of Heruka and Vajrayogini and their places—the Pure Lands of Keajra—pervade everywhere throughout this world.

The people of this world have a special karmic connection with Heruka and Vajrayogini.

The first lineage holder of these instructions on Heruka body mandala is the great Yogi Ghantapa. He received the empowerment and instructions of Heruka body mandala directly from Heruka. Ghantapa lived deep in a forest in Odivisha (present-day Orissa), in India, where he engaged in intensive meditation on Heruka and Vajrayogini. Since he was living in such an isolated place his diet was poor and his body became emaciated. One day the king of Odivisha was out hunting in the forest when he came across Ghantapa. Seeing how thin and weak he was, the king asked Ghantapa why he lived in the forest on such a poor diet, and encouraged him to return with him to the city where he would give him food and shelter. Ghantapa replied that just as a great elephant could not be led from the forest by a fine thread, so he could not be tempted to leave the forest by the riches of a king. Angered by Ghantapa's refusal, the king returned to his palace threatening revenge.

The king's anger was so great that he summoned a number of women from the city and told them about the arrogant monk in the forest. He offered great wealth to any one of them who could seduce him and force him to break his vows of celibacy. One woman, a wine-seller, boasted that she could do this and she set out for the forest to look for Ghantapa. When she eventually found him she asked if she could become his servant. Ghantapa had no need of a servant, but he realized that they had a strong relationship from previous lives and so he allowed her to stay. Ghantapa gave her spiritual instructions and empowerments and they engaged sincerely in meditation. After twelve years they both attained the Union of No More Learning, full enlightenment.

One day Ghantapa and the former wine-seller decided to encourage the people of the city to develop a greater interest in Dharma. Accordingly, the woman returned to the king and reported that she had seduced the monk. At first the king doubted the truth of her story, but when she explained that she and Ghantapa now had two children, a son and a daughter, the king was delighted with the news and told her to bring Ghantapa to the city on a particular day. He then issued a proclamation disparaging Ghantapa, and ordered his subjects to assemble on the appointed day to insult and humiliate the monk.

When the day came, Ghantapa and the woman left the forest with their children, the son on Ghantapa's right and the daughter on his left. As they entered the city Ghantapa was walking as if he were drunk, holding a bowl into which the woman was pouring wine. All the people who had gathered laughed and jeered, hurling abuse and insults at him. "Long ago," they taunted him, "our king invited you to the city but you arrogantly refused his invitation. Now you come drunk and with a wine-seller. What a bad example of a Buddhist and a monk!" When they had finished, Ghantapa appeared to become angry and threw his bowl to the ground. The bowl sank into the earth, splitting the ground and causing a spring of water to appear. Ghantapa immediately transformed into Heruka and the woman into Vajrayogini. The boy transformed into a vajra which Ghantapa held in his right hand, and the girl into a bell which he held in his left hand. Ghantapa and his consort then embraced and flew into the sky.

The people were astonished and immediately developed deep regret for their disrespect. They prostrated to Ghantapa, begging him and the emanation of Vajrayogini to return. Ghantapa and his consort refused, but told the people that if their regret was sincere they should make confession to Mahakaruna, the embodiment of Buddha's great compassion. Through the deep remorse of the people of Odivisha and the force of their prayers a statue of Mahakaruna arose from the spring water. The people of Odivisha became very devoted Dharma practitioners and many of them gained realizations. The statue of Mahakaruna can still be seen today.

Because of Ghantapa's pure practice of Heruka and Vajrayogini in the forest, Vajrayogini saw that it was the right time for him to receive her blessings and so she manifested as the wine-seller. Through living with her Ghantapa attained the state of full enlightenment.

In this modern age, people find it difficult to believe that human beings are able to fly, but such things were very common in ancient times when people had strong potentialities for spiritual attainments. Milarepa was a great practitioner of Heruka and Vajrayogini, and—as explained in his life story—at one time he told a large assembly of his disciples how he had gained the ability to fly. Through various methods, including his tummo meditation, he had released the central channel knots at his heart, navel, and below the navel, and because of this he developed a very special physical suppleness that pervaded his body. This made his body extremely light, like a soft feather. At first he could only levitate but gradually he was able to move through space until finally he was able to fly like an eagle. One day Milarepa was flying above a small town called Longda, near where a father and son were plowing a field. First the son saw Milarepa flying and said, "Father, look in the sky. There's a man flying!" The father looked carefully, and realizing that it was Milarepa, told his son, "This man is called Milarepa. He is an evil person who killed many people through his black magic." However, the son deeply appreciated what he saw and said, "There is no sight more amazing than a human being flying through the sky." Milarepa attained the enlightened state of Buddha Heruka through the practice of Heruka body mandala, and many of his disciples including Rechungpa attained the Pure Land of Keajra without abandoning their human body. We can understand this from his collection of songs called *gur bum* in Tibetan. Shortly before he intended to pass away, Milarepa gave advice to his assembled disciples, finally

Milarepa attained the enlightened state of Buddha Heruka.

saying, "We will meet in the Pure Land of Keajra." The actual method to attain the Pure Land of Keajra is qualified meditation on the self-generation of Heruka and Vajrayogini.

Milarepa and his root Guru Marpa, and Je Tsongkhapa and his heart disciple Khedrubje have a special connection. It is said that Marpa is one of Je Tsongkhapa's former incarnations, and Milarepa is one of Khedrubje's former incarnations. Through this we can understand the great kindness of these holy beings who, by changing their physical aspect, continually benefit the people of this world from generation to generation.

The Pure Land of Keajra is the Pure Land of Heruka. It is sometimes also called *Akanishta*, which means the "Highest" Pure Land, and *Pure Dakini Land*, indicating that it is also the Pure Land of Vajrayogini. In general, when an ordinary person takes rebirth in any of the Pure Lands of Buddha he or she is permanently freed from all sufferings and will never again take rebirth within samsara, a contaminated rebirth. Therefore taking rebirth in the Pure Land of Buddha is like attaining liberation or nirvana. For this reason, when an ordinary person takes rebirth in a Pure Land of Buddha through the practice of transference of consciousness, or powa, it is called *attaining enlightenment in one moment*. However, this is only similar to the attainment of enlightenment and is not the actual attainment.

The Pure Land of Keajra is unequalled among all the other Pure Lands of Buddhas. Living beings who abide in other Pure Lands, such as Sukhavati and Tushita, do not have the opportunity to practice completion stage Tantra. Because their bodies have no channels, drops, and inner fire (tummo), they are unable to meditate on the central channel, drops, and inner fire. However, living beings who dwell in the Pure Land of Keajra have bodies that possess channels, drops, and inner fire. These have the nature of light, but they function in the same way as the channels, drops, and inner fire of human beings. They can therefore meditate on the central channel, indestructible drop, and indestructible wind and mind, and in this way they can accomplish the realizations of meaning clear light and pure illusory body, and attain enlightenment within one single life. This is the special good fortune of living beings who dwell in the Pure Land of Keajra. This shows the special power of the instructions on the practices of Heruka and Vajrayogini. It is through practicing these instructions that living beings who dwell in the Pure Land of Keajra have this special good fortune.

The extensive sadhana of Heruka body mandala lists thirty-nine lineage holder Teachers, or *lineage Gurus*, from Ghantapa to Heruka Losang Yeshe, Trijang Rinpoche. All of these spiritual Teachers and many of their disciples attained the realization of Highest Yoga Tantra through practicing Heruka body mandala and Vajrayogini. We should therefore engage in our practice of Heruka body mandala and Vajrayogini with confidence.

WHAT IS THE HERUKA BODY MANDALA?

In this context, "body" refers to our *subtle body*—our channels and drops; and "mandala" means an assembly of enlightened Deities. Our channels and drops are called our *subtle body* because they are parts of our body that are not easy to recognize. The Heruka body mandala is the assembly of the imagined Heruka (ourself) with the consort Vajravarahi (who is the same as Vajrayogini)—the nature of our purified indestructible white and red drops—and our imagined retinue (the Heroes and Heroines)—the nature of our purified channels and drops—in the imagined Pure Land of Keajra. Generally, "mandala" refers to either a "supporting" mandala, which means the world, environment, and palace of an enlightened Deity or Deities, or a "supported" mandala, which means an assembly of enlightened Deities.

The purpose of meditating on Heruka body mandala is to receive the powerful blessings of Buddha Heruka and his retinue within our channels and drops. Through these blessings we can be freed from any obstacles within our channels and drops, and our meditation on the central channel, indestructible drop, and indestructible wind and mind will be successful. Because of this we will easily develop and make progress in the five stages of completion stage mentioned above, and through this fulfill our final goal.

The explanation of how to generate the Heruka body mandala and how to meditate on it given in this book is simple but presents the very essence. I have prepared this for those who are unable to practice the extensive sadhana of Heruka body mandala. In this practice, we need to visualize thirty-six channels of our body—which are the twenty-four channels of the twenty-four places of our body, the four channels of our heart channel wheel, and the eight channels of our eight sense doors. We also visualize the white indestructible drop and the red indestructible drop at our heart, and the twenty-four drops that are contained within the twenty-four channels of the twenty-four places of our body. We then need to receive the powerful blessings of Heruka Father and Mother and his retinue of Heroes and Heroines within these channels and drops.

The twenty-four places of our body represent the twenty-four places of Heruka in the world. The twenty-four places of our body are (1) the hairline, (2) the crown, (3) the right ear, (4) the back of the neck, (5) the left ear, (6) the point between the eyebrows, (7) the two eyes, (8) the two shoulders, (9) the two armpits, (10) the two breasts, (11) the navel, (12) the tip of the nose, (13) the mouth, (14) the throat, (15) the heart, (16) the two testicles, (17) the tip of the sex organ, (18) the anus, (19) the two thighs, (20) the two calves, (21) the eight fingers and eight toes, (22) the tops of the feet, (23) the two thumbs and two big toes, and (24) the two knees.

When we meditate on Heruka body mandala we meditate on ourself as Heruka with our consort Vajravarahi, surrounded in concentric circles by the four Yoginis of the great bliss wheel, the eight Heroes and Heroines of the heart wheel, the eight Heroes and Heroines of the speech wheel, the eight Heroes and Heroines of the body wheel, and the eight Heroines of the commitment wheel. In this way we meditate on the assembly of sixty-two enlightened Deities. Ourself Heruka, and Vajravarahi, are included within the Deities of the great bliss wheel, and are the principal Deities.

While meditating on the assembly of sixty-two enlightened Deities we should believe that ourself Heruka is the nature of our purified indestructible white drop and Vajravarahi is the nature of our purified indestructible red drop. The four Yoginis of the great bliss wheel are the nature of our purified four channels in the cardinal directions of the heart channel wheel. The twenty-four Heroines of the heart, speech, and body wheels are the nature of our purified twenty-four channels of the twenty-four places of our body. The twenty-four Heroes of the heart, speech, and body wheels are the nature of our purified twenty-four drops that are contained inside the twenty-four channels of the twenty-four places of our body. The eight Heroines of the commitment wheel are the nature of our purified eight channels of the eight sense doors.

If we continually meditate in this way on this assembly of the sixty-two enlightened Deities every day with strong faith and conviction, we will definitely receive the powerful blessings of these enlightened Deities within our channels and drops, we will be free from obstacles of the channels and drops, and our meditations on completion stage will therefore be effective. This means that through these meditations we will attain meaning clear light, pure illusory body, and finally enlightenment in this short life.

Many completion stage practitioners experience difficulties in gathering and dissolving their inner winds into the central channel through meditation, and in developing qualified clear light and bliss. This is because their channels and drops do not function correctly, and may even give rise to physical pain. Through sincerely practicing the meditations on Heruka body mandala we will be freed from all these obstacles.

Within the sixty-two enlightened Deities, Heruka and Vajravarahi are the principal and the others are their retinue. The four Yoginis of the great bliss wheel are Dakini, Lama, Khandarohi, and Rupini, and their function is to bestow on us spontaneous great bliss. The eight Heroes and Heroines of the heart wheel are Khandakapala and Partzandi, Mahakankala and Tzändriakiya, Kankala and Parbhawatiya, Vikatadamshtri and Mahanasa, Suraberi and Biramatiya, Amitabha and Karwariya, Vajraprabha and Lamkeshöriya, Vajradeha and Drumatzaya, and their function

Through sincerely practicing the meditations on Heruka body mandala we will be freed from all obstacles.

is to bestow on us the attainment of Buddha's holy mind. The eight Heroes and Heroines of the speech wheel are Ankuraka and Airawatiya, Vajrajatila and Mahabhairawi, Mahavira and Bayubega, Vajrahumkara and Surabhakiya, Subhadra and Shamadewi, Vajrabhadra and Suwatre, Mahabhairawa and Hayakarne, Virupaksha and Khaganane, and their function is to bestow on us the attainment of Buddha's holy speech. The eight Heroes and Heroines of the body wheel are Mahabala and Tzatrabega, Ratnavajra and Khandarohi, Hayagriva and Shaundini, Akashagarbha and Tzatrawarmini, Shri Heruka and Subira, Pämanarteshvara and Mahabala, Vairochana and Tzatrawartini, Vajrasattva and Mahabire, and their function is to bestow on us the attainment of Buddha's holy body. Our present body, speech, and mind are contaminated by the poison of delusions, so they act as the basis of all suffering. We therefore need to attain a Buddha's holy body, speech, and mind. The eight Heroines of the commitment wheel are Kakase, Ulukase, Shönase, Shukarase, Yamadhathi, Yamaduti, Yamadangtrini, and Yamamatani, and their function and commitment is to pacify our obstacles. The Heroes and Heroines of the five wheels are so called because they are victorious over the enemies of ordinary appearance and conceptions.

THE PRELIMINARY PRACTICES

The following explanation of how to practice Heruka body mandala is based on the instructions of the Ganden Oral Lineage. It is simple but very profound. Following these instructions we should practice Heruka body mandala in conjunction with the sadhana, or ritual prayer, called *The Yoga of Buddha Heruka* (see Appendix V). As this sadhana implies, there are six stages to practicing

Heruka body mandala: (1) training in going for refuge, (2) training in renunciation, (3) training in bodhichitta, (4) training in Guru yoga, (5) training in the generation stage of Heruka body mandala, and (6) training in completion stage.

The first four trainings are preliminary practices and the remaining two are the actual practice of Heruka body mandala. Just as a vehicle depends on its four wheels, so the precious vehicle of Heruka body mandala practice depends on the four wheels of training in going for refuge, renunciation, bodhichitta, and Guru yoga. Training in going for refuge is the gateway through which we enter Buddhism; renunciation is the gateway through which we enter the path to liberation; bodhichitta is the gateway through which we enter the path to enlightenment; and Guru yoga is the gateway through which the blessings of all the Buddhas will enter our mind. These are the basic foundations that make the practice of Heruka body mandala effective.

TRAINING IN GOING FOR REFUGE

In this training we should remember and contemplate the following, as explained in Part One:

I want to protect and liberate myself permanently from the sufferings of this life and countless future lives. I can accomplish this only by receiving Buddha's blessings, putting Dharma into practice, and receiving help from Sangha—the supreme spiritual friends.

Thinking deeply in this way, we first make the strong determination and then the promise to seek refuge sincerely in Buddha, Dharma, and Sangha throughout our life. We should meditate on this determination every day and maintain our promise continually for the rest of our life. As the principal commitment of our refuge vow we should always apply effort to receive Buddha's blessings, to put Dharma into practice, and to receive help from Sangha, our pure spiritual friends including our Spiritual Teacher. This is how we go for refuge to Buddha, Dharma, and Sangha. Through this we will accomplish our goal—permanent liberation from all the sufferings of this life and countless future lives, the real meaning of our human life.

To maintain our promise to go for refuge to Buddha, Dharma, and Sangha throughout our life, and so that we and all living beings may receive Buddha's blessings and protection, we recite the following refuge prayer from the sadhana *The Yoga of Buddha Heruka* every day with strong faith:

I and all sentient beings, until we achieve enlightenment,
Go for refuge to Buddha, Dharma, and Sangha.

TRAINING IN RENUNCIATION

In this training we remember and contemplate how we will experience unbearable suffering in our countless future lives, as explained in detail in Part One. Then from the depths of our heart, we should think:

There is no benefit in denying the sufferings of future lives; when they actually descend on me it will be too late to protect myself from them. Therefore I definitely need to prepare protection now, while I have this human life that gives me the opportunity to liberate myself permanently from the sufferings of my countless future lives. If I do not apply effort to accomplish this, but allow my human life to become empty of meaning, there is no greater deception and no greater foolishness. I must put effort now into liberating myself permanently from the sufferings of my countless future lives.

We meditate on this determination continually until we develop the spontaneous wish to liberate ourself permanently from the sufferings of countless future lives.

TRAINING IN BODHICHITTA

In this training we should maintain the practice of the five stages of training in bodhichitta that was explained in detail in Part One. In conclusion, we think:

I should not be content with seeking merely my own liberation; I must consider the welfare of other living beings. They are all my mothers, and they are drowning in the vast and deep ocean of samsara, experiencing unbearable suffering in life after life, without end. While I am just one single person, other living beings are countless in number; the happiness and freedom of others are therefore much more important than my own. I cannot bear that my countless mothers are experiencing unbearable physical suffering and mental pain in this life and in their countless future lives; I must permanently liberate them all from their suffering, and for this purpose I will make great effort to become an enlightened Buddha.

We should maintain this supreme good heart of bodhichitta, continually day and night. All our meditations on generation and completion stages should be motivated by this supreme good heart, and we should always remember that all our meditations on generation and completion stages are methods to fulfill our bodhichitta wishes. To generate bodhichitta we recite from the sadhana:

Through the virtues I collect by giving and other perfections,
May I become a Buddha for the benefit of all.

TRAINING IN GURU YOGA

The term *Guru* is a Sanskrit word that means "Spiritual Guide." A Spiritual Guide can be Eastern, Western, male, female, ordained, or lay. Our Spiritual Guide is any Spiritual Teacher who leads us into correct paths to liberation and enlightenment by giving teachings and showing a good example. Guru yoga is a special training in relying on our Spiritual Guide; in this context, *yoga* means training in spiritual paths, not physical training. The sadhana *The Yoga of Buddha Heruka* in Appendix V presents the Guru yoga of Je Tsongkhapa inseparable from our root Guru, Buddha Shakyamuni, and Heruka, who is known as Guru Sumati Buddha Heruka. In this context, *root Guru* refers to our Spiritual Guide from whom we have received the instructions, transmission, and empowerment of Heruka body mandala. The name Guru Sumati Buddha Heruka implies that our root *Guru*, Je Tsongkhapa (or *Sumati* Kirti, Sanskrit for Je Tsongkhapa's ordained name), *Buddha* Shakyamuni, and *Heruka* are one person but have different aspects. We need to maintain this recognition at all times for our practice of Heruka body mandala to be effective. To benefit each and every living being directly every day, definitive Heruka emanated Buddha Shakyamuni, who in turn emanated Je Tsongkhapa, who in turn emanated our Spiritual Guide; they are like one actor showing different aspects at different times.

The purpose of this Guru yoga practice is:

1. To accumulate a great collection of merit, or good fortune. Because of our lack of merit it is difficult for us to fulfill our wishes and we experience many obstacles to accomplishing spiritual attainments.

2. To purify negativity, or non-virtuous actions. When we purify the countless potentialities of our non-virtuous actions we purify our mind. As mentioned above, by purifying our mind we will attain full enlightenment.

3. To receive the powerful blessings of all the Buddhas. We have the seed of the realizations of Highest Yoga Tantra in general and Heruka body mandala in particular, which is part of our Buddha nature. However, without receiving the powerful blessings of all Buddhas through our Spiritual Guide, who is their representative, our seed of the realization of Highest Yoga Tantra will never ripen.

4. To generate the experience of great bliss and emptiness. This practice is a powerful method to ripen our seed of the realization of Mahamudra Tantra.

Through accomplishing these four necessary conditions we can easily make progress in the main practice of this sadhana, which is training in generation and completion stages.

Je Sherab Senge, one of Je Tsongkhapa's heart disciples, received the special instructions of the Guru yoga of Je Tsongkhapa from

Je Tsongkhapa himself. This is called the *Guru yoga of the Segyu lineage*, now known as the Guru yoga of *Heart Jewel*. The instructions of the Guru yoga of *Heart Jewel* were originally only given as oral instructions. Later the great Yogi Palden Sangpo composed a sadhana based on these oral instructions, and since then it has been practiced publicly. The Guru yoga of *Heart Jewel* can be practiced either according to Sutra tradition or according to Highest Yoga Tantra tradition. The sadhana, *The Yoga of Buddha Heruka*, presents the practice of the Guru yoga of *Heart Jewel* according to Highest Yoga Tantra. Those who have the commitment to practice *Heart Jewel* can add prayers to Dorje Shugden just before the dedication verses of *The Yoga of Buddha Heruka*.

The practice of this Guru yoga has five stages: (1) visualization and meditation, (2) inviting the wisdom beings, (3) the practice of the seven limbs, (4) making special requests, and (5) generating the experience of great bliss and emptiness.

VISUALIZATION AND MEDITATION

We recite the following from the sadhana, while concentrating on its meaning:

In the space before me is Guru Sumati Buddha Heruka—Je Tsongkhapa inseparable from my root Guru, Buddha Shakyamuni, and Heruka—surrounded by all the Buddhas of the ten directions.

While we visualize this we think and contemplate:

Je Tsongkhapa attained enlightenment to lead all living beings to the liberating path through his emanations. Who is his emanation now leading me to the liberating path? It is definitely my Spiritual Guide from whom I have received instructions, transmission, and empowerment of Heruka body mandala, and who shows a qualified example.

Thinking in this way we should strongly believe that our Spiritual Guide is an emanation of Je Tsongkhapa, and then meditate on this belief single-pointedly. We should practice this meditation continually.

INVITING THE WISDOM BEINGS

We recite the following verse from the sadhana, while concentrating on its meaning:

From the heart of the Protector of the hundreds of Deities of the Joyful Land,
To the peak of a cloud which is like a cluster of fresh, white curd,
All-knowing Losang Dragpa, King of the Dharma,
Please come to this place together with your Sons.

The "Protector of the hundreds of Deities of the Joyful Land" refers to Buddha Maitreya. We believe that wisdom being Je Tsongkhapa together with his retinue dissolves into the assembly of Guru Sumati Buddha Heruka visualized in front of us, and they become non-dual.

We also recite the following request from the sadhana:

In the space before me on a lion throne lotus and moon,
The venerable Gurus smile with delight.

O Supreme Field of Merit for my mind of faith,
Please remain for a hundred eons to spread the doctrine.

THE PRACTICE OF THE SEVEN LIMBS

With strong faith in our Spiritual Guide, Guru Sumati Buddha Heruka, we should sincerely engage every day in the practice of the seven limbs. These are (1) prostration, (2) offerings, (3) purification, (4) rejoicing, (5) requesting the turning of the Wheel of Dharma, (6) beseeching the Spiritual Guides to remain for a long time, and (7) dedication. In this context, the actual practice of Heruka body mandala is like the main body, and the seven limbs are like the limbs that support the main body. Just as our body is able to function in dependence upon its limbs, so the effectiveness of our training in Heruka body mandala depends on our practice of the seven limbs.

PROSTRATION

Making prostrations to enlightened beings is a powerful method for purifying negative karma, sickness, and obstacles, and for increasing our merit, our happiness, and our Dharma realizations. Temporarily, prostrations improve our physical health and make our mind happy; and ultimately, they cause us to attain a Buddha's Form Body. Generating faith in the holy beings is mental prostration, reciting praises to them is verbal prostration, and showing respect to them with our body is physical prostration. We can make physical prostrations by respectfully prostrating our entire body on the ground; by respectfully touching our knees, palms, and forehead to the ground; or by respectfully placing our palms together at the level of our heart.

To make powerful prostrations to the holy beings, we imagine that from every pore of our body we emanate another body, and from every pore of these bodies we emanate yet more bodies, until our emanated bodies fill the entire world. Then, while reciting the following verse, we strongly believe that all these countless bodies make prostrations to Guru Sumati Buddha Heruka and all the Buddhas of the ten directions:

Your mind of wisdom realizes the full extent of objects of
    knowledge,
Your eloquent speech is the ear-ornament of the fortunate,
Your beautiful body is ablaze with the glory of renown,
I prostrate to you, whom to see, to hear, and to remember is
    so meaningful.

We should do this practice of prostration every day. As a preliminary guide for our actual practice of Heruka body mandala, we can collect a hundred thousand prostrations, either throughout our daily life or in retreat.

OFFERINGS

From the depths of our heart we make the following determination:

To liberate all living beings from suffering permanently
I make excellent offerings to the supreme holy being
Guru Sumati Buddha Heruka,
And to all the other holy beings.

However many flowers and fruits there are,
And all the different types of medicine;

All the jewels there are in the world,
And all the pure, refreshing waters;

Mountains of jewels, forest groves,
And quiet and joyful places;
Heavenly trees adorned with flowers,
And trees whose branches hang with delicious fruits;

Scents that come from the celestial realms,
Incense, wish-granting trees, and jeweled trees;
Harvests that need no cultivation,
And all ornaments that are suitable to be offered;

Lakes and pools adorned with lotuses,
And the beautiful call of wild geese;
Everything that is unowned
Throughout all worlds as extensive as space—

Holding these in my mind, I offer them well
To you, the supreme beings, the Buddhas and
    Bodhisattvas.
O Compassionate Ones, holy objects of offering,
Think of me kindly and accept what I offer.

Eternally I will offer all my bodies
To you, the Buddhas and Bodhisattvas.
Out of respect, I will become your servant;
Please accept me, O Supreme Heroes.

While we imagine making all of these offerings, we can recite the
following short verse:

Pleasing water offerings, various flowers,
Sweet-smelling incense, lights, scented water, and so forth,
A vast cloud of offerings both set out and imagined,
I offer to you, O Supreme Field of Merit.

In Buddhism an offering is anything that delights the enlightened beings. Our main offering is our practice of compassion, because this gives enlightened beings the greatest delight. Therefore, our motivation for making offerings should be compassion for all living beings—our sincere wish to liberate all living beings from suffering permanently.

In summary, we should always regard all our daily Dharma practices as unsurpassed offerings to Guru Sumati Buddha Heruka—the synthesis of our Spiritual Guide, Je Tsongkhapa, Buddha Shakyamuni, and Heruka—and to all the other enlightened beings. In this way we can accumulate immeasurable merit, or good fortune.

PURIFICATION

Purification is the supreme method to prevent future suffering and to remove obstacles to our Dharma practice, especially to the practice of Heruka body mandala. It makes our actions pure so that we ourselves become pure. Since our body is not our self, cleaning our body alone is not enough; we need to clean our self through purification practice.

What is it that we need to purify? We need to purify our nonvirtuous and inappropriate actions. In our countless previous lives we performed many actions that caused other living beings to experience suffering and problems, and as a result of these non-virtuous actions, we now experience suffering and many different problems. Although the actions themselves have ceased, their potential to give rise to suffering and problems still remains on our subtle consciousness, and will remain for life after life until it ripens. Therefore, on our root consciousness there are infinite negative potentials, which function to lead us into wrong paths and cause us to experience endless suffering. These are serious obstacles to our Dharma practice in general, and to our practice of Heruka body mandala in particular.

We can understand how our non-virtuous potentials are the main obstacle to our Dharma practice through contemplating the following:

In our previous lives we performed actions that rejected holy Dharma, and denied rebirth, karma, and the attainment of liberation and enlightenment. As a result of this we now experience (1) difficulties developing the intention to practice Dharma; (2) difficulties believing Dharma teachings, such as karma; and (3) difficulties making progress in our Dharma practice.

Purification practice is very simple. All we need to do is contemplate the great disadvantages of the non-virtuous actions that we have performed since beginningless time. Then with strong regret we confess all these non-virtuous actions, as well as transgressions of our vows and commitments, to Guru Sumati Buddha Heruka, and to all the other holy beings, while reciting the following verse:

Whatever non-virtues of body, speech, and mind
I have accumulated since time without beginning,
Especially transgressions of my three vows,
With great remorse I confess each one from the depths of my
heart.

We should repeat this practice many times. At the end of each session we make a strong determination not to perform any non-virtuous action or to transgress any of our vows and commitments. As the great preliminary guide for our Heruka body mandala practice, we can collect a hundred thousand recitations of this verse—concentrating strongly on its meaning. Alternatively we can collect a hundred thousand recitations of Vajrasattva's mantra.

REJOICING

We should learn to rejoice in others' virtuous actions, happiness, good qualities, and good fortune. Normally we do the opposite and develop jealousy. Jealousy is very harmful for individuals and society. In an instant it can destroy our own and others' happiness and harmony, and lead to fighting, or even war. In everyday life we can see how people react with jealousy in regard to relationships, business, position, and religious views, causing suffering to so many people. Our problems of jealousy can be solved simply by learning to rejoice in others' happiness and goodness. This can be practiced even while we are lying down, relaxing, or going about our daily activities.

With very little effort we can accumulate immeasurable good fortune simply by rejoicing in the excellent deeds of Buddhas such

Buddha Vajradhara

as Je Tsongkhapa. We can do this while reciting the following verse with strong concentration on the meaning:

In this degenerate age you strove for much learning and
accomplishment.
Abandoning the eight worldly concerns, you made your
freedom and endowment meaningful.
O Protector, from the very depths of my heart,
I rejoice in the great wave of your deeds.

REQUESTING THE TURNING OF
THE WHEEL OF DHARMA

We begin this practice by thinking:

I have the opportunity to listen to, understand, and practice
holy Dharma, and therefore the good fortune to enter, make
progress on, and complete the path to enlightenment. It would
be so wonderful if all other living beings could enjoy the same
good fortune!

From the depths of our heart we then repeatedly request Guru Sumati Buddha Heruka to emanate countless Spiritual Teachers to teach holy Dharma and guide all living beings to the state of ultimate happiness, enlightenment, while reciting the following verse:

From the billowing clouds of wisdom and compassion
In the space of your Truth Body, O Venerable and holy Gurus,
Please send down a rain of vast and profound Dharma
Appropriate to the disciples of this world.

BESEECHING THE SPIRITUAL GUIDES TO REMAIN FOR A LONG TIME

In this practice we think:

If the Spiritual Teachers who have been emanated by holy beings remain in this world for many eons, all living beings will gradually have the opportunity to listen to, understand, and practice Dharma. In this way, eventually all living beings without exception will attain enlightenment.

We then request Guru Sumati Buddha Heruka that his emanations who are teaching Dharma will remain in this world until samsara ends, while reciting the following verse:

From your actual deathless body, born from meaning clear light,
Please send countless emanations throughout the world
To spread the oral lineage of the Ganden doctrine;
And may they remain for a very long time.

DEDICATION

Whenever we perform any virtuous actions, we should dedicate them to the attainment of enlightenment and to the flourishing of Buddha's doctrine, which benefits all living beings. The great Master Atisha said:

Dedicate your virtues throughout the day and the night, and always watch your mind.

If we dedicate our virtuous actions in this way, their potentialities will never be destroyed by anger and wrong views but instead will increase in strength. The practice of dedication makes our virtuous actions effective. We can engage in this practice while reciting the following verse:

Through the virtues I have accumulated here,
May the doctrine and all living beings receive every benefit.
Especially may the essence of the doctrine
Of Venerable Losang Dragpa shine forever.

In summary, while practicing each of the seven limbs we should apply effort to making the sun of our faith shine continually on the snow mountain of our Spiritual Guide—Guru Sumati Buddha Heruka—and make strong requests. Through this, the blessing waters of all the Buddhas of the ten directions will flow down, our very subtle body will receive a special power that transforms it into an enlightened body, and our very subtle mind will receive a special power that transforms it into an enlightened mind.

MAKING SPECIAL REQUESTS

To make this special request, we first offer the entire universe, regarding it as the Pure Land of Buddha, to Guru Sumati Buddha Heruka and all the Buddhas of the ten directions. This offering is called a *mandala offering*, a detailed explanation of which can be found in *Guide to Dakini Land*. Then while concentrating on its meaning, we recite three times the following request prayer from the sadhana:

O Guru Sumati Buddha Heruka, from now until I attain
enlightenment,
I shall seek no refuge other than you.

Please pacify my obstacles and bestow upon me
The two attainments of liberating and ripening.
Please bless me so that I will become definitive Heruka,
In which state I shall experience all phenomena as purified
and gathered into emptiness, inseparable from great bliss.

This prayer has the same meaning as the essence mantra of Heruka. Through completing the meditations on generation and completion stages, we abandon all our subtle mistaken appearances; this abandonment is the attainment of "liberating." And due to ripening our Buddha nature completely, we experience ourself as a real Buddha, and our world, enjoyments, and activities as those of a Buddha; this experience is the attainment of "ripening." By accomplishing these two attainments we become definitive Heruka; that is, Heruka imputed on Buddha's Truth Body, or Dharmakaya. At the same time we experience all phenomena as purified, which means that we have purified the subtle mistaken appearance of all phenomena; and we experience all phenomena gathered into emptiness, which means we realize that all phenomena are not other than emptiness. These two experiences of "purified" and "gathered" imply that we have realized the union of the two truths directly and simultaneously; this realization is actual enlightenment. With this prayer we are requesting Guru Sumati Buddha Heruka to bestow all these attainments upon us.

As ordinary beings we have only one body that we can use, and in reality this is part of our parents' bodies. Buddhas, however, possess four bodies simultaneously: the two Truth Bodies, which are the Wisdom Truth Body and Nature Truth Body; and the two Form Bodies, which are the Enjoyment Body and Emanation

Body. Buddha's mind is the Wisdom Truth Body and the emptiness of Buddha's mind is the Nature Truth Body; together they are called the *Truth Body* or *Dharmakaya*. Buddha's bodies that possess form are called Form Bodies. Buddha's subtle Form Body is called the Enjoyment Body, and Buddha's gross Form Body is called the Emanation Body. A Buddha's Truth Body is extremely subtle and therefore can be seen only by Buddhas and not by others. A Buddha's Enjoyment Body can be seen by Superior Bodhisattvas, and a Buddha's Emanation Body can be seen by ordinary beings who have a pure mind.

GENERATING THE EXPERIENCE OF GREAT BLISS AND EMPTINESS

After we have recited the special request prayer three times sincerely from our heart, we then think and imagine:

Due to my making requests in this way, all the Buddhas of the ten directions dissolve into Je Tsongkhapa who is inseparable from my root Guru, he dissolves into Buddha Shakyamuni at his heart, and Buddha Shakyamuni dissolves into Heruka at his heart. With delight, Guru Heruka, who is the nature of the union of great bliss and emptiness, enters my body through my crown, and dissolves into my mind at my heart. Because Heruka, who is the nature of the union of great bliss and emptiness, becomes inseparable from my mind, I experience spontaneous great bliss and emptiness. I perceive nothing other than the emptiness of all phenomena, the mere absence of all phenomena that I normally see or perceive. My subtle mistaken appearance of all phenomena, including the channels and drops of my body, is purified.

Holding this belief, we meditate on the emptiness of all phenomena while experiencing great bliss.

TRAINING IN THE GENERATION STAGE OF HERUKA BODY MANDALA

There are five stages to training in the generation stage of Heruka body mandala, the actual self-generation practice of Heruka body mandala: (1) generating the body mandala of Heruka, (2) training in clear appearance, (3) training in divine pride, (4) training in non-dual appearance and emptiness, and (5) training in mantra recitation.

GENERATING THE BODY MANDALA OF HERUKA

While meditating on the emptiness of all phenomena, perceiving nothing other than emptiness, we think and imagine:

In the vast space of emptiness of all phenomena, the nature of my purified mistaken appearance of all phenomena—which is the Pure Land of Keajra—I appear as Buddha Heruka with a blue-colored body, four faces, and twelve arms, the nature of my purified white indestructible drop. I am embracing Vajravarahi, the nature of my purified red indestructible drop. I am surrounded by the Heroes and Heroines of the five wheels, who are the nature of my purified subtle body—the channels and drops. I reside in the mandala, the celestial mansion, which is the nature of my purified gross body. Although I have this appearance it is not other than the emptiness of all phenomena.

At this point, (1) while experiencing great bliss and emptiness, (2) we meditate on the clear appearance of the mandala and

Deities with divine pride, while (3) recognizing that the Deities are the nature of our purified channels and drops, which are our subtle body, and that the mandala is the nature of our purified gross body.

In this way we train sincerely in one single meditation on generation stage possessing these three characteristics. Holding the third characteristic—recognizing the Deities as the nature of our purified subtle body, and the mandala as the nature of our purified gross body—makes this concentration an actual body mandala meditation.

TRAINING IN CLEAR APPEARANCE

For our meditation on the body mandala of Heruka to be qualified we need to train in clear appearance. We think and imagine deeply, as above:

In the vast space of emptiness of all phenomena, the nature of my purified mistaken appearance of all phenomena—which is the Pure Land of Keajra—I appear as Buddha Heruka with a blue-colored body, four faces, and twelve arms, the nature of my purified white indestructible drop. I am embracing Vajravarahi, the nature of my purified red indestructible drop. I am surrounded by the Heroes and Heroines of the five wheels, who are the nature of my purified subtle body—the channels and drops. I reside in the mandala, the celestial mansion, which is the nature of my purified gross body. Although I have this appearance it is not other than the emptiness of all phenomena.

We mentally repeat this contemplation again and again until we perceive clearly the object of our meditation—the Heruka

Buddha Vajradharma

body mandala, which is the assembly of imagined Heruka (ourself) with consort Vajravarahi, the nature of our purified white and red indestructible drops, and our imagined retinue of Heroes and Heroines, who are the nature of our purified channels and drops, in the imagined Pure Land of Keajra. When we perceive the assembly of this supporting mandala and supported Deities—the Heruka body mandala—we hold it without forgetting and remain on it single-pointedly for as long as possible.

We should repeat this meditation again and again, until we are able to maintain our concentration clearly for one minute every time we meditate on it. Our concentration that has this ability is called *concentration of placing the mind*. In the second stage, with the concentration of placing the mind, we meditate on the Heruka body mandala continually until we are able to maintain our concentration clearly for five minutes every time we meditate on it. Our concentration that has this ability is called *concentration of continual placement*. In the third stage, with the concentration of continual placement, we meditate on the Heruka body mandala continually until we are able to remember immediately our object of meditation—the Heruka body mandala—whenever we lose it during meditation. Our concentration that has this ability is called *concentration of replacement*. In the fourth stage, with the concentration of replacement, we meditate on the Heruka body mandala continually until we are able to maintain our concentration clearly throughout our whole meditation session without forgetting every time we meditate on it. Our concentration that has this ability is called *concentration of close placement*. At this stage we have very stable and clear concentration focused on the Heruka body mandala.

Then, with the concentration of close placement, we meditate on the Heruka body mandala continually until finally we attain the concentration of tranquil abiding focused on the Heruka body mandala, which causes us to experience special physical and mental suppleness and bliss. Through this concentration of tranquil abiding focused on the Heruka body mandala, we will definitely attain the Pure Land of Keajra in this life or in our next life.

TRAINING IN DIVINE PRIDE

Through perceiving our imagined Heruka's body and mind we develop the thought, "I am Heruka"—this thought is divine pride. It is a correct thought or belief because it arises from wisdom that realizes correct reasons. Generally, if we improve our clear appearance of perceiving the Heruka body mandala through the practice of concentration mentioned above, this makes it easier for us to develop and increase divine pride. This is because clear appearance reduces our ordinary appearance, and this makes it easier for us to develop and increase the thought, "I am Heruka." However, we can train in divine pride by contemplating correct reasons why it is necessary for us to change the basis of imputation for our self from a contaminated body and mind to the uncontaminated body and mind of Heruka. How we can do this has already been explained in the chapter *The Tantra of Generation Stage*.

TRAINING IN NON-DUAL
APPEARANCE AND EMPTINESS

This is a very profound practice of generation stage. The explanation of this practice presented in this book is based on the instructions of the Ganden Oral Lineage. With respect to the term *non-dual appearance and emptiness*: "appearance" refers to the Heruka body mandala, which is the assembly of the supporting mandala and supported Deities of Heruka body mandala, the nature of our purified gross and subtle bodies; "emptiness" refers to the emptiness of all phenomena; and "non-dual" means that the Heruka body mandala and emptiness are one object but have different names. When we perceive and realize this non-dual Heruka body mandala and emptiness we have found the object of our meditation; we should hold this object without forgetting, and remain on it single-pointedly for as long as possible. We should practice this meditation continually and sincerely, without distraction. By doing this, initially we will realize appearance (the Heruka body mandala), which is the conventional truth, and emptiness, which is the ultimate truth, simultaneously with our gross mind. Finally we will realize these two truths directly and simultaneously with our very subtle mind. Our very subtle mind that realizes these two truths directly and simultaneously is the state of enlightenment.

When we first meditate on Heruka body mandala we have a strong perception of the Heruka body mandala that we normally perceive. This perception is our mistaken appearance of the Heruka body mandala. It is mistaken because the Heruka body mandala that we normally perceive does not exist, even if we perceive it. The strong perception of the Heruka body mandala that we normally perceive, directly interferes with our understanding that the Heruka body mandala and the emptiness of all phenomena are non-dual. However, through meditating on the emptiness of all phenomena with strong concentration, the strong perception of the Heruka body mandala that we normally perceive will cease during meditation. We will then automatically realize that the Heruka body mandala and the emptiness of all phenomena are non-dual. This can be illustrated by the analogy of seeing two empty glasses in front of us. At first we would perceive the spaces inside the two glasses as different, but if we broke the two glasses we would realize that the spaces inside them were non-dual.

In the sadhana, the words, "Although I have this appearance it is not other than the emptiness of all phenomena," reveal the training in non-dual appearance and emptiness. If we understand clearly the meaning of the union of the two truths (explained in detail in the chapter "Training in Ultimate Bodhichitta" in Part One) it will not be difficult to understand the meaning of non-dual appearance and emptiness that is explained in this section.

THE ACTUAL MEDITATION ON NON-DUAL APPEARANCE AND EMPTINESS

Having accomplished clear appearance and divine pride through training in them as explained above, we then think and contemplate:

Since all phenomena that I normally perceive do not exist, the Heruka body mandala that I normally perceive does not exist. Heruka body mandala is a mere name, which means that it is not other than the emptiness of all phenomena. The emptiness of all phenomena and Heruka body mandala are non-dual; they are not two different objects but one object with different names.

Thinking in this way, when we perceive as non-dual the assembly of the supporting mandala and supported Deities of the Heruka body mandala existing as mere name, and the emptiness of all phenomena, we meditate on this non-dual Heruka body mandala and emptiness single-pointedly with the experience of great bliss. As mentioned above, through continually practicing this meditation, initially we will realize the Heruka body mandala, which is the conventional truth, and emptiness, which is the ultimate truth, simultaneously with our gross mind. Finally we will realize these two truths directly and simultaneously with our very subtle mind. Our very subtle mind that realizes these two truths directly and simultaneously is actual enlightenment. It is a wisdom that is permanently free from the mistaken appearance of all phenomena; such a wisdom is possessed only by fully enlightened Buddhas. Through this we can understand that this training in non-dual appearance and emptiness is a powerful method to attain enlightenment very quickly and easily. This training is the very essence practice of the instructions of the Ganden Oral Lineage. Through this training Gyalwa Ensapa and many of his disciples began, made progress on, and completed the Vajrayana path; and in this way they attained enlightenment within three years.

Through this training Gyalwa Ensapa and many of his disciples attained enlightenment within three years.

TRAINING IN MANTRA RECITATION

The Sanskrit word *mantra* means protection of mind. Through reciting the mantras of Heruka Father and Mother and their retinue with strong faith we can protect ourself from being harmed by inanimate objects such as earthquakes, floods, hurricanes, and fire, and by animate objects such as humans and non-humans; we can pacify our sickness, untimely death, and other adverse conditions; we can increase our good fortune, lifespan, and especially our internal qualities of faith, correct view, correct intention, and other spiritual realizations; we can control our delusions such as anger; we can benefit others through performing various kinds of actions including wrathful actions; and especially we can lead ourself and others to the supreme happiness of enlightenment.

We recite the following mantras as a request to bestow these attainments on us, while recognizing and believing that the wisdom beings of Heruka Father and Mother and their retinues are inseparable from the imagined Heruka (ourself) and consort Vajravarahi, and our retinue of Heroes and Heroines.

THE ESSENCE MANTRA OF HERUKA

We recite the following, while concentrating on the meaning:

At my heart is wisdom being Buddha Heruka, definitive Heruka.

O Glorious Vajra Heruka, you who enjoy
The divine illusory body and mind of clear light,
Please pacify my obstacles and bestow upon me
The two attainments of liberating and ripening.
Please bless me so that I will become definitive Heruka,
In which state I shall experience all phenomena as purified
*   and gathered into emptiness, inseparable from great bliss.*

OM SHRI VAJRA HE HE RU RU KAM HUM HUM PHAT
DAKINI DZALA SHAMBARAM SÖHA

We can recite this mantra twenty-one times, a hundred times, or as many times as we wish.

THE THREE-OM MANTRA OF VAJRAYOGINI

We recite the following, while concentrating on the meaning:

At the heart of imagined Vajrayogini (Vajravarahi) is wisdom being Buddha Vajrayogini, definitive Vajrayogini.

OM OM OM SARWA BUDDHA DAKINIYE VAJRA WARNANIYE VAJRA BEROTZANIYE HUM HUM HUM PHAT PHAT PHAT SÖHA

We should recite at least as many three-OM mantras as we promised to recite when we received a Vajrayogini empowerment.

The *three*-OM mantra is the union of the essence and close essence mantras of Vajravarahi. The meaning of this mantra is as follows. With OM OM OM we are calling Vajrayogini—the principal Deity—and her retinue of Heroines of the three wheels (the body, speech, and mind wheels). SARWA BUDDHA DAKINIYE means that Vajrayogini is the synthesis of the minds of all Buddhas, VAJRA WARNANIYE means that she is the synthesis of the speech of all Buddhas, and VAJRA BEROTZANIYE means that she is the synthesis of the bodies of all Buddhas. With HUM HUM HUM we are requesting Vajrayogini and her retinues to bestow upon us the attainments of the body, speech, and mind of all the Buddhas. With PHAT PHAT PHAT we are requesting them to pacify our main obstacle—the subtle mistaken appearance of our body, speech, and mind; and SÖHA means "please build the basic foundation for all these attainments within me."

As mentioned above, because our present body, speech, and mind are contaminated by the poison of delusions they act as the basis of all suffering. We therefore need to attain a Buddha's holy body, speech, and mind.

THE CONDENSED MANTRA OF THE SIXTY-TWO DEITIES OF HERUKA BODY MANDALA

We recite the following, while concentrating on the meaning:

At the heart of each of the sixty-two Deities is their individual wisdom being, their own definitive Deity.

OM HUM BAM RIM RIM LIM LIM, KAM KHAM GAM GHAM NGAM, TSAM TSHAM DZAM DZHAM NYAM, TrAM THrAM DrAM DHrAM NAM, TAM THAM DAM DHAM NAM, PAM PHAM BAM BHAM, YAM RAM LAM WAM, SHAM KAM SAM HAM HUM HUM PHAT

We can recite this mantra seven times, twenty-one times, one hundred times, or more.

When we recite this mantra we are making requests to wisdom being Buddha Heruka with Vajravarahi, and his retinue of Heroes and Heroines of the five wheels, to pacify our obstacle of subtle mistaken appearance and to bestow on us the attainments of outer and inner Dakini Land. Outer Dakini Land is the Pure Land of Keajra and inner Dakini Land is meaning clear light. The moment our mind is free from subtle mistaken appearance, we open the door through which we can see all enlightened Deities directly. For as long as our mind remains polluted by subtle mistaken appearance this door is closed. The meaning of subtle mistaken appearance has already been explained.

After mantra recitation, we conclude our practice of *The Yoga of Buddha Heruka* sadhana by reciting dedication and auspicious prayers.

Those who wish to perform a close retreat of Heruka body mandala can do so in conjunction with the sadhana *Blissful Journey: How to Engage in a Close Retreat of Heruka Body Mandala* found in Appendix VI.

TRAINING IN COMPLETION STAGE

Training in completion stage is the method for completely releasing our mind from subtle mistaken appearance. We will finally attain enlightenment by completely abandoning the subtle mistaken appearance of all phenomena through our realization of completion stage. Developing the realization of completion stage depends on the inner winds entering, abiding, and dissolving within the central channel through the force of meditation. The objects of these meditations are the central channel, indestructible drop, and the indestructible wind and mind. Therefore, in this context, training in completion stage means training in meditation on the central channel, indestructible drop, and the indestructible wind and mind.

In the scriptures it is said that meditation on the central channel is like a wishfulfilling cow. Just as a wishfulfilling cow provides milk unceasingly, so meditation on the central channel will enable us to experience great bliss unceasingly, and the meditations on the indestructible drop and on the indestructible wind and mind will enable us to experience the fully qualified clear light of bliss, which has the function of releasing our mind permanently from subtle mistaken appearance. A detailed explanation of the channels, drops, and winds, how to meditate on the central channel, indestructible drop, and indestructible wind and mind, and how to make progress in realizing the five stages of completion stage has already been given.

The Instructions of Vajrayogini

THE YOGAS OF SLEEPING, RISING, AND EXPERIENCING NECTAR

Vajrayogini is a female enlightened Deity of Highest Yoga Tantra who is the manifestation of the wisdom of all Buddhas. Her function is to guide all living beings to the Pure Land of Keajra, or Pure Dakini Land. The instructions of Vajrayogini were taught by Buddha in *Root Tantra of Heruka*. The great Yogi Naropa received these instructions directly from Vajrayogini, and passed them to Pamtingpa—one of his heart disciples. Pamtingpa then passed these instructions to the Tibetan translator Sherab Tseg, and from Sherab Tseg these instructions have been passed down in an unbroken lineage to Je Phabongkhapa, and then to the most venerable Kyabje Trijang Rinpoche, holder of the lineage. It is from this great master that I, the author of this book, received these precious instructions.

Highest Yoga Tantra can be divided into Father Tantra and Mother Tantra. Mother Tantras principally reveal the training in clear light, which is the main cause of attaining Buddha's holy mind; and Father Tantras such as Guhyasamaja Tantra principally reveal the training in the illusory body, which is the main cause

Venerable Vajrayogini

of attaining Buddha's holy body. Because Vajrayogini Tantra is Mother Tantra, the main body of Vajrayogini practice is training in clear light. This main body has eleven limbs, which are called the *eleven yogas*. In this context, *yoga* means training in spiritual paths. For example, training in a spiritual path in conjunction with sleep is called the *yoga of sleeping*.

When the eleven yogas are listed in the scriptures, the first is the yoga of sleeping. This indicates that we should begin the practice of Vajrayogini with the yoga of sleeping. As already mentioned, the main body of Vajrayogini practice is training in clear light. Clear light naturally manifests during sleep; we therefore have the opportunity to train in recognizing it during sleep. When we recognize and realize clear light directly, we will have attained meaning clear light, the realization of the fourth of the five stages of completion stage.

What is clear light? It is the very subtle mind that manifests when the inner winds enter, abide, and dissolve within the central channel. Clear light is the eighth sign of the dissolution of inner winds within the central channel, and it perceives emptiness. There are three different types of clear light: (1) the clear light of sleep, (2) the clear light of death, and (3) the realization of clear light.

During sleep our very subtle mind manifests because our inner winds naturally enter and dissolve within our central channel. This very subtle mind is the clear light of sleep. It perceives emptiness, but we cannot recognize the clear light itself or emptiness because our memory cannot function during sleep. In a similar way, during our death, our very subtle mind manifests because our inner winds enter and dissolve within the central channel. This very subtle mind is the clear light of death. It perceives emptiness, but we cannot recognize the clear light itself or emptiness because our memory cannot function during death.

During waking, if we are able to cause our inner winds to enter, abide, and dissolve within the central channel through the power of meditation, we experience a deep dissolution of our inner winds into the central channel, and through this our very subtle mind will manifest. This very subtle mind is the realization of clear light. Its nature is a bliss arisen from the melting of the drops inside the central channel, and its function is to prevent mistaken appearance. It is also the realization of the clear light of bliss, which is the very essence of Highest Yoga Tantra and the actual quick path to enlightenment.

In conclusion, the main body of Vajrayogini practice is training in clear light of bliss. This can be divided into two: (1) training in bliss, and (2) training in clear light. Before training in bliss we should know what it is. This bliss is not sexual bliss; we do not need to train in sexual bliss because anyone, even an animal, can experience this without training. The bliss that we are training in is the bliss that Buddha explains in Highest Yoga Tantra. It is called *great bliss*, and possesses two special characteristics: (1) its nature is a bliss arisen from the melting of the drops inside the central channel, and (2) its function is to prevent subtle mistaken appearance. Ordinary beings cannot experience such bliss. As mentioned earlier, the sexual bliss of ordinary beings arises from the melting of the drops inside the left channel, not the central channel.

If you realize your own mind you will become a Buddha; you should not seek Buddhahood elsewhere.

In the *Condensed Heruka Root Tantra* Buddha says:

The supreme secret of great bliss
Arises through melting the drops inside the central
    channel;
Thus it is hard to find in the world
A person who experiences such bliss.

Such a great bliss is experienced only by someone who is able to
cause their inner winds to enter, abide, and dissolve within their
central channel through the power of meditation. Because this
great bliss prevents subtle mistaken appearance, when we experience this bliss our ignorance of self-grasping and all distracting
conceptual thoughts cease, and we experience a deep inner peace,
which is superior to the supreme inner peace of nirvana explained
by Buddha in Sutra teachings.

HOW TO PRACTISE THE YOGA OF SLEEPING

Every night when we are about to sleep we should think:

To benefit all living beings
I will become the enlightened Buddha Vajrayogini.
For this purpose I will accomplish the realization of the clear
    light of bliss.

We then recollect that our body, our self, and all other phenomena that we normally perceive do not exist. We try to perceive
the mere absence of all phenomena that we normally see, the
emptiness of all phenomena, and we meditate on this emptiness.
Then we think and imagine:

In the vast space of emptiness of all phenomena—the Pure Land of Keajra—I appear as Vajrayogini surrounded by the enlightened Heroines and Heroes. Although I have this appearance it is not other than the emptiness of all phenomena.

We meditate on this self-generation.

We should train in this profound self-generation meditation while we are sleeping, but not in deep sleep. Through training in this practice each and every night with continual effort, gradually our memory will be able to function during sleep. Because of this, when our very subtle mind manifests during sleep we will be able to recognize or realize it. Through further training we will realize our very subtle mind directly. When this happens our mind will mix with the emptiness of all phenomena, like water mixing with water. Because of this our subtle mistaken appearance will quickly and permanently cease, and we will become an enlightened being, a Buddha. As Buddha said, "If you realize your own mind you will become a Buddha; you should not seek Buddhahood elsewhere." With regard to this accomplishment our sleep has so much meaning.

HOW TO PRACTISE THE YOGA OF RISING

We should try to practice the yoga of sleeping throughout the night, and throughout the day we should try to practice the yoga of rising. Every day, in the early morning, we should first meditate on the mere absence of all phenomena that we normally see or perceive, the emptiness of all phenomena. Then we think and imagine:

In the vast space of emptiness of all phenomena—the Pure Land of Keajra—I appear as Vajrayogini surrounded by the

enlightened Heroines and Heroes. Although I have this appear-
ance it is not other than the emptiness of all phenomena.

We meditate on this self-generation.

We should repeat this meditation practice again and again, throughout the day. This is the yoga of rising. Then at night we again practice the yoga of sleeping. Through continually practicing the cycle of the yogas of sleeping and rising, our ordinary appearances and conceptions, which are the root of our suffering, will cease.

HOW TO PRACTISE THE YOGA OF EXPERIENCING NECTAR

Whenever we eat or drink, we should first understand and think:

For enlightened beings all food and drink are supreme nectar,
which possesses three special qualities: (1) it is medicine nectar
that cures sickness, (2) it is life nectar that prevents death, and
(3) it is wisdom nectar that pacifies delusions.

With this recognition, whenever we eat or drink we should offer our pleasure in these objects of desire to ourself, the self-generated Vajrayogini. Through practicing in this way we can transform our daily experience of eating and drinking into a spiritual path that accumulates a great collection of merit, or good fortune. In the same way, whenever we enjoy seeing attractive forms or beautiful things, enjoy hearing beautiful sounds such as music or songs, enjoy smelling beautiful scents, and enjoy touching tangible objects, we should offer our pleasure in these objects of desire to ourself, the self-generated Vajrayogini. In this way we can transform all our daily experiences of objects of desire into a spiritual path that leads us to the attainment of the enlightened state of Vajrayogini.

In summary, we should recognize that in the vast space of emptiness of all phenomena—the Pure Land of Keajra—is ourself Vajrayogini surrounded by the enlightened Heroines and Heroes. We should maintain this recognition throughout the day and night, except

Attaining enlightenment is very simple; all we need to do is apply effort to purifying our mind.

when we are concentrating on common paths, such as going for refuge, training in renunciation and bodhichitta, and engaging in purification practices.

This way of practicing the yogas of sleeping, rising, and experiencing nectar is simple but very profound. There are also other ways of practicing these yogas, which are explained in *Guide to Dakini Land.*

THE REMAINING EIGHT YOGAS

The remaining eight yogas from the yoga of immeasurables to the yoga of daily actions should be practiced in conjunction with the sadhana *Quick Path to Great Bliss* composed by Je Phabongkhapa (see Appendix VII). This sadhana is very blessed and precious. A detailed explanation of how to practice each yoga can be found in *Guide to Dakini Land*, but the following is a brief explanation of their essence.

THE YOGA OF IMMEASURABLES

Going for refuge, generating bodhichitta, and meditation and recitation of Vajrasattva are called the *yoga of immeasurables* because they are trainings in spiritual paths that will bring us immeasurable benefit in this life and countless future lives.

The meditation and recitation of Vajrasattva gives us the great opportunity to purify our mind quickly, so that we can attain enlightenment more quickly. As mentioned above, attaining enlightenment is very simple; all we need to do is apply effort to purifying our mind.

THE YOGA OF THE GURU

In this Guru yoga practice, to receive the blessings of all the Buddhas' speech we visualize our root Guru in the aspect of Buddha Vajradharma. Vajradharma, Vajradhara, Vajrasattva, and Heruka are different aspects of one enlightened being. The function of Buddha Vajradharma is to bestow the blessings of all the Buddhas' speech. Through receiving these blessings, our speech will be very powerful whenever we explain Dharma instructions. In this way we can fulfill the wishes of countless living beings and purify or heal their mental continuums through the nectar of our speech.

This Guru yoga contains a practice called *kusali tsog offering*, which has the same function as the *chod* or *cutting* practice. It also contains a practice of receiving the blessings of the four empowerments, which will give us great confidence in accomplishing the realizations of generation and completion stages.

THE YOGA OF SELF-GENERATION

This yoga includes the practices of bringing death, the intermediate state (bardo), and rebirth into the paths of the Truth Body, Enjoyment Body, and Emanation Body.

Mandala of Vajrayogini

In this practice, the supporting mandala is visualized in the aspect of a double tetrahedron, which symbolizes the emptiness of all phenomena; and the supported Deities are ourself, the imagined Vajrayogini, and our retinue of Heroines.

THE YOGA OF PURIFYING MIGRATORS

In this practice, having generated ourself as the enlightened Buddha Vajrayogini, we imagine ourself giving blessings that liberate all living beings from suffering and negativities and transform them into the state of Vajrayogini—the state of ultimate happiness. This is a special practice of taking and giving according to Highest Yoga Tantra. It causes our potential to directly benefit each and every living being to ripen, and it also fulfills the commitment we made when we took the Highest Yoga Tantra empowerment in which we promised to benefit all living beings.

THE YOGA OF BEING BLESSED BY
HEROES AND HEROINES

In this practice, through meditating on the body mandala of Vajrayogini, our channels and drops will receive powerful blessings directly from the thirty-seven Heroines—the female enlightened Deities of the Vajrayogini body mandala—and indirectly from their consorts, the Heroes. Also, through inviting all Heroines and Heroes (female and male enlightened beings) from the ten directions in the aspect of Vajrayogini and dissolving them into us, we will receive the blessings of all Heroes and Heroines.

The meditation on Vajrayogini's body mandala is very profound. Although it is a generation stage practice it functions to cause the inner winds to enter, abide, and dissolve within the central channel. Je Phabongkhapa highly praised the practice of Vajrayogini body mandala.

THE YOGA OF VERBAL AND MENTAL RECITATION

By concentrating on verbal recitation of the Vajrayogini mantra (the *three-OM mantra*) we can accomplish the pacifying, increasing, controlling, wrathful, and supreme attainments, which are mentioned in the section *Training in Mantra Recitation*. The practice of mental recitation presents two completion stage meditations, both of which are the very essence of Vajrayogini practice. These two meditations are clearly explained in *Guide to Dakini Land*.

THE YOGA OF INCONCEIVABILITY

As described in the sadhana *Quick Path to Great Bliss* (see Appendix VII), having dissolved everything, from the formless realm to the nada, into emptiness, we imagine that we experience the clear light of bliss, and with this experience we meditate on the emptiness of all phenomena—the mere absence of all phenomena that we normally perceive. This meditation is training in the clear light of bliss, the main body of Vajrayogini practice. Through continually practicing this meditation, gradually we will experience meaning clear light—the union of great bliss and emptiness—which is the actual inconceivability. In this context, *inconceivability* means that it cannot be experienced by those who have not attained meaning clear light.

THE YOGA OF DAILY ACTIONS

The yoga of daily actions is a method for transforming all our daily actions such as eating, sleeping, working, and talking into profound spiritual paths, and thus extracting great meaning from every moment of our life.

Dedication

Through the great collection of virtue that I have accumulated by composing this book, may each and every living being have the opportunity to listen to and practice the precious teachings of Sutra and Tantra, and thereby experience the pure and everlasting happiness of enlightenment.

Appendix I

Liberating Prayer

PRAISE TO BUDDHA SHAKYAMUNI

O Blessed One, Shakyamuni Buddha,
Precious treasury of compassion,
Bestower of supreme inner peace,

You, who love all beings without exception,
Are the source of happiness and goodness;
And you guide us to the liberating path.

Your body is a wishfulfilling jewel,
Your speech is supreme, purifying nectar,
And your mind is refuge for all living beings.

With folded hands I turn to you,
Supreme unchanging friend,
I request from the depths of my heart:

Please give me the light of your wisdom
To dispel the darkness of my mind
And to heal my mental continuum.

Please nourish me with your goodness,
That I in turn may nourish all beings
With an unceasing banquet of delight.

Through your compassionate intention,
Your blessings and virtuous deeds,
And my strong wish to rely upon you,

May all suffering quickly cease
And all happiness and joy be fulfilled;
And may holy Dharma flourish for evermore.

Colophon: This prayer was composed by Venerable Geshe Kelsang Gyatso and is recited at the beginning of teachings, meditations, and prayers in Kadampa Buddhist Centers throughout the world.

Appendix II

Prayers for Meditation

BRIEF PREPARATORY PRAYERS FOR MEDITATION

Introduction

We all have the potential to gain realizations of all the stages of the path to enlightenment. These potentials are like seeds in the field of our mind, and our meditation practice is like cultivating these seeds. However, our meditation practice will be successful only if we make good preparations in advance.

If we want to cultivate external crops, we begin by making careful preparations. First, we remove anything from the soil that might obstruct their growth, such as stones and weeds. Second, we enrich the soil with compost or fertilizer to give it the strength to sustain growth. Third, we provide warm, moist conditions to enable the seeds to germinate and the plants to grow. In the same way, to cultivate our inner crops of Dharma realizations we also need to begin by making careful preparations.

First, we must purify our mind to eliminate the negative karma we have accumulated in the past, because if we do not purify this karma it will obstruct the growth of Dharma realizations. Second, we need to give our mind the strength to support the growth of Dharma realizations by accumulating merit. Third, we need to activate and sustain the growth of Dharma realizations by receiving the blessings of the holy beings.

The brief prayers that follow contain the essence of these three preparations. For more information on them, see *The New Meditation Handbook* or *Joyful Path of Good Fortune*.

Geshe Kelsang Gyatso
1987

Prayers for Meditation

Going for refuge

I and all sentient beings, until we achieve enlightenment,
Go for refuge to Buddha, Dharma, and Sangha.

(3x, 7x, 100x, or more)

Generating bodhichitta

Through the virtues I collect by giving and other perfections,
May I become a Buddha for the benefit of all.   (3x)

Generating the four immeasurables

May everyone be happy,
May everyone be free from misery,
May no one ever be separated from their happiness,
May everyone have equanimity, free from hatred and attachment.

Visualizing the Field for Accumulating Merit

In the space before me is the living Buddha Shakyamuni surrounded by all the Buddhas and Bodhisattvas, like the full moon surrounded by stars.

Prayer of seven limbs

With my body, speech, and mind, humbly I prostrate,
And make offerings both set out and imagined.
I confess my wrong deeds from all time,
And rejoice in the virtues of all.
Please stay until samsara ceases,
And turn the Wheel of Dharma for us.
I dedicate all virtues to great enlightenment.

Offering the mandala

The ground sprinkled with perfume and spread with flowers,
The Great Mountain, four lands, sun, and moon,
Seen as a Buddha Land and offered thus,
May all beings enjoy such Pure Lands.

I offer without any sense of loss
The objects that give rise to my attachment, hatred, and confusion,
My friends, enemies, and strangers, our bodies and enjoyments;
Please accept these and bless me to be released directly from the
    three poisons.

IDAM GURU RATNA MANDALAKAM NIRYATAYAMI

Prayer of the Stages of the Path

The path begins with strong reliance
On my kind Teacher, source of all good;
O Bless me with this understanding
To follow him with great devotion.

This human life with all its freedoms,
Extremely rare, with so much meaning;
O Bless me with this understanding
All day and night to seize its essence.

My body, like a water bubble,
Decays and dies so very quickly;
After death come results of karma,
Just like the shadow of a body.

With this firm knowledge and remembrance
Bless me to be extremely cautious,
Always avoiding harmful actions
And gathering abundant virtue.

Samsara's pleasures are deceptive,
Give no contentment, only torment;
So please bless me to strive sincerely
To gain the bliss of perfect freedom.

O Bless me so that from this pure thought
Come mindfulness and greatest caution,
To keep as my essential practice
The doctrine's root, the Pratimoksha.

Just like myself all my kind mothers
Are drowning in samsara's ocean;
O So that I may soon release them,
Bless me to train in bodhichitta.

But I cannot become a Buddha
By this alone without three ethics;
So bless me with the strength to practice
The Bodhisattva's ordination.

By pacifying my distractions
And analyzing perfect meanings,
Bless me to quickly gain the union
Of special insight and quiescence.

When I become a pure container
Through common paths, bless me to enter
The essence practice of good fortune,
The supreme vehicle, Vajrayana.

The two attainments both depend on
My sacred vows and my commitments;
Bless me to understand this clearly
And keep them at the cost of my life.

By constant practice in four sessions,
The way explained by holy Teachers,
O Bless me to gain both the stages,
Which are the essence of the Tantras.

May those who guide me on the good path,
And my companions all have long lives;
Bless me to pacify completely
All obstacles, outer and inner.

May I always find perfect Teachers,
And take delight in holy Dharma,
Accomplish all grounds and paths swiftly,
And gain the state of Vajradhara.

Receiving blessings and purifying

From the hearts of all the holy beings, streams of light and nectar
flow down, granting blessings and purifying.

*At this point, we begin the actual contemplation and meditation.
After the meditation, we dedicate our merit while reciting the
following prayers:*

Dedication prayers

Through the virtues I have collected
By practicing the stages of the path,
May all living beings find the opportunity
To practice in the same way.

May everyone experience
The happiness of humans and gods,
And quickly attain enlightenment,
So that samsara is finally extinguished.

Prayers for the Virtuous Tradition

So that the tradition of Je Tsongkhapa,
The King of the Dharma, may flourish,
May all obstacles be pacified
And may all favorable conditions abound.

Through the two collections of myself and others
Gathered throughout the three times,
May the doctrine of Conqueror Losang Dragpa
Flourish for evermore.

The nine-line *Migtsema* prayer

Tsongkhapa, crown ornament of the scholars of the Land of the
Snows,
You are Buddha Shakyamuni and Vajradhara, the source of all
attainments,
Avalokiteshvara, the treasury of unobservable compassion,
Manjushri, the supreme stainless wisdom,
And Vajrapani, the destroyer of the hosts of maras.

O Venerable Guru-Buddha, synthesis of all Three Jewels,
With my body, speech, and mind, respectfully I make requests:
Please grant your blessings to ripen and liberate myself and others,
And bestow the common and supreme attainments.

(3x)

Colophon: These prayers were compiled from traditional
sources by Venerable Geshe Kelsang Gyatso.

Appendix III

An Explanation of Channels

There are three main channels: the central channel, the right channel, and the left channel. The central channel is like the pole of an umbrella, running through the center of each of the channel wheels, and the other two run on either side of it. The central channel is pale blue and has four attributes: (1) it is very straight, like the trunk of a plantain tree; (2) inside it has an oily red color, like pure blood; (3) it is very clear and transparent, like a candle flame; and (4) it is very soft and flexible, like a lotus petal.

The central channel is located exactly midway between the left and right halves of the body, but is closer to the back than the front. Immediately in front of the spine, there is the life channel, which is quite thick; and in front of this is the central channel. As mentioned before, it begins at the point between the eyebrows, from where it ascends in an arch to the crown of the head and then descends in a straight line to the tip of the sex organ. Although its most common name is the central channel, it is also known as the *two abandonments* because gathering the winds into this channel causes the negative activity associated with the winds of the right and left channels to be abandoned. It is also known as the *mind channel* and as *Rahu*.

On either side of the central channel, with no intervening space, are the right and left channels. The right channel is red in color and the left is white. The right channel begins at the tip of the right nostril and the left channel at the tip of the left nostril. From there they both ascend in an arch to the crown of the head, on either side of the central channel. From the crown of the head down to the navel, these three major channels are straight and adjacent to one another. As the left channel continues down below the level of the navel, it curves a little to the right, separating slightly from the central channel and rejoining it at the tip of the sex organ. There it functions to hold and release sperm, blood, and urine. As the right channel continues down below the level of the navel, it curves a little to the left and terminates at the tip of the anus, where it functions to hold and release feces and so forth.

Other names for the right channel are the *sun channel*, the *speech channel*, and the *channel of the subjective holder*. This last title indicates that the winds flowing through this channel cause the generation of conceptions developed in terms of the subjective mind. Other names for the left channel are the *moon channel*, the *body channel*, and the *channel of the held object*, with the last title indicating that the winds flowing through this channel cause the generation of conceptions developed in terms of the object.

The right and left channels coil around the central channel at various places, thereby forming the so-called *channel knots*. The four places where these knots occur are, in ascending order, the navel channel wheel, the heart channel wheel, the throat channel wheel, and the crown channel wheel. At each of these places, except at the heart level, there is one two-fold knot formed by a single coil of the right channel and a single coil of the left. As the right and left channels ascend to these places, they coil around the central channel by crossing in front and then looping around it. They then continue upward to the level of the next knot. At the heart level, the same thing happens, except that here there is a six-fold knot formed by three overlapping loops of each of the flanking channels.

The four places where these knots occur are four of the six major channel wheels. At each of the six major channel wheels, a different number of spokes, or petals, branch off from the central channel in the same way that the ribs of an umbrella appear to branch off from the central pole. Thus, at the crown channel wheel (known as the *great bliss wheel*) there are thirty-two such petals or channel spokes, all of them white in color. The center is triangular with the apex facing forward. (This refers to the shape of the coiled knot through which the spokes emanate, as seen from the top.) These thirty-two spokes arch downward, like the ribs of an upright umbrella. A description of this and the three other major channel wheels where knots occur is given in Table 1, below.

These four channel wheels contain a total of one hundred and twenty spokes. As for the remaining two major channel wheels, the channel wheel at the secret place has thirty-two red-colored spokes arching downward and the jewel channel wheel has eight white spokes arching upward. It should also be noted that according to some texts the spokes at the crown, navel, and secret place can be visualized as having various colors.

Since the heart channel wheel is of particular importance, it will now be described in more detail. Its eight spokes, or petals, are arranged in the cardinal and intermediate directions with the front being the east. In each spoke, there flows mainly the supporting wind of a particular element as indicated in Table 2.

Table 1 The Four Major Channel Wheels

location	name	shape of center	number of spokes	color	direction of arching
crown	great bliss wheel	triangular	thirty-two	white	downward
throat	enjoyment wheel	circular	sixteen	red	upward
heart	Dharma wheel	circular	eight	white	downward
navel	emanation wheel	triangular	sixty-four	red	upward

Table 2 The Spokes of the Heart Channel Wheel

direction	supporting wind
east	of the earth element
north	of the wind element
west	of the fire element
south	of the water element
south-east	of the element of form
south-west	of the element of smell
north-west	of the element of taste
north-east	of the element of touch

From each of these eight petals or channel spokes of the heart, three channels split off, making twenty-four channels in all. These are the channels of the twenty-four places. They are all included in three groups of eight: the channels of the mind wheel, which are blue and contain mainly winds; the channels of the speech wheel, which are red and contain mostly red drops; and the channels of the body wheel, which are white and contain mostly white drops. Each channel goes to a different place in the body. These places are the twenty-four inner places. When we practice the extensive Heruka sadhana, we visualize the Deities of the body mandala at these places.

The outer tips of the eight channels of the mind wheel terminate at (1) the hairline, (2) the crown, (3) the right ear, (4) the back of the neck, (5) the left ear, (6) the brow (the place between the eyebrows), (7) the two eyes, and (8) the two shoulders. Those of the speech wheel terminate at (9) the two armpits, (10) the two breasts, (11) the navel, (12) the tip of the nose, (13) the mouth, (14) the throat, (15) the heart (the area midway between the two breasts), and (16) the two testicles or the two sides of the vagina. Finally, those of the body wheel terminate at (17) the tip of the sex organ, (18) the anus, (19) the two thighs, (20) the two calves, (21) the eight fingers and eight lesser toes, (22) the tops of the feet, (23) the two thumbs and the two big toes, and (24) the two knees.

Each of these twenty-four channels splits into three branches, which are distinguished by the principal elements—winds, red drops, and white drops—that flow through them. Each of these seventy-two channels then splits into a thousand, making seventy-two thousand channels in all. It is important for a Highest Yoga

Tantric practitioner to be familiar with the arrangement of the channels, since it is through gaining control over the winds and drops flowing through these channels that the union of spontaneous great bliss and emptiness is accomplished.

The winds in the body of an ordinary person flow through most of these channels except the central channel. Because these winds are impure, the various minds that they support are also impure, and so for as long as these winds continue to flow through the peripheral channels they will continue to support the various negative conceptions that keep us trapped in samsara. Through the force of meditation, however, these winds can be brought into the central channel, where they are no longer able to support the development of gross conceptions of dualistic appearance. With a mind free from dualistic appearances, we will be able to gain a direct realization of ultimate truth, emptiness.

Corresponding to the twenty-four inner places of the Heruka body mandala are the *twenty-four outer places*, which are located at various points throughout this world. Practitioners with pure karma can see these outer places of Heruka as Pure Lands, but people with impure karma see them only as ordinary places.

Appendix IV

An Explanation of Inner Winds

The definition of wind is any of the four elements that is light in weight and moving. Winds can be divided into external and internal winds, and into gross and subtle winds. Gross external wind is the wind we experience on a windy day. Subtle external wind is much more difficult to detect. It is the energy that makes plants grow and exists even inside rocks and mountains. It is with the help of subtle winds that plants draw up water, grow new leaves, and so forth. Such winds are the life-force of plants. Indeed, in some Tantric texts wind is called *life* or *life-force*. Thus, although it is incorrect to say that plants are alive in the sense of being conjoined with consciousness, we can say that they are alive in this sense.

Internal winds are the winds in the continuum of a person that flow through the channels of the body. The main function of internal winds is to move the mind to its object. The function of the mind is to apprehend objects, but without a wind to act as its mount it cannot move toward, or establish a connection with, its object. Mind is sometimes likened to a lame person who can see, and wind to a blind person with legs. It is only by operating together with internal winds that minds can function.

There are many different winds flowing through the channels of the body, but all are included within the five root winds and the five branch winds. The five root winds are (1) the life-supporting wind, (2) the downward-voiding wind, (3) the upward-moving wind, (4) the equally-abiding wind, and (5) the pervading wind.

Each of the five root winds has six characteristics by which it can be recognized: (1) its color, (2) its associated Buddha family, (3) an element for which it serves as the support, (4) its principal seat or fundamental location, (5) its function, and (6) its direction (how it leaves the nostrils on exhalation). These are summarized in Table 1 on page 282.

The life-supporting wind is called the *Akshobya wind*, because when it is completely purified, it transforms into the nature of Akshobya. Right now our life-supporting wind is like the seed of Akshobya's Form Body, but not Akshobya himself. The main function of the life-supporting wind is to support life by maintaining the connection between body and mind. The stronger the life-supporting wind, the longer we will live. Another function of this wind is to support the water element of our body and to cause it to increase. The life-supporting wind is white in color and its principal location is at the heart. When we exhale, it leaves from both nostrils, flowing gently downward.

The downward-voiding wind is the seed of Ratnasambhava's Form Body and is associated with the earth element. It is yellow in color and it functions to release urine, feces, sperm, and menstrual blood. Its principal locations are at the anus and the sex organ, and when we exhale, it leaves horizontally from both nostrils, flowing heavily forward.

The upward-moving wind is the seed of Amitabha's Form Body and is associated with the fire element. It is red in color and it functions to enable us to swallow food and drink, to speak, to cough, and so forth. Its principal location is at the throat, and when we exhale it leaves from the right nostril, flowing violently upward.

The equally-abiding wind is the seed of Amoghasiddhi's Form Body and is associated with the wind element. It is greenish-yellow in color and it functions to cause the inner fire to blaze, and to digest food and drink by separating the nutrients from waste matter. Its principal location is at the navel, and when we exhale it leaves from the left nostril, moving to the left and the right from the edge of the nostril.

The pervading wind is the seed of Vairochana's Form Body and is associated with the space element. It is pale blue in color, and as its name suggests, it pervades the entire body, particularly the three hundred and sixty joints. It functions to enable the body to move. Without this wind we would be completely immobile, like a stone. This wind does not flow through the nostrils except at the moment of death.

Generally speaking, at any one time, one of the winds is flowing more strongly through the nostrils than the other winds. If, for example, the life-supporting wind is flowing strongly, the other winds (except the pervading wind) are flowing gently. Unless we observe our breath very carefully, it is difficult to notice the different movements of the four winds, but they definitely flow through our nostrils whenever we breathe.

Table 1 The Root Winds

	life-supporting	downward-voiding	upward-moving	equally-abiding	pervading
color	white	yellow	red	green/yellow	pale blue
Buddha family	Akshobya	Ratnasambhava	Amitabha	Amoghasiddhi	Vairochana
element	water	earth	fire	wind	space
seat	heart	the two lower doors: the anus and the sex organ	throat	navel	both the upper and lower parts of the body, mainly the 360 joints
function	to support and maintain life	to retain and release urine, feces, semen, blood, etc.	to speak, swallow, etc.	to cause the inner fire to blaze, to digest food and drink, etc.	to enable the body to come and go; to allow movement, lifting, and placing
direction	from both nostrils, gently downward	from both nostrils, horizontally heavily forward	from the right nostril, violently upward	from the left nostril, moving to the left and the right from the edge of this nostril	this wind does not flow through the nostrils except at the moment of death

The five branch winds are (1) the moving wind, (2) the intensely-moving wind, (3) the perfectly-moving wind, (4) the strongly-moving wind, and (5) the definitely-moving wind

The five branch winds are so called because they branch off from the life-supporting wind, which resides in the heart center. The main location of these winds is in the four channel spokes of the heart channel wheel, from where they flow through our channels to the five doors of the sense powers. Because they function to enable sense awarenesses to develop, the five branch winds are also called the *five winds of the sense powers*. The color and function of each branch wind are summarized in Table 2.

Table 2 The Branch Winds

name	*color*	*function*
the moving wind	red	to enable the eye awareness to move to visual forms
the intensely-moving wind	blue	to enable the ear awareness to move to sounds
the perfectly-moving wind	yellow	to enable the nose awareness to move to smells
the strongly-moving wind	white	to enable the tongue awareness to move to tastes
the definitely-moving wind	green	to enable the body awareness to move to tactile objects

The first wind, the moving wind, flows from the heart through the door of the eyes to enable the eye awareness to move to its object, visual forms. Without the moving wind, eye awareness would be powerless to contact visual forms. The reason we cannot see when we are asleep is that the moving wind has withdrawn from the door of the eye sense power back to its seat at the heart.

The intensely-moving wind flows from the heart to the ears, enabling the ear awareness to move to sounds. The perfectly-moving wind flows from the heart to the nostrils, enabling the nose awareness to move to smells. The strongly-moving wind flows from the heart to the tongue, enabling the tongue awareness to move to tastes. And the definitely-moving wind flows from the heart all over the body, enabling the body awareness to move to tactile objects.

The downward-voiding wind, the upward-moving wind, the equally-abiding wind, the pervading wind, and the five branch winds are all gross internal winds. The life-supporting wind has three levels: gross, subtle, and very subtle. Most mounted winds of conceptual thoughts are gross life-supporting winds; the mounted winds of the minds of white appearance, red increase, and black near-attainment are subtle life-supporting winds; and the mounted wind of the mind of clear light is a very subtle life-supporting wind.

The life-supporting wind is very extensive. If a defiled life-supporting wind manifests, negative conceptual thoughts will develop, but if the life-supporting wind is purified, negative conceptual thoughts will be pacified. All meditations use the mental awareness, and the mounted wind of mental awareness is necessarily a life-supporting wind.

Each of the five winds of the sense powers and the gross life-supporting wind has two parts: a wind that develops the specific type of awareness, and a wind that moves the awareness toward its object. These twelve winds normally flow through the right and left channels, and are the principal objects to be purified by means of vajra recitation, as explained in *Tantric Grounds and Paths* and *Essence of Vajrayana*. If we want to overcome distractions, it is very important to cause these twelve winds to enter, abide, and dissolve within the central channel.

Naropa

Appendix V

The Yoga of Buddha Heruka

THE BRIEF SELF-GENERATION SADHANA OF HERUKA BODY MANDALA & CONDENSED SIX-SESSION YOGA

Tantric commitment objects:
inner offering in kapala, vajra, bell, damaru, mala

Introduction

Those who have received the empowerment of Heruka body mandala, but who are unable to practice the extensive sadhana, *Essence of Vajrayana*, can practice this short sadhana, which contains the very essence of Heruka body mandala practice.

It is very important to improve our understanding of and faith in this precious practice through sincerely studying its commentary as presented in the chapter "The Practice of Heruka Body Mandala." Having understood the meaning clearly and with strong faith we can enter, make progress on, and complete the quick path to the enlightened state of Buddha Heruka.

Geshe Kelsang Gyatso
April 2010

Je Phabongkhapa

The Yoga of Buddha Heruka

PRELIMINARIES

Going for refuge

I and all sentient beings, until we achieve enlightenment,
Go for refuge to Buddha, Dharma, and Sangha.　　(3x)

Generating the supreme good heart, bodhichitta

Through the virtues I collect by giving and other perfections,
May I become a Buddha for the benefit of all.　　(3x)

Guru yoga

VISUALIZATION AND MEDITATION

In the space before me is Guru Sumati Buddha Heruka—Je
Tsongkhapa inseparable from my root Guru, Buddha
Shakyamuni, and Heruka—surrounded by all the Buddhas of
the ten directions.

INVITING THE WISDOM BEINGS

From the heart of the Protector of the hundreds of Deities of the
    Joyful Land,
To the peak of a cloud which is like a cluster of fresh, white curd,
All-knowing Losang Dragpa, King of the Dharma,
Please come to this place together with your Sons.

> *At this point we imagine that wisdom being Je Tsongkhapa together
> with his retinue dissolves into the assembly of Guru Sumati
> Buddha Heruka, and they become non-dual.*

THE PRACTICE OF THE SEVEN LIMBS

In the space before me on a lion throne, lotus, and moon,
The venerable Gurus smile with delight.
O Supreme Field of Merit for my mind of faith,
Please remain for a hundred eons to spread the doctrine.

Your mind of wisdom realizes the full extent of objects of
    knowledge,
Your eloquent speech is the ear-ornament of the fortunate,
Your beautiful body is ablaze with the glory of renown,
I prostrate to you, whom to see, to hear, and to remember is so
    meaningful.

Pleasing water offerings, various flowers,
Sweet-smelling incense, lights, scented water, and so forth,
A vast cloud of offerings both set out and imagined,
I offer to you, O Supreme Field of Merit.

Whatever non-virtues of body, speech, and mind
I have accumulated since time without beginning,
Especially transgressions of my three vows,
With great remorse I confess each one from the depths of my heart.

In this degenerate age you strove for much learning and
  accomplishment.
Abandoning the eight worldly concerns, you made your freedom
  and endowment meaningful.
O Protector, from the very depths of my heart,
I rejoice in the great wave of your deeds.

From the billowing clouds of wisdom and compassion
In the space of your Truth Body, O Venerable and holy Gurus,
Please send down a rain of vast and profound Dharma
Appropriate to the disciples of this world.

From your actual deathless body, born from meaning clear light,
Please send countless emanations throughout the world
To spread the oral lineage of the Ganden doctrine;
And may they remain for a very long time.

Through the virtues I have accumulated here,
May the doctrine and all living beings receive every benefit.
Especially may the essence of the doctrine
Of Venerable Losang Dragpa shine forever.

OFFERING THE MANDALA

The ground sprinkled with perfume and spread with flowers,
The Great Mountain, four lands, sun, and moon,
Seen as a Buddha Land and offered thus,
May all beings enjoy such Pure Lands.

I offer without any sense of loss
The objects that give rise to my attachment, hatred, and confusion,
My friends, enemies, and strangers, our bodies and enjoyments;
Please accept these and bless me to be released directly from the
  three poisons.

IDAM GURU RATNA MANDALAKAM NIRYATAYAMI

MAKING SPECIAL REQUESTS

O Guru Sumati Buddha Heruka, from now until I attain
   enlightenment,
I shall seek no refuge other than you.
Please pacify my obstacles and bestow upon me
The two attainments of liberating and ripening.
Please bless me so that I will become definitive Heruka,
In which state I shall experience all phenomena as purified and
   gathered into emptiness, inseparable from great bliss.   (3x)

GENERATING THE EXPERIENCE OF GREAT BLISS AND EMPTINESS

Due to my making requests in this way, all the Buddhas of the ten
directions dissolve into Je Tsongkhapa who is inseparable from
my root Guru, he dissolves into Buddha Shakyamuni at his heart,
and Buddha Shakyamuni dissolves into Heruka at his heart. With
delight, Guru Heruka, who is the nature of the union of great bliss
and emptiness, enters my body through my crown, and dissolves
into my mind at my heart. Because Heruka, who is the nature of
the union of great bliss and emptiness, becomes inseparable from
my mind, I experience spontaneous great bliss and emptiness. I
perceive nothing other than the emptiness of all phenomena, the
mere absence of all phenomena that I normally see or perceive. My
subtle mistaken appearance of all phenomena, including the channels, winds, and drops of my body, is purified.

*At this point we meditate briefly on the emptiness of all phenomena
while experiencing great bliss.*

THE ACTUAL SELF GENERATION

In the vast space of emptiness of all phenomena, the nature of my
purified mistaken appearance of all phenomena—which is the Pure
Land of Keajra—I appear as Buddha Heruka with a blue-colored

body, four faces, and twelve arms, the nature of my purified white indestructible drop. I am embracing Vajravarahi, the nature of my purified red indestructible drop. I am surrounded by the Heroes and Heroines of the five wheels, who are the nature of my purified subtle body—the channels and drops. I reside in the mandala, the celestial mansion, which is the nature of my purified gross body. Although I have this appearance it is not other than the emptiness of all phenomena.

At this point, (1) while experiencing great bliss and emptiness, (2) we meditate on the clear appearance of the mandala and Deities with divine pride, while (3) recognizing that the Deities are the nature of our purified channels and drops, which are our subtle body, and that the mandala is the nature of our purified gross body.

In this way we train sincerely in one single meditation on generation stage possessing these three characteristics. Holding the third characteristic—recognizing the Deities as the nature of our purified subtle body, and the mandala as the nature of our purified gross body—makes this concentration an actual body mandala meditation.

If we wish to practice completion stage meditation, we should change ourself through imagination from Heruka with four faces and twelve arms into Heruka with one face and two arms. We then engage in the meditations on the central channel, indestructible drop, indestructible wind, tummo, and so forth.

Then, when we need to rest from meditation, we can practice mantra recitation.

Reciting the mantras

THE ESSENCE MANTRA OF HERUKA

At my heart is wisdom being Buddha Heruka, definitive Heruka.

O Glorious Vajra Heruka, you who enjoy
The divine illusory body and mind of clear light,
Please pacify my obstacles and bestow upon me
The two attainments of liberating and ripening.
Please bless me so that I will become definitive Heruka,
In which state I shall experience all phenomena as purified and
    gathered into emptiness, inseparable from great bliss.

OM SHRI VAJRA HE HE RU RU KAM HUM HUM PHAT DAKINI
    DZALA SHAMBARAM SÖHA   (21x, 100x, etc.)

THE THREE-OM MANTRA OF VAJRAYOGINI

At the heart of imagined Vajrayogini (Vajravarahi) is wisdom being
Buddha Vajrayogini, definitive Vajrayogini.

OM OM OM SARWA BUDDHA DAKINIYE VAJRA WARNANIYE VAJRA
    BEROTZANIYE HUM HUM HUM PHAT PHAT PHAT SÖHA

Recite at least as many mantras as you have promised.

The three-OM *mantra is the union of the essence and close essence
mantras of Vajravarahi. The meaning of this mantra is as follows.
With* OM OM OM *we are calling Vajrayogini—the principal
Deity—and her retinue of Heroines of the three wheels.* SARWA
BUDDHA DAKINIYE *means that Vajrayogini is the synthesis of the
minds of all Buddhas,* VAJRA WARNANIYE *means that she is the
synthesis of the speech of all Buddhas, and* VAJRA BEROTZANIYE
means that she is the synthesis of the bodies of all Buddhas. With
HUM HUM HUM *we are requesting Vajrayogini and her retinues
to bestow upon us the attainments of the body, speech, and mind of*

all the Buddhas. With PHAT PHAT PHAT we are requesting them to pacify our main obstacle—the subtle mistaken appearance of our body, speech, and mind; and SÖHA means "please build within me the basic foundation for all these attainments."

THE CONDENSED MANTRA OF THE SIXTY-TWO DEITIES OF HERUKA BODY MANDALA

At the heart of each of the sixty-two Deities is their individual wisdom being, their own definitive Deity.

OM HUM BAM RIM RIM LIM LIM, KAM KHAM GAM GHAM NGAM, TSAM TSHAM DZAM DZHAM NYAM, TrAM THrAM DrAM DHrAM NAM, TAM THAM DAM DHAM NAM, PAM PHAM BAM BHAM, YAM RAM LAM WAM, SHAM KAM SAM HAM HUM HUM PHAT

(7x, 21x, 100x, etc.)

When we recite this mantra we are making requests to wisdom being Buddha Heruka with Vajravarahi, and his retinue of Heroes and Heroines of the five wheels, to pacify our obstacle of subtle mistaken appearance and to bestow on us the attainments of outer and inner Dakini Land. Outer Dakini Land is the Pure Land of Keajra and inner Dakini Land is meaning clear light. The moment our mind is free from subtle mistaken appearance we open the door through which we can directly see all enlightened Deities. For as long as our mind remains polluted by subtle mistaken appearance this door is closed.

Dedication

Thus, through my virtues from correctly performing the offerings,
    praises, recitations, and meditations
Of the generation stage of Glorious Heruka,
May I complete all the stages
Of the common and uncommon paths.

For the sake of all living beings
May I become Heruka;
And then lead every living being
To Heruka's supreme state.

And if I do not attain this supreme state in this life,
At my deathtime may I be met by the venerable Father and Mother
    and their retinue,
With clouds of breathtaking offerings, heavenly music,
And many excellent, auspicious signs.

Then, at the end of the clear light of death,
May I be led to the Pure Land of Keajra,
The abode of the Knowledge Holders who practice the supreme
    path;
And there may I swiftly complete this profound path.

May the most profound practice and instruction of Heruka,
Practiced by millions of powerful Yogis, greatly increase;
And may it remain for a very long time without degenerating,
As the main gateway for those seeking liberation.

May the Heroes, Dakinis, and their retinues
Abiding in the twenty-four supreme places of this world,
Who possess unobstructed power for accomplishing this method,
Never waver from always assisting practitioners.

Auspicious prayers

May there be the auspiciousness of a great treasury of blessings
Arising from the excellent deeds of all the root and lineage Gurus,
Who have accomplished the supreme attainment of Buddha
    Heruka
By relying upon the excellent, secret path of the King of Tantras.

May there be the auspiciousness of the great excellent deeds of the
Three Jewels—
The holy Buddha Jewel, the pervading nature Heruka, definitive
Heruka;
The ultimate, great, secret Dharma Jewel, the scriptures and realiza-
tions of Heruka Tantra;
And the supreme Sangha Jewel, the assemblies of Heruka's retinue
Deities.

Through all the great good fortune there is
In the precious, celestial mansions as extensive as the three thou-
sand worlds,
Adorned with ornaments like the rays of the sun and the moon,
May all worlds and their beings have happiness, goodness, glory,
and prosperity.

Prayers for the Virtuous Tradition

So that the tradition of Je Tsongkhapa,
The King of the Dharma, may flourish,
May all obstacles be pacified
And may all favorable conditions abound.

Through the two collections of myself and others
Gathered throughout the three times,
May the doctrine of Conqueror Losang Dragpa
Flourish for evermore.

The nine-line *Migtsema* prayer

Tsongkhapa, crown ornament of the scholars of the Land of the
Snows,
You are Buddha Shakyamuni and Vajradhara, the source of all
attainments,
Avalokiteshvara, the treasury of unobservable compassion,
Manjushri, the supreme stainless wisdom,
And Vajrapani, the destroyer of the hosts of maras.
O Venerable Guru-Buddha, synthesis of all Three Jewels,
With my body, speech, and mind, respectfully I make requests:
Please grant your blessings to ripen and liberate myself and others,
And bestow the common and supreme attainments.

(3x)

Condensed Six-session Yoga

Everyone who has received a Highest Yoga Tantra empowerment has a commitment to practice six-session yoga. If we are very busy, we can fulfill our six-session commitment by doing the following practice six times each day. First we recall the nineteen commitments of the five Buddha families that are listed below, and then, with a strong determination to keep these commitments purely, we recite the Condensed Six-session Yoga *that follows.*

THE NINETEEN COMMITMENTS OF THE FIVE BUDDHA FAMILIES

The six commitments of the family of Buddha Vairochana:

1. To go for refuge to Buddha
2. To go for refuge to Dharma
3. To go for refuge to Sangha
4. To refrain from non-virtue
5. To practice virtue
6. To benefit others

301

The four commitments of the family of Buddha Akshobya:

1. To keep a vajra to remind us to emphasize the development of great bliss through meditation on the central channel
2. To keep a bell to remind us to emphasize meditation on emptiness
3. To generate ourself as the Deity while realizing all things that we normally see do not exist
4. To rely sincerely upon our Spiritual Guide, who leads us to the practice of the pure moral discipline of the Pratimoksha, Bodhisattva, and Tantric vows

The four commitments of the family of Buddha Ratnasambhava:

1. To give material help
2. To give Dharma
3. To give fearlessness
4. To give love

The three commitments of the family of Buddha Amitabha:

1. To rely upon the teachings of Sutra
2. To rely upon the teachings of the two lower classes of Tantra
3. To rely upon the teachings of the two higher classes of Tantra

The two commitments of the family of Buddha Amoghasiddhi:

1. To make offerings to our Spiritual Guide
2. To strive to maintain purely all the vows we have taken

CONDENSED SIX-SESSION YOGA

I go for refuge to the Guru and Three Jewels.
Holding vajra and bell I generate as the Deity and make offerings.
I rely upon the Dharmas of Sutra and Tantra and refrain from all
  non-virtuous actions.
Gathering all virtuous Dharmas, I help all living beings through
  the practice of the four givings.

All nineteen commitments are referred to in this verse. The words
"I go for refuge to the . . . Three Jewels," *refer to the first three*
commitments of the family of Buddha Vairochana—to go for
refuge to Buddha, to go for refuge to Dharma, and to go for refuge
to Sangha. The word "Guru" *refers to the fourth commitment of*
the family of Buddha Akshobya—to rely sincerely on our Spiritual
Guide.

The words "Holding vajra and bell I generate as the Deity," *refer*
to the first three commitments of the family of Buddha Akshobya—
to keep a vajra to remind us of great bliss, to keep a bell to remind
us of emptiness, and to generate ourself as the Deity. The words
"and make offerings," *refer to the first commitment of the family*
of Buddha Amoghasiddhi—to make offerings to our Spiritual
Guide.

The words "I rely upon the Dharmas of Sutra and Tantra,"
refer to the three commitments of Buddha Amitabha—to rely on
the teachings of Sutra, to rely on the teachings of the two lower
classes of Tantra, and to rely on the teachings of the two higher
classes of Tantra. The words "and refrain from all non-virtuous
actions," *refer to the fourth commitment of the family of Buddha*
Vairochana—to refrain from non-virtue.

The words "Gathering all virtuous Dharmas," *refer to the fifth commitment of the family of Buddha Vairochana—to practice virtue. The words* "I help all living beings," *refer to the sixth commitment of the family of Buddha Vairochana—to benefit others. The words* "through the practice of the four givings," *refer to the four commitments of the family of Buddha Ratnasambhava—to give material help, to give Dharma, to give fearlessness, and to give love.*

Finally, the entire verse refers to the second commitment of the family of Buddha Amoghasiddhi—to strive to maintain purely all the vows we have taken.

More detail on the vows and commitments of Secret Mantra can be found in the book Tantric Grounds and Paths.

Colophon: This sadhana was compiled from traditional sources by Venerable Geshe Kelsang Gyatso, June 2009, and revised April 2010.

Appendix VI

Blissful Journey

HOW TO ENGAGE IN A CLOSE RETREAT
OF HERUKA BODY MANDALA

Kyabje Trijang Rinpoche

Introduction

Sincere practitioners of *The Yoga of Buddha Heruka* sadhana can perform a close retreat of Heruka body mandala in accordance with the following instructions.

Having set out ritual objects, and torma and other offerings, in either a traditional or simple manner, in the evening of the first day on which the retreat begins you should engage in the practice of *The Yoga of Buddha Heruka* from "Going for refuge" up to and including "Reciting the mantras"; then perform torma and tsog offerings as presented below. The session should be concluded by reciting the "Dedication" and remaining prayers from the sadhana.

Beginning on the second day, if you intend to do four sessions of retreat each day, in the first three sessions you should engage in the practice of *The Yoga of Buddha Heruka* from "Going for refuge" up to and including reciting the "Dedication" and remaining prayers, without any additions. In the fourth or last session you should engage in the practice of *The Yoga of Buddha Heruka* from "Going for refuge" up to and including "Reciting the mantras," and then perform the torma offerings as presented below. This session should be concluded by reciting the "Dedication" and remaining prayers from the sadhana.

Having collected 100,000 recitations of the essence mantra of Heruka, 100,000 recitations of the three-OM Mantra of Vajrayogini, and 10,000 recitations of the condensed mantra of the sixty-two Deities of Heruka body mandala you then need to perform a fire puja, or burning offering. This practice and its explanation can be found in the book *Essence of Vajrayana*. In this way your close retreat of Heruka body mandala will be completed. Until the fire puja is completed you should engage in at least two sessions of *The Yoga of Buddha Heruka* each day, making torma offerings in the last session.

Once you have completed the close retreat of Heruka body mandala you can engage in the practice of Heruka body mandala self-initiation, which can be found in the sadhana *Union of No More Learning*. It is most important that whenever you recite the sadhana *The Yoga of Buddha Heruka* you should strongly concentrate on its meaning, free from distraction and impure motivation. Between sessions you should carefully read the commentary to this sadhana presented in the chapter "The Practice of Heruka Body Mandala."

Geshe Kelsang Gyatso
April 2010

Blissful Journey

TORMA OFFERING

Having engaged in the practice of The Yoga of Buddha Heruka *from "Going for refuge" up to and including "Reciting the mantras," now perform the torma offering.*

Blessing the inner offering

OM KHANDAROHI HUM HUM PHAT
OM SÖBHAWA SHUDDHA SARWA DHARMA SÖBHAWA
     SHUDDHO HAM
Everything becomes emptiness.

From the state of emptiness, from YAM comes wind, from RAM comes fire, from AH a grate of three human heads. Upon this from AH appears a broad and expansive skullcup. Inside from OM, KHAM, AM, TRAM, HUM come the five nectars; from LAM, MAM, PAM, TAM, BAM come the five meats, each marked by these letters. The wind blows, the fire blazes, and the substances inside the skull-cup melt. Above them from HUM there arises a white, upside-down khatanga, which falls into the skullcup and melts whereby the substances take on the color of mercury. Above them three rows of vowels and consonants, standing one above the other, transform into OM AH HUM. From these, light rays draw the nectar of exalted wisdom from the hearts of all the Tathagatas, Heroes, and Yoginis of the ten directions. When this is added the contents increase and become vast.

OM AH HUM   (3x)

Blessing the outer offerings

OM KHANDAROHI HUM HUM PHAT
OM SÖBHAWA SHUDDHA SARWA DHARMA SÖBHAWA
    SHUDDHO HAM
Everything becomes emptiness.

From the state of emptiness, from KAMs come broad and expansive skullcups, inside which from HUMs come water for drinking, water for bathing, water for the mouth, flowers, incense, lights, perfume, food, and music. By nature emptiness, they have the aspect of the individual offering substances, and function as objects of enjoyment of the six senses to bestow special, uncontaminated bliss.

OM AHRGHAM AH HUM
OM PADÄM AH HUM
OM ÄNTZAMANAM AH HUM
OM VAJRA PUPE AH HUM
OM VAJRA DHUPE AH HUM
OM VAJRA DIWE AH HUM
OM VAJRA GÄNDHE AH HUM
OM VAJRA NEWIDE AH HUM
OM VAJRA SHAPTA AH HUM

Blessing the tormas

OM KHANDAROHI HUM HUM PHAT
OM SÖBHAWA SHUDDHA SARWA DHARMA SÖBHAWA
    SHUDDHO HAM
Everything becomes emptiness.

From the state of emptiness, from YAM comes wind, from RAM comes fire, from AH a grate of three human heads. Upon this from AH appears a broad and expansive skullcup. Inside from OM, KHAM, AM, TRAM, HUM come the five nectars; from LAM, MAM, PAM, TAM, BAM come the five meats, each marked by these letters. The wind blows, the fire blazes, and the substances inside the skull-cup melt. Above them from HUM there arises a white, upside-down khatanga, which falls into the skullcup and melts whereby the substances take on the color of mercury. Above them three rows of vowels and consonants, standing one above the other, transform into OM AH HUM. From these, light rays draw the nectar of exalted wisdom from the hearts of all the Tathagatas, Heroes, and Yoginis of the ten directions. When this is added the contents increase and become vast.

OM AH HUM   (3x)

Inviting the guests of the tormas

PHAIM

Light rays radiate from the letter HUM on the sun seat at my heart and invite to the space before me the entire assembly of the Deities of Chakrasambara together with his mundane retinues, such as the directional guardians who reside in the eight charnel grounds.

OM AHRGHAM PARTITZA SÖHA
OM PADÄM PARTITZA SÖHA
OM VAJRA PUPE AH HUM SÖHA
OM VAJRA DHUPE AH HUM SÖHA
OM VAJRA DIWE AH HUM SÖHA
OM VAJRA GÄNDHE AH HUM SÖHA
OM VAJRA NEWIDE AH HUM SÖHA
OM VAJRA SHAPTA AH HUM SÖHA

From a white HUM in the tongue of each guest, there arises a white, three-pronged vajra, through which they partake of the essence of the torma by drawing it through straws of light the thickness of only a grain of barley.

Offering the principal torma

OM VAJRA AH RA LI HO: DZA HUM BAM HO: VAJRA DAKINI
SAMAYA TÖN TRISHAYA HO　　(3x)

With the first recitation, offer the torma to the Principal Father, with the second to the Principal Mother, and with the third to the four Yoginis, beginning in the east and offering counterclockwise.

Offering the torma to the Deities of the heart wheel, speech wheel, and body wheel

OM KARA KARA, KURU KURU, BÄNDHA BÄNDHA, TrASAYA TrASAYA, KYOMBHAYA KYOMBHAYA, HROM HROM, HRAH HRAH, PHAIM PHAIM, PHAT PHAT, DAHA DAHA, PATSA PATSA, BHAKYA BHAKYA BASA RUDHI ÄNTRA MALA WALAMBINE, GRIHANA GRIHANA SAPTA PATALA GATA BHUDZAMGAM SARWAMPA TARDZAYA TARDZAYA, AKANDYA AKANDYA, HRIM HRIM, GYÖN GYÖN, KYAMA KYAMA, HAM HAM, HIM HIM, HUM HUM, KILI KILI, SILI SILI, HILI HILI, DHILI DHILI, HUM HUM PHAT

Offering the torma to the Deities of the commitment wheel

OM VAJRA AH RA LI HO: DZA HUM BAM HO: VAJRA DAKINI
SAMAYA TÖN TRISHAYA HO　　(2x)

Outer offerings

OM AHRGHAM PARTITZA SÖHA
OM PADÄM PARTITZA SÖHA
OM VAJRA PUPE AH HUM SÖHA
OM VAJRA DHUPE AH HUM SÖHA
OM VAJRA DIWE AH HUM SÖHA
OM VAJRA GÄNDHE AH HUM SÖHA
OM VAJRA NEWIDE AH HUM SÖHA
OM VAJRA SHAPTA AH HUM SÖHA

OM AH VAJRA ADARSHE HUM
OM AH VAJRA WINI HUM
OM AH VAJRA GÄNDHE HUM
OM AH VAJRA RASE HUM
OM AH VAJRA PARSHE HUM
OM AH VAJRA DHARME HUM

Inner offering

OM HUM BAM RIM RIM LIM LIM, KAM KHAM GAM GHAM
NGAM, TSAM TSHAM DZAM DZHAM NYAM, TrAM THrAM
DrAM DHrAM NAM, TAM THAM DAM DHAM NAM, PAM
PHAM BAM BHAM, YAM RAM LAM WAM, SHAM KAM SAM
HAM HUM HUM PHAT OM AH HUM

Secret and thatness offerings

Through Father and Mother uniting in embrace, all the principal
and retinue Deities enjoy a special experience of great bliss and
emptiness.

Eight lines of praise to the Father

OM I prostrate to the Blessed One, Lord of the Heroes HUM HUM PHAT

OM To you with a brilliance equal to the fire of the great eon HUM HUM PHAT

OM To you with an inexhaustible topknot HUM HUM PHAT

OM To you with a fearsome face and bared fangs HUM HUM PHAT

OM To you whose thousand arms blaze with light HUM HUM PHAT

OM To you who hold an axe, an uplifted noose, a spear, and a khatanga HUM HUM PHAT

OM To you who wear a tiger-skin garment HUM HUM PHAT

OM I bow to you whose great smoke-colored body dispels obstructions HUM HUM PHAT

Eight lines of praise to the Mother

OM I prostrate to Vajravarahi, the Blessed Mother HUM HUM PHAT

OM To the Superior and powerful Knowledge Lady unconquered by the three realms HUM HUM PHAT

OM To you who destroy all fears of evil spirits with your great vajra HUM HUM PHAT

OM To you with controlling eyes who remain as the vajra seat unconquered by others HUM HUM PHAT

OM To you whose wrathful fierce form desiccates Brahma HUM HUM PHAT

OM To you who terrify and dry up demons, conquering those in other directions HUM HUM PHAT

OM To you who conquer all those who make us dull, rigid, and confused HUM HUM PHAT

OM I bow to Vajravarahi, the Great Mother, the Dakini consort who fulfills all desires HUM HUM PHAT

Requesting the fulfillment of wishes

You who have destroyed equally attachment to samsara and solitary
    peace, as well as all conceptualizations,
Who see all things that exist throughout space;
O Protector endowed with strong compassion, may I be blessed by
    the waters of your compassion,
And may the Dakinis take me into their loving care.

Offering the torma to the mundane Deities

The directional guardians, regional guardians, nagas, and so forth,
who reside in the eight great charnel grounds, instantly enter into
the clear light, and arise in the form of the Deities of Heruka in the
aspect of Father and Mother. From a white HUM in the tongue of
each guest, there arises a white, three-pronged vajra, through which
they partake of the essence of the torma by drawing it through
straws of light the thickness of only a grain of barley.

OM KHA KHA, KHAHI KHAHI, SARWA YAKYA RAKYASA, BHUTA,
TRETA, PISHATSA, UNATA, APAMARA, VAJRA DAKA, DAKI NÄDAYA,
IMAM BALING GRIHANTU, SAMAYA RAKYANTU, MAMA SARWA
SIDDHI METRA YATZANTU, YATIPAM, YATETAM, BHUDZATA,
PIWATA, DZITRATA, MATI TRAMATA, MAMA SARWA KATAYA,
SÄDSUKHAM BISHUDHAYE, SAHAYEKA BHAWÄNTU, HUM HUM
PHAT PHAT SÖHA   (2x)

> *With the first recitation, offer the torma to the guests in the cardinal
> directions, and with the second to the guests in the intermediate
> directions.*

Outer offerings

OM AHRGHAM PARTITZA SÖHA
OM PADÄM PARTITZA SÖHA

OM VAJRA PUPE AH HUM SÖHA
OM VAJRA DHUPE AH HUM SÖHA
OM VAJRA DIWE AH HUM SÖHA
OM VAJRA GÄNDHE AH HUM SÖHA
OM VAJRA NEWIDE AH HUM SÖHA
OM VAJRA SHAPTA AH HUM SÖHA

Inner offering

To the mouths of the directional guardians, regional guardians, nagas, and so forth, OM AH HUM

Requests

You the entire gathering of gods,
The entire gathering of nagas,
The entire gathering of givers of harm,
The entire gathering of cannibals,
The entire gathering of evil spirits,
The entire gathering of hungry ghosts,
The entire gathering of flesh-eaters,
The entire gathering of crazy-makers,
The entire gathering of forgetful-makers,
The entire gathering of dakas,
The entire gathering of female spirits,
All of you without exception
Please come here and listen to me.
O Glorious attendants, swift as thought,
Who have taken oaths and heart commitments
To guard the doctrine and benefit living beings,
Who subdue the malevolent and destroy the dark forces
With terrifying forms and inexhaustible wrath,
Who grant results to yogic actions,

And who have inconceivable powers and blessings,
To you eight types of guest I prostrate.

I request all of you together with your consorts, children, and
    servants
To grant me the fortune of all the attainments.
May I and other practitioners
Have good health, long life, power,
Glory, fame, fortune,
And extensive enjoyments.
Please grant me the attainments
Of pacifying, increasing, controlling, and wrathful actions.
O Guardians, always assist me.
Eradicate all untimely death, sicknesses,
Harm from spirits, and hindrances.
Eliminate bad dreams,
Ill omens, and bad actions.

May there be happiness in the world, may the years be good,
May crops increase, and may Dharma flourish.
May all goodness and happiness come about,
And may all wishes be accomplished.

*At this point you can, if you wish, make the tsog offering. This
starts on page 319.*

Purifying any mistakes made during this practice with the hundred-letter mantra of Heruka

OM VAJRA HERUKA SAMAYA, MANU PALAYA, HERUKA TENO
PATITA, DRIDHO ME BHAWA, SUTO KAYO ME BHAWA, SUPO KAYO
ME BHAWA, ANURAKTO ME BHAWA, SARWA SIDDHI ME PRAYATZA,
SARWA KARMA SUTZA ME, TZITAM SHRIYAM KURU HUM, HA HA
HA HA HO BHAGAWÄN, VAJRA HERUKA MA ME MUNTSA, HERUKA

317

BHAWA, MAHA SAMAYA SATTÖ AH HUM PHAT

OM YOGA SHUDDHA SARWA DHARMA YOGA SHUDDHO HAM

VAJRA MU

The mundane beings return to their own places, and the assembly of the Deities of the in-front-generation dissolve into me.

Dissolution and generating the action Deities

The charnel grounds and protection circle dissolve into the celestial mansion. The celestial mansion dissolves into the Deities of the commitment wheel. They dissolve into the Deities of the body wheel. They dissolve into the Deities of the speech wheel. They dissolve into the Deities of the heart wheel. They dissolve into the four Yoginis of the great bliss wheel. They dissolve into me, the Principal Deity Father and Mother, the nature of the white and red indestructible drop. I, the Principal Deity Father and Mother, also melt into light and dissolve into the letter HUM at my heart, in nature the emptiness of the Dharmakaya.

From the state of emptiness our world arises as Heruka's Pure Land, Keajra. I and all sentient beings arise as the Blessed One Heruka, with a blue-colored body, one face, and two arms embracing Vajravarahi.

The session should be concluded by reciting the "Dedication" and remaining prayers from the sadhana The Yoga of Buddha Heruka.

THE TSOG OFFERING TO
HERUKA BODY MANDALA

Blessing the outer and inner offerings, the environment and beings, and the substances of the tsog offering

OM AH HUM   (3x)

By nature exalted wisdom, having the aspect of the inner offering and the individual offering substances, and functioning as objects of enjoyment of the six senses to generate a special, exalted wisdom of bliss and emptiness, inconceivable clouds of outer, inner, and secret offerings, commitment substances and attractive offerings, cover all the ground and fill the whole of space.

EH MA HO Great manifestation of exalted wisdom.
All realms are vajra realms
And all places are great vajra palaces
Endowed with vast clouds of Samantabhadra's offerings,
An abundance of all desired enjoyments.
All beings are actual Heroes and Heroines.
Everything is immaculately pure,
Without even the name of mistaken impure appearance.

HUM All elaborations are completely pacified in the state of the Truth Body. The wind blows and the fire blazes. Above, on a grate of three human heads, AH within a qualified skullcup, OM the individual substances blaze. Above these stand OM AH HUM, each ablaze with its brilliant color. Through the wind blowing and the fire blazing, the substances melt. Boiling, they swirl in a great vapor. Masses of light rays from the three letters radiate to the ten directions and invite the three vajras together with nectars. These dissolve separately into the three letters. Melting into nectar, they blend with the mixture. Purified, transformed, and increased,

EH MA HO They become a blazing ocean of magnificent delights.

OM AH HUM   (3x)

Inviting the guests of the tsog offering

PHAIM

From the sacred palace of the Dharmakaya,
Great Master, holder of the supreme lineage of the Vajrayana,
Who fulfill our hopes for all the attainments,
O Assembly of root and lineage Gurus, please come to this place.

From the twenty-four holy places throughout the world,
O Glorious Heruka, whose nature is the compassion of all the
     Buddhas,
And all the Heroes and Heroines of these places,
Please come here to bestow the attainments that we long for.

From the pure and impure lands of the ten directions,
O Assembly of Yidams, Buddhas, Bodhisattvas, and Dharma
     Protectors,
And all the beings of samsara and nirvana,
Please come here as guests of this tsog offering.

OM GURU VAJRADHARA CHAKRASAMBARA SÄMANDALA DEWA
SARWA BUDDHA BODHISATTÖ SAPARIWARA EH HAYE HI VAJRA
SAMAYA DZA DZA

PÄMA KAMALAYE TÖN

Making the tsog offering

HO This ocean of tsog offering of uncontaminated nectar,
Blessed by concentration, mantra, and mudra,
I offer to please my kind root Guru, Guru Sumati Buddha Heruka.

OM AH HUM
Delighted by enjoying these magnificent objects of desire,
EH MA HO
Please bless me so that I may attain outer and inner Dakini Land.

HO This ocean of tsog offering of uncontaminated nectar,
Blessed by concentration, mantra, and mudra,
I offer to please the four Yoginis of the great bliss wheel.
OM AH HUM
Delighted by enjoying these magnificent objects of desire,
EH MA HO
Please bless me so that I may attain spontaneous great bliss.

HO This ocean of tsog offering of uncontaminated nectar,
Blessed by concentration, mantra, and mudra,
I offer to please the Heroes and Heroines of the vajra mind.
OM AH HUM
Delighted by enjoying these magnificent objects of desire,
EH MA HO
Please bless me so that I may experience delight with the messen-
gers of the vajra mind family.

HO This ocean of tsog offering of uncontaminated nectar,
Blessed by concentration, mantra, and mudra,
I offer to please the Heroes and Heroines of the vajra speech.
OM AH HUM
Delighted by enjoying these magnificent objects of desire,
EH MA HO
Please bless me so that I may experience delight with the messen-
gers of the vajra speech family.

HO This ocean of tsog offering of uncontaminated nectar,
Blessed by concentration, mantra, and mudra,
I offer to please the Heroes and Heroines of the vajra body.

OM AH HUM
Delighted by enjoying these magnificent objects of desire,
EH MA HO
Please bless me so that I may experience delight with the messengers of the vajra body family.

HO This ocean of tsog offering of uncontaminated nectar,
Blessed by concentration, mantra, and mudra,
I offer to please the Deities of the commitment wheel.
OM AH HUM
Delighted by enjoying these magnificent objects of desire,
EH MA HO
Please bless me so that I may pacify all obstacles.

HO This ocean of tsog offering of uncontaminated nectar,
Blessed by concentration, mantra, and mudra,
I offer to please all other Yidams, Buddhas, Bodhisattvas, and
    Dharma Protectors.
OM AH HUM
Delighted by enjoying these magnificent objects of desire,
EH MA HO
Please bless me so that I may attain all the realizations of Sutra and
    Tantra.

HO This ocean of tsog offering of uncontaminated nectar,
Blessed by concentration, mantra, and mudra,
I offer to please the assembly of mother sentient beings.
OM AH HUM
Delighted by enjoying these magnificent objects of desire,
EH MA HO
May suffering and mistaken appearance be pacified.

Outer offerings

OM AHRGHAM PARTITZA SÖHA
OM PADÄM PARTITZA SÖHA
OM VAJRA PUPE AH HUM SÖHA
OM VAJRA DHUPE AH HUM SÖHA
OM VAJRA DIWE AH HUM SÖHA
OM VAJRA GÄNDHE AH HUM SÖHA
OM VAJRA NEWIDE AH HUM SÖHA
OM VAJRA SHAPTA AH HUM SÖHA

Inner offering

OM HUM BAM RIM RIM LIM LIM, KAM KHAM GAM GHAM NGAM,
TSAM TSHAM DZAM DZHAM NYAM, TrAM THrAM DrAM DHrAM
NAM, TAM THAM DAM DHAM NAM, PAM PHAM BAM BHAM, YAM
RAM LAM WAM, SHAM KAM SAM HAM HUM HUM PHAT OM AH
HUM

Secret and thatness offerings

Through Father and Mother uniting in embrace, all the principal
and retinue Deities enjoy a special experience of great bliss and
emptiness.

Eight lines of praise to the Father

OM I prostrate to the Blessed One, Lord of the Heroes HUM HUM
   PHAT
OM To you with a brilliance equal to the fire of the great eon HUM
   HUM PHAT
OM To you with an inexhaustible topknot HUM HUM PHAT
OM To you with a fearsome face and bared fangs HUM HUM PHAT
OM To you whose thousand arms blaze with light HUM HUM PHAT

OM To you who hold an axe, an uplifted noose, a spear, and a khatanga HUM HUM PHAT

OM To you who wear a tiger-skin garment HUM HUM PHAT

OM I bow to you whose great smoke-colored body dispels obstructions HUM HUM PHAT

Eight lines of praise to the Mother

OM I prostrate to Vajravarahi, the Blessed Mother HUM HUM PHAT

OM To the Superior and powerful Knowledge Lady unconquered by the three realms HUM HUM PHAT

OM To you who destroy all fears of evil spirits with your great vajra HUM HUM PHAT

OM To you with controlling eyes who remain as the vajra seat unconquered by others HUM HUM PHAT

OM To you whose wrathful fierce form desiccates Brahma HUM HUM PHAT

OM To you who terrify and dry up demons, conquering those in other directions HUM HUM PHAT

OM To you who conquer all those who make us dull, rigid, and confused HUM HUM PHAT

OM I bow to Vajravarahi, the Great Mother, the Dakini consort who fulfills all desires HUM HUM PHAT

Making the tsog offering to the Vajra Master

EH MA HO Great circle of tsog!
O Great Hero we understand
That, following in the path of the Sugatas of the three times,
You are the source of all attainments.
Forsaking all minds of conceptualization
Please continuously enjoy this circle of tsog.
AH LA LA HO

The Master's reply

OM With a nature inseparable from the three vajras
I generate as the Guru-Deity.
AH This nectar of uncontaminated exalted wisdom and bliss,
HUM Without stirring from bodhichitta,
I partake to delight the Deities dwelling in my body.
AH HO MAHA SUKHA

Song of the Spring Queen

HUM All you Tathagatas,
Heroes, Yoginis,
Dakas, and Dakinis,
To all of you I make this request:
O Heruka who delight in great bliss,
You engage in the Union of spontaneous bliss,
By attending the Lady intoxicated with bliss
And enjoying in accordance with the rituals.
AH LA LA, LA LA HO, AH I AH, AH RA LI HO
May the assembly of stainless Dakinis
Look with loving affection and accomplish all deeds.

HUM All you Tathagatas,
Heroes, Yoginis,
Dakas, and Dakinis,
To all of you I make this request:
With a mind completely aroused by great bliss
And a body in a dance of constant motion,
I offer to the hosts of Dakinis
The great bliss from enjoying the lotus of the mudra.
AH LA LA, LA LA HO, AH I AH, AH RA LI HO
May the assembly of stainless Dakinis
Look with loving affection and accomplish all deeds.

HUM All you Tathagatas,
Heroes, Yoginis,
Dakas, and Dakinis,
To all of you I make this request:
You who dance with a beautiful and peaceful manner,
O Blissful Protector and the hosts of Dakinis,
Please come here before me and grant me your blessings,
And bestow upon me spontaneous great bliss.
AH LA LA, LA LA HO, AH I AH, AH RA LI HO
May the assembly of stainless Dakinis
Look with loving affection and accomplish all deeds.

HUM All you Tathagatas,
Heroes, Yoginis,
Dakas, and Dakinis,
To all of you I make this request:
You who have the characteristic of the liberation of great bliss,
Do not say that deliverance can be gained in one lifetime
Through various ascetic practices having abandoned great bliss,
But that great bliss resides in the center of the supreme lotus.
AH LA LA, LA LA HO, AH I AH, AH RA LI HO
May the assembly of stainless Dakinis
Look with loving affection and accomplish all deeds.

HUM All you Tathagatas,
Heroes, Yoginis,
Dakas, and Dakinis,
To all of you I make this request:
Like a lotus born from the center of a swamp,
This method, though born from attachment, is unstained by the
    faults of attachment.
O Supreme Dakini, through the bliss of your lotus,
Please quickly bring liberation from the bonds of samsara.

AH LA LA, LA LA HO, AH I AH, AH RA LI HO
May the assembly of stainless Dakinis
Look with loving affection and accomplish all deeds.

HUM All you Tathagatas,
Heroes, Yoginis,
Dakas, and Dakinis,
To all of you I make this request:
Just as the essence of honey in the honey source
Is drunk by swarms of bees from all directions,
So through your broad lotus with six characteristics
Please bring satisfaction with the taste of great bliss.
AH LA LA, LA LA HO, AH I AH, AH RA LI HO
May the assembly of stainless Dakinis
Look with loving affection and accomplish all deeds.

Blessing the remaining tsog offering

HUM Impure mistaken appearances are purified in emptiness,
AH Great nectar accomplished from exalted wisdom,
OM It becomes a vast ocean of desired enjoyment.
OM AH HUM   (3x)

Giving the remaining tsog offering to the spirits

HO This ocean of remaining tsog offering of uncontaminated
    nectar,
Blessed by concentration, mantra, and mudra,
I offer to please the assembly of oath-bound guardians.
OM AH HUM
Delighted by enjoying these magnificent objects of desire,
EH MA HO
Please perform perfect actions to help practitioners.

Send out the remainder of the tsog offering to the spirits.

HO
O Guests of the remainder together with your retinues
Please enjoy this ocean of remaining tsog offering.
May those who spread the precious doctrine,
The holders of the doctrine, their benefactors, and others,
And especially I and other practitioners
Have good health, long life, power,
Glory, fame, fortune,
And extensive enjoyments.
Please grant me the attainments
Of pacifying, increasing, controlling, and wrathful actions.
You who are bound by oaths please protect me
And help me to accomplish all the attainments.
Eradicate all untimely death, sicknesses,
Harm from spirits, and hindrances.
Eliminate bad dreams,
Ill omens, and bad actions.

May there be happiness in the world, may the years be good,
May crops increase, and may Dharma flourish.
May all goodness and happiness come about,
And may all wishes be accomplished.

By the force of this bountiful giving
May I become a Buddha for the sake of living beings;
And through my generosity may I liberate
All those not liberated by previous Buddhas.

Colophon: This sadhana was compiled from traditional sources by Venerable Geshe Kelsang Gyatso, April 2010.

Appendix VII

Quick Path to Great Bliss

VAJRAYOGINI SELF-GENERATION SADHANA

by Je Phabongkhapa

Introduction

The instructions on the Highest Yoga Tantra practice of Venerable Vajrayogini were taught by Buddha Vajradhara in the forty-seventh and forty-eighth chapters of the *Condensed Root Tantra of Heruka*. This particular lineage of instructions, the Narokhacho lineage, was passed directly from Vajrayogini to Naropa, and from him through an unbroken lineage of realized practitioners to the present-day Teachers.

After Buddha Vajradharma had taught the practice he left the mandalas of Heruka and Vajrayogini intact in twenty-four auspicious places in this world. Thus even to this day there are countless manifestations of Vajrayogini in this world who help sincere practitioners gain realizations by blessing their mental continuum.

In many respects the practice of Vajrayogini is ideally suited to the present day. By relying on this practice sincerely, with a good heart and a mind of faith, it is definitely possible to attain full enlightenment; but to accomplish such results we must practice the extensive sadhana regularly.

This particular sadhana, *Quick Path to Great Bliss*, was composed by the great Lama Phabongkha Rinpoche. Compared to other sadhanas it is not very long, but it contains all the essential practices of Secret Mantra. To practice the sadhana successfully we should first receive the empowerment of Vajrayogini, and then study authentic instructions on the practice such as those found in the commentary *Guide to Dakini Land*. This sadhana is suitable both for our regular daily practice and for retreat; and we can practice it alone or in a group.

Geshe Kelsang Gyatso
1985

Quick Path to Great Bliss

THE YOGA OF IMMEASURABLES

Going for refuge

In the space before me appear Guru Chakrasambara Father and Mother, surrounded by the assembly of root and lineage Gurus, Yidams, Three Jewels, Attendants, and Protectors.

Imagining yourself and all sentient beings going for refuge, recite three times:

I and all sentient beings, the migrators as extensive as space, from this time forth until we reach the essence of enlightenment,
Go for refuge to the glorious, sacred Gurus,
Go for refuge to the complete Buddhas, the Blessed Ones,
Go for refuge to the sacred Dharmas,
Go for refuge to the superior Sanghas.

(3x)

Generating bodhichitta

Generate bodhichitta and the four immeasurables while reciting three times:

Once I have attained the state of a complete Buddha, I shall free all sentient beings from the ocean of samsara's suffering and lead them to the bliss of full enlightenment. For this purpose I shall practice the stages of Vajrayogini's path.   (3x)

Receiving blessings

Now with your palms pressed together, recite:

I prostrate and go for refuge to the Gurus and Three Precious Jewels. Please bless my mental continuum.

Due to reciting this:

The objects of refuge before me melt into the form of white, red, and dark blue rays of light. These dissolve into me and I receive their blessings of body, speech, and mind.

Instantaneous self-generation

In an instant I become Venerable Vajrayogini.

Blessing the inner offering

Purify the inner offering either with the mantra emanating from the four mouths or with the following:

OM KHANDAROHI HUM HUM PHAT
OM SÖBHAWA SHUDDHA SARWA DHARMA SÖBHAWA
    SHUDDHO HAM
Everything becomes emptiness.

From the state of emptiness, from YAM comes wind, from RAM comes fire, from AH a grate of three human heads. Upon this from AH appears a broad and expansive skullcup. Inside from OM, KHAM, AM, TRAM, HUM come the five nectars; from LAM, MAM, PAM, TAM, BAM come the five meats, each marked by these letters. The wind blows, the fire blazes, and the substances inside the skullcup melt. Above them from HUM there arises a white, upside-down khatanga which falls into the skullcup and melts whereby the substances take on the color of mercury. Above them three rows of vowels and consonants, standing one above the other, transform into OM AH HUM. From these, light rays draw the nectar of exalted wisdom from the hearts of all the Tathagatas, Heroes, and Yoginis of the ten directions. When this is added the contents increase and become vast.

OM AH HUM   (3x)

Blessing the outer offerings

Now bless the two waters, flowers, incense, lights, perfume, food, and music.

OM KHANDAROHI HUM HUM PHAT
OM SÖBHAWA SHUDDHA SARWA DHARMA SÖBHAWA
    SHUDDHO HAM
Everything becomes emptiness.

From the state of emptiness, from KAM come skullcup vessels inside which from HUM come offering substances. By nature emptiness, they have the aspect of the individual offering substances and function as objects of enjoyment of the six senses to bestow special, uncontaminated bliss.

OM AHRGHAM AH HUM
OM PADÄM AH HUM

OM VAJRA PUPE AH HUM
OM VAJRA DHUPE AH HUM
OM VAJRA DIWE AH HUM
OM VAJRA GÄNDHE AH HUM
OM VAJRA NEWIDE AH HUM
OM VAJRA SHAPTA AH HUM

Meditation and recitation of Vajrasattva

On my crown, on a lotus and moon seat, sit Vajrasattva Father and Mother embracing each other. They have white-colored bodies, one face, and two hands, and hold vajra and bell and curved knife and skullcup. The Father is adorned with six mudras, the Mother with five. They sit in the vajra and lotus postures. On a moon in his heart is a HUM encircled by the mantra rosary. From this a stream of white nectar descends, cleansing all sickness, spirits, negativities, and obstructions.

OM VAJRA HERUKA SAMAYA, MANU PALAYA, HERUKA TENO PATITA, DRIDHO ME BHAWA, SUTO KAYO ME BHAWA, SUPO KAYO ME BHAWA, ANURAKTO ME BHAWA, SARWA SIDDHI ME PRAYATZA, SARWA KARMA SUTZA ME, TZITAM SHRIYAM KURU HUM, HA HA HA HA HO BHAGAWÄN, VAJRA HERUKA MA ME MUNTSA, HERUKA BHAWA, MAHA SAMAYA SATTÖ AH HUM PHAT

Recite the mantra twenty-one times and then contemplate:

Vajrasattva Father and Mother dissolve into me and my three doors become inseparable from the body, speech, and mind of Vajrasattva.

THE YOGA OF THE GURU

Visualization

In the space before me arising from the appearance of the exalted wisdom of non-dual purity and clarity is a celestial mansion which is square with four doorways, ornaments, and archways, and complete with all the essential features. In the center on a jeweled throne supported by eight great lions, on a seat of a lotus of various colors, a sun, and a moon, sits my kind root Guru in the aspect of Buddha Vajradharma. He has a red-colored body, one face, and two hands which are crossed at his heart and hold a vajra and bell. His hair is tied up in a topknot and he sits with his legs crossed in the vajra posture. He assumes the form of a sixteen-year-old in the prime of his youth, adorned with silks and all the bone and jeweled ornaments.

Beginning in front of him and circling counter-clockwise are all the lineage Gurus from Buddha Vajradhara to my root Guru. They are in the aspect of Hero Vajradharma with red-colored bodies, one face, and two hands. Their right hands play damarus which reverberate with the sound of bliss and emptiness. Their left hands hold at their hearts skullcups filled with nectar, and their left elbows hold khatangas. They sit with their legs crossed in the vajra posture. In the prime of their youth, they are adorned with six bone ornaments.

The Principal and all of his retinue have at their foreheads OM, at their throats AH, and at their hearts HUM. From the HUM at their hearts light rays radiate and invite from their natural abodes the Gurus, Yidams, hosts of mandala Deities, and the assembly of Buddhas, Bodhisattvas, Heroes, Dakinis, Dharmapalas, and Protectors.

OM VAJRA SAMADZA DZA HUM BAM HO
Each becomes a nature which is the synthesis of all objects of refuge.

Prostration

With your palms pressed together, recite:

Vajra Holder, my jewel-like Guru,
Through whose kindness I can accomplish
The state of great bliss in an instant,
At your lotus feet humbly I bow.

Offering goddesses emanate from my heart and perform the offerings.

Outer offerings

OM AHRGHAM PARTITZA SÖHA
OM PADÄM PARTITZA SÖHA
OM VAJRA PUPE AH HUM SÖHA
OM VAJRA DHUPE AH HUM SÖHA
OM VAJRA DIWE AH HUM SÖHA
OM VAJRA GÄNDHE AH HUM SÖHA
OM VAJRA NEWIDE AH HUM SÖHA
OM VAJRA SHAPTA AH HUM SÖHA

OM AH VAJRA ADARSHE HUM
OM AH VAJRA WINI HUM
OM AH VAJRA GÄNDHE HUM
OM AH VAJRA RASE HUM
OM AH VAJRA PARSHE HUM
OM AH VAJRA DHARME HUM

Inner offering

OM GURU VAJRA DHARMA SAPARIWARA OM AH HUM

Secret offering

Contemplate that innumerable knowledge goddesses such as Pemachen emanate from your heart and assume the form of Vajrayogini. Guru Father and Mother embrace and experience uncontaminated bliss.

And I offer most attractive illusory mudras,
A host of messengers born from places, born from mantra, and
    spontaneously born,
With slender bodies, skilled in the sixty-four arts of love,
And possessing the splendor of youthful beauty.

Thatness offering

Remember that the three circles of the offering are indivisible bliss and emptiness.

I offer you the supreme, ultimate bodhichitta,
A great, exalted wisdom of spontaneous bliss free from obstructions,
Inseparable from the nature of all phenomena, the sphere of free-
    dom from elaboration,
Effortless, and beyond words, thoughts, and expressions.

Offering our spiritual practice

I go for refuge to the Three Jewels
And confess individually all negative actions.
I rejoice in the virtues of all beings
And promise to accomplish a Buddha's enlightenment.

I go for refuge until I am enlightened
To Buddha, Dharma, and the Supreme Assembly,
And to accomplish the aims of myself and others
I shall generate the mind of enlightenment.

Having generated the mind of supreme enlightenment,
I shall invite all sentient beings to be my guests
And engage in the pleasing, supreme practices of enlightenment.
May I attain Buddhahood to benefit migrators.

Kusali tsog offering

My own mind, the powerful Lady of Dakini Land, the size of only
a thumb, leaves through the crown of my head and comes face to
face with my root Guru. Once again I return, and slicing the skull
from my old body, place it upon a grate of three human heads
which has arisen instantaneously. I chop up the rest of my flesh,
blood, and bones, and heap it inside. By staring with wide open
eyes I purify, transform, and increase it into an ocean of nectar.
OM AH HUM HA HO HRIH   (3x)

Innumerable offering goddesses holding skullcups emanate from
my heart. With the skullcups they scoop up nectar and offer it to
the guests, who partake by drawing it through their tongues which
are straws of vajra-light.

I offer this nectar of commitment substance
To my root Guru, the nature of the four [Buddha] bodies;
May you be pleased.
OM AH HUM   (7x)

I offer this nectar of commitment substance
To the lineage Gurus, the source of attainments;
May you be pleased.
OM AH HUM

I offer this nectar of commitment substance
To the assembly of Gurus, Yidams, Three Jewels, and Protectors;
May you be pleased.
OM AH HUM

I offer this nectar of commitment substance
To the guardians who reside in the local places and in the regions;
May you assist me.
OM AH HUM

I offer this nectar of commitment substance
To all sentient beings in the six realms and the intermediate state;
May you be freed.
OM AH HUM

Through this offering all the guests are satiated with an uncontaminated bliss
And the sentient beings attain the Truth Body free from obstructions.
The three circles of the offering are the nature of non-dual bliss and emptiness,
Beyond words, thoughts, and expressions.

Offering the mandala

OM VAJRA BHUMI AH HUM
Great and powerful golden ground,
OM VAJRA REKHE AH HUM
At the edge the iron fence stands around the outer circle.
In the center Mount Meru the king of mountains,
Around which are four continents:
In the east, Purvavideha, in the south, Jambudipa,
In the west, Aparagodaniya, in the north, Uttarakuru.
Each has two sub-continents:

Deha and Videha, Tsamara and Abatsamara,
Satha and Uttaramantrina, Kurava and Kaurava.
The mountain of jewels, the wish-granting tree,
The wish-granting cow, and the harvest unsown.
The precious wheel, the precious jewel,
The precious queen, the precious minister,
The precious elephant, the precious supreme horse,
The precious general, and the great treasure vase.
The goddess of beauty, the goddess of garlands,
The goddess of music, the goddess of dance,
The goddess of flowers, the goddess of incense,
The goddess of light, and the goddess of scent.
The sun and the moon, the precious umbrella,
The banner of victory in every direction.
In the center all treasures of both gods and men,
An excellent collection with nothing left out.
I offer this to you my kind root Guru and lineage Gurus,
To all of you sacred and glorious Gurus;
Please accept with compassion for migrating beings,
And having accepted please grant us your blessings.

O Treasure of Compassion, my Refuge and Protector,
I offer you the mountain, continents, precious objects, treasure
    vase, sun, and moon,
Which have arisen from my aggregates, sources, and elements
As aspects of the exalted wisdom of spontaneous bliss and
    emptiness.

I offer without any sense of loss
The objects that give rise to my attachment, hatred, and confusion,
My friends, enemies, and strangers, our bodies and enjoyments;

Please accept these and bless me to be released directly from the
three poisons.

IDAM GURU RATNA MANDALAKAM NIRYATAYAMI

Requesting the lineage Gurus

Vajradharma, Lord of the family of the ocean of Conquerors,
Vajrayogini, supreme Mother of the Conquerors,
Naropa, powerful Son of the Conquerors,
I request you, please bestow the spontaneously born exalted
   wisdom.

Pamtingpa, holder of the explanations of the great secrets for
   disciples,
Sherab Tseg, you are a treasure of all the precious secrets,
Malgyur Lotsawa, lord of the ocean of Secret Mantra,
I request you, please bestow the spontaneously born exalted
   wisdom.

Great Sakya Lama, you are powerful Vajradhara,
Venerable Sonam Tsemo, supreme vajra son,
Dragpa Gyaltsen, crown ornament of the vajra holders,
I request you, please bestow the spontaneously born exalted
   wisdom.

Great Sakya Pandita, master scholar of the Land of the Snows,
Drogon Chogyal Pagpa, crown ornament of all beings of the three
   grounds,
Shangton Choje, holder of the Sakya doctrine,
I request you, please bestow the spontaneously born exalted
   wisdom.

Nasa Dragpugpa, powerful accomplished one,
Sonam Gyaltsen, navigator of scholars and supremely accomplished ones,
Yarlungpa, lord of the whispered lineage of the family of accomplished ones,
I request you, please bestow the spontaneously born exalted wisdom.

Gyalwa Chog, refuge and protector of all migrators, both myself and others,
Jamyang Namka, you are a great being,
Lodro Gyaltsen, great being and lord of the Dharma,
I request you, please bestow the spontaneously born exalted wisdom.

Jetsun Doringpa, you are unequalled in kindness,
Tenzin Losel, you have practiced in accordance with the [Guru's] words,
Kyentse, the expounder of the great, secret lineage of words,
I request you, please bestow the spontaneously born exalted wisdom.

Labsum Gyaltsen, holder of the mantra families,
Glorious Wangchug Rabten, all-pervading lord of the hundred families,
Jetsun Kangyurpa, principal of the families,
I request you, please bestow the spontaneously born exalted wisdom.

Shaluwa, all-pervading lord of the ocean of mandalas,
Kyenrabje, principal of all the mandalas,
Morchenpa, lord of the circle of mandalas,
I request you, please bestow the spontaneously born exalted wisdom.

Nesarpa, navigator of the ocean of whispered lineages,
Losel Phuntsog, lord of the whispered lineages,
Tenzin Trinlay, scholar who furthered the whispered lineages,
I request you, please bestow the spontaneously born exalted
    wisdom.

Kangyurpa, all-pervading lord upholding the Ganden doctrine,
Ganden Dargyay, friend of migrators in degenerate times,
Dharmabhadra, holder of the Ganden tradition,
I request you, please bestow the spontaneously born exalted
    wisdom.

Losang Chopel, lord of the Sutras and Tantras,
You have completed the essence of the paths of all the Sutras and
    Tantras.
Jigme Wangpo, scholar who furthered the Sutras and Tantras,
I request you, please bestow the spontaneously born exalted
    wisdom.

Dechen Nyingpo, you have the blessings of Naropa
To explain perfectly in accordance with Naropa
The essence of the excellent ripening and liberating paths of the
    Naro Dakini,
I request you, please bestow the spontaneously born exalted
    wisdom.

Losang Yeshe, Vajradhara,
You are a treasury of instructions on the ripening and liberating
    [paths] of the Vajra Queen,
The supreme, quick path for attaining the vajra state,
I request you, please bestow the spontaneously born exalted
    wisdom.

Kelsang Gyatso, you have completed all the profound and essential
    exalted states,
You are the compassionate Refuge and Protector of mother sentient
    beings,
You reveal the unmistaken path,
I request you, please bestow the spontaneously born exalted
    wisdom.

My kind root Guru, Vajradharma,
You are the embodiment of all the Conquerors,
Who grant the blessings of all Buddhas' speech,
I request you, please bestow the spontaneously born exalted
    wisdom.

Please bless me so that through the force of meditation
On the Dakini yoga of the profound generation stage,
And the central channel yoga of completion stage,
I may generate the exalted wisdom of spontaneous great bliss and
    attain the enlightened Dakini state.

Receiving the blessings of the four empowerments

I request you O Guru incorporating all objects of refuge,
Please grant me your blessings,
Please grant me the four empowerments completely,
And bestow on me, please, the state of the four bodies.   (3x)

Contemplate that as a result of your requests:

White light rays and nectars radiate from the OM at the forehead of
    my Guru.
They dissolve into my forehead, purifying the negativities and
    obstructions of my body.
I receive the vase empowerment, and the blessings of my Guru's
    body enter my body.

Red light rays and nectars radiate from the AH at the throat of my
Guru.

They dissolve into my throat, purifying the negativities and obstructions of my speech.

I receive the secret empowerment, and the blessings of my Guru's
speech enter my speech.

Blue light rays and nectars radiate from the HUM at the heart of my
Guru.

They dissolve into my heart, purifying the negativities and obstructions of my mind.

I receive the wisdom-mudra empowerment, and the blessings of
my Guru's mind enter my mind.

White, red, and blue light rays and nectars radiate from the letters
at my Guru's three places.

They dissolve into my three places, purifying the negativities and
obstructions of my body, speech, and mind.

I receive the fourth empowerment, the precious word empowerment, and the blessings of my Guru's body, speech, and mind
enter my body, speech, and mind.

Brief request

I request you my precious Guru, the essence of all Buddhas of the
three times, please bless my mental continuum.   (3x)

Absorbing the Gurus

Requested in this way, the encircling lineage Gurus dissolve into
my root Guru in the center. My root Guru too, out of affection
for me, melts into the form of red light, and entering through the
crown of my head, mixes inseparably with my mind in the aspect
of a red letter BAM at my heart.

THE YOGA OF SELF-GENERATION

Bringing death into the path of the Truth Body

This very letter BAM expands and spreads to the ends of space whereby all worlds and their beings become the nature of bliss and emptiness. Once again, contracting gradually from the edges, it becomes an extremely minute letter BAM which dissolves in stages from the bottom up into the nada. Then even the nada disappears and becomes the Truth Body of inseparable bliss and emptiness. OM SHUNYATA GYANA VAJRA SÖBHAWA ÄMAKO HAM

Bringing the intermediate state into the path of the Enjoyment Body

From the state of emptiness where all appearance has gathered like this there appears a red letter BAM standing upright in space, in essence an aspect of my own mind, the exalted wisdom of non-dual bliss and emptiness.

Bringing rebirth into the path of the Emanation Body

From the state of emptiness, from EH EH comes a red phenomena source, a double tetrahedron. Inside from AH comes a moon mandala, white with a shade of red. Upon this standing in a circle counter-clockwise rests the mantra OM OM OM SARWA BUDDHA DAKINIYE VAJRA WARNANIYE VAJRA BEROTZANIYE HUM HUM HUM PHAT PHAT PHAT SÖHA. I, the letter BAM in space, see the moon, and motivated to take rebirth in its center, enter the center of the moon.

Light rays radiate from the moon, letter BAM, and mantra rosary making all worlds and beings of samsara and nirvana into the nature of Venerable Vajrayogini. These gather back and dissolve into the letter BAM and mantra rosary which change completely into the supported and supporting mandala, fully and all at once.

Checking meditation on the mandala and the beings within it

Furthermore, there is the vajra ground, fence, tent, and canopy, outside of which a mass of five-colored fires blaze, swirling counter-clockwise. Inside these is the circle of the eight great charnel grounds, the Ferocious One, and so forth. In the center of these is a red phenomena source, a double tetrahedron, with its broad neck facing upwards and its fine tip pointing downwards. Except for the front and back, each of the other four corners is marked by a pink joy swirl whirling counter-clockwise.

Inside the phenomena source, in the center of an eight-petalled lotus of various colors, is a sun mandala. Upon this I arise in the form of Venerable Vajrayogini. My outstretched right leg treads on the breast of red Kalarati. My bent left leg treads on the head of black Bhairawa, which is bent backwards. I have a red-colored body which shines with a brilliance like that of the fire of the eon. I have one face, two hands, and three eyes looking towards the Pure Land of the Dakinis. My right hand, outstretched and point-ing downwards, holds a curved knife marked with a vajra. My left holds up a skullcup filled with blood which I partake of with my upturned mouth. My left shoulder holds a khatanga marked with a vajra from which hang a damaru, bell, and triple banner. My black hair hanging straight covers my back down to my waist. In the prime of my youth, my desirous breasts are full and I show the manner of generating bliss. My head is adorned with five human skulls and I wear a necklace of fifty human skulls. Naked, I am adorned with five mudras and stand in the center of a blazing fire of exalted wisdom.

THE YOGA OF PURIFYING MIGRATORS

At my heart inside a red phenomena source, a double tetrahedron, is a moon mandala. In the center of this is a letter BAM encircled by a mantra rosary. From these light rays radiate, leaving through the pores of my skin. Touching all sentient beings of the six realms, they purify their negativities and obstructions together with their imprints and transform them all into the form of Vajrayogini.

THE YOGA OF BEING BLESSED BY HEROES AND HEROINES

Meditation on the body mandala

At my heart, in the center of a phenomena source and moon seat, is a letter BAM which is the nature of the four elements. By splitting it changes into the four letters YA, RA, LA, WA which are the seeds of the four elements. They are the nature of the heart channel petals of the four directions such as the Desirous One. These transform starting from the left into Lama, Khandarohi, Rupini, and Dakini. In the center, the crescent moon, drop, and nada of the letter BAM, whose nature is the union of my very subtle red and white drops, transform into Venerable Vajrayogini.

Outside these in sequence are the channels such as the Unchanging One of the twenty-four places of the body, such as the hairline and crown, and the twenty-four elements from which come the nails, teeth, and so forth. These channels and elements, which are by nature inseparable, become the nature of the twenty-four letters of the mantra, OM OM and so forth, standing in a circle counter-clockwise from the east. These transform into the eight Heroines of the heart family: Partzandi, Tzändriakiya, Parbhawatiya, Mahanasa, Biramatiya, Karwariya, Lamkeshöriya, and Drumatzaya; the eight Heroines of the speech family: Airawatiya, Mahabhairawi, Bayubega, Surabhakiya, Shamadewi, Suwatre, Hayakarne, and Khaganane; and the eight Heroines of the body family: Tzatrabega, Khandarohi, Shaundini, Tzatrawarmini, Subira, Mahabala, Tzatrawartini, and Mahabire. These are the actual Yoginis who are non-dual with the Heroes of the twenty-four external places such as Puliramalaya. The channels and elements of the eight doors such as the mouth, by nature inseparable from the eight letters HUM HUM and so forth, transform into Kakase, Ulukase, Shönase, Shukarase, Yamadhathi, Yamaduti, Yamadangtrini, and Yamamatani. They all have the bodily form of the Venerable Lady, complete with ornaments and details.

Absorbing the wisdom beings and mixing the three messengers

Perform the blazing mudra and recite:

PHAIM
Light rays radiate from the letter BAM at my heart, and leaving from between my eyebrows, go to the ten directions. They invite all the Tathagatas, Heroes, and Yoginis of the ten directions in the aspect of Vajrayogini.
DZA HUM BAM HO

The wisdom beings are summoned, dissolve, remain firm, and are delighted. Now with the lotus-turning mudra followed by the embracing mudra, recite:

OM YOGA SHUDDHA SARWA DHARMA YOGA SHUDDHO HAM
I am the nature of the yoga of the complete purity of all phenomena.

Contemplate divine pride.

Putting on the armor

At places in my body arise moon mandalas upon which at my navel is red OM BAM, Vajravarahi; at my heart blue HAM YOM, Yamani; at my throat white HRIM MOM, Mohani; at my forehead yellow HRIM HRIM, Sachalani; at my crown green HUM HUM, Samtrasani; at all my limbs smoke-colored PHAT PHAT, essence of Chandika.

Granting empowerment and adorning the crown

PHAIM
Light rays radiate from the letter BAM at my heart and invite the empowering Deities, the supported and supporting mandala of Glorious Chakrasambara.

O, all you Tathagatas, please grant the empowerment.

Requested in this way, the eight Goddesses of the doorways drive away hindrances, the Heroes recite auspicious verses, the Heroines sing vajra songs, and the Rupavajras and so forth make offerings. The Principal mentally resolves to grant the empowerment and the four Mothers together with Varahi, holding jeweled vases filled with the five nectars, confer the empowerment through the crown of my head.

"Just as all the Tathagatas granted ablution
At the moment of [Buddha's] birth,
Likewise do we now grant ablution
With the pure water of the gods.

OM SARWA TATHAGATA ABHIKEKATA SAMAYA SHRIYE HUM"

Saying this, they grant the empowerment. My whole body is filled, all stains are purified, and the excess water remaining on my crown changes into Vairochana-Heruka, together with the Mother, who adorn my crown.

Offerings to the self-generation

If you are doing self-generation in conjunction with self-initiation it is necessary to bless the outer offerings at this point.

Offering goddesses emanate from my heart and perform the offerings.

Outer offerings

OM AHRGHAM PARTITZA SÖHA
OM PADÄM PARTITZA SÖHA
OM VAJRA PUPE AH HUM SÖHA
OM VAJRA DHUPE AH HUM SÖHA
OM VAJRA DIWE AH HUM SÖHA
OM VAJRA GÄNDHE AH HUM SÖHA
OM VAJRA NEWIDE AH HUM SÖHA
OM VAJRA SHAPTA AH HUM SÖHA

OM AH VAJRA ADARSHE HUM
OM AH VAJRA WINI HUM
OM AH VAJRA GÄNDHE HUM
OM AH VAJRA RASE HUM
OM AH VAJRA PARSHE HUM
OM AH VAJRA DHARME HUM

Inner offering

OM OM OM SARWA BUDDHA DAKINIYE VAJRA WARNANIYE VAJRA
BEROTZANIYE HUM HUM HUM PHAT PHAT PHAT SÖHA OM AH
HUM

Secret and thatness offerings

To perform the secret and thatness offerings either imagine:

I, Vajrayogini, stand in union with Chakrasambara, who has transformed from my khatanga, and generate spontaneous bliss and emptiness.

or imagine that as Vajrayogini you transform into Heruka and with divine pride perform the secret and thatness offerings:

With the clarity of Vajrayogini I give up my breasts and develop a penis. In the perfect place in the center of my vagina the two walls transform into two bell-like testicles and the stamen into the penis itself. Thus I take on the form of Great Joy Heruka together with the Secret Mother Vajrayogini who is by nature the synthesis of all Dakinis.

From the sphere of the unobservability of the secret place of the Father, from a white HUM there arises a white, five-pronged vajra, and from a red BÄ there arises a red jewel with a yellow BÄ marking its tip.

From the sphere of the unobservability of the secret place of the Mother, from an AH there arises a red, three-petalled lotus, and from a white DÄ there arises a white stamen, signifying white bodhichitta, with a yellow DÄ marking its tip.

OM SHRI MAHA SUKHA VAJRA HE HE RU RU KAM AH HUM HUM
PHAT SÖHA

Through Father and Mother being absorbed in union, the bodhichitta melts. When from my crown it reaches my throat [I experience] joy. When from my throat it reaches my heart

[I experience] supreme joy. When from my heart it reaches my navel [I experience] extraordinary joy. When from my navel it reaches the tip of my jewel I generate a spontaneous exalted wisdom whereby I remain absorbed in the concentration of inseparable bliss and emptiness. Thus, through this bliss inseparably joined with emptiness remaining in single-pointed absorption on the thatness that is the lack of inherent existence of the three circles of the offering, I delight in the secret and thatness offerings.

Then contemplate:

Once again I become Venerable Vajrayogini.

Eight lines of praise to the Mother

OM NAMO BHAGAWATI VAJRA VARAHI BAM HUM HUM PHAT

OM NAMO ARYA APARADZITE TRE LOKYA MATI BIYE SHÖRI
  HUM HUM PHAT

OM NAMA SARWA BUTA BHAYA WAHI MAHA VAJRE
  HUM HUM PHAT

OM NAMO VAJRA SANI ADZITE APARADZITE WASHAM KARANITRA
  HUM HUM PHAT

OM NAMO BHRAMANI SHOKANI ROKANI KROTE KARALENI
  HUM HUM PHAT

OM NAMA DRASANI MARANI PRABHE DANI PARADZAYE
  HUM HUM PHAT

OM NAMO BIDZAYE DZAMBHANI TAMBHANI MOHANI
  HUM HUM PHAT

OM NAMO VAJRA VARAHI MAHA YOGINI KAME SHÖRI KHAGE
  HUM HUM PHAT

THE YOGA OF VERBAL AND MENTAL RECITATION

Verbal recitation

At my heart inside a red phenomena source, a double tetrahedron, in the center of a moon mandala, is a letter BAM encircled by a red-colored mantra rosary standing counter-clockwise. From these, immeasurable rays of red light radiate. They purify the negativities and obstructions of all sentient beings and make offerings to all the Buddhas. All the power and force of their blessings is invoked in the form of rays of red light, which dissolve into the letter BAM and mantra rosary, blessing my mental continuum.

OM OM OM SARWA BUDDHA DAKINIYE VAJRA WARNANIYE VAJRA BEROTZANIYE HUM HUM HUM PHAT PHAT PHAT SÖHA

Recite at least as many mantras as you have promised to.

Mental recitation

(1) Sit in the sevenfold posture and bring the phenomena source, moon, and mantra letters from the heart down to the secret place if you want to generate bliss, or to the navel if you want to generate a non-conceptual mind, and enclose them with the winds. As if mentally reading the mantra rosary, which stands counter-clockwise in a circle, collect just three, five, or seven recitations. Then, while holding your breath, focus your mind on the pink joy swirls spinning counter-clockwise in the four corners of the phenomena source other than the front and the back, and especially on the nada of the BAM in the center, which is about to blaze.

(2) The red joy swirl at the upper tip of the central channel and the white joy swirl at the lower tip, each the size of only a grain

of barley, travel to the heart while spinning furiously counter-clockwise. At the heart they mix and gradually diminish into emptiness. Place your mind in absorption on bliss and emptiness.

THE YOGA OF INCONCEIVABILITY

From the letter BAM and the mantra rosary at my heart, light rays radiate and pervade all three realms. The formless realm dissolves into the upper part of my body in the aspect of rays of blue light. The form realm dissolves into the middle part of my body in the aspect of rays of red light. The desire realm dissolves into the lower part of my body in the aspect of rays of white light. I, in turn, gradually melt into light from below and above and dissolve into the phenomena source. That dissolves into the moon. That dissolves into the thirty-two Yoginis. They dissolve into the four Yoginis, and they dissolve into the Principal Lady of the body mandala. The Principal Lady, in turn, gradually melts into light from below and above and dissolves into the phenomena source. That dissolves into the moon. That dissolves into the mantra rosary. That dissolves into the letter BAM. That dissolves into the head of the BAM. That dissolves into the crescent moon. That dissolves into the drop. That dissolves into the nada, and that, becoming smaller and smaller, dissolves into clear light emptiness.

THE YOGA OF DAILY ACTIONS

From the state of emptiness in an instant I become Venerable Vajrayogini. At places in my body arise moon mandalas upon which at my navel is red OM BAM, Vajravarahi; at my heart blue HAM YOM, Yamani; at my throat white HRIM MOM, Mohani; at my forehead yellow HRIM HRIM, Sachalani; at my crown green HUM HUM, Samtrasani; at all my limbs smoke-colored PHAT PHAT, essence of Chandika.

To protect the main directions and intermediate directions recite twice:

OM SUMBHANI SUMBHA HUM HUM PHAT
OM GRIHANA GRIHANA HUM HUM PHAT
OM GRIHANA PAYA GRIHANA PAYA HUM HUM PHAT
OM ANAYA HO BHAGAWÄN VAJRA HUM HUM PHAT

The yoga of the tormas

Set up offerings in the traditional manner and then purify them in the following way:

OM KHANDAROHI HUM HUM PHAT
OM SÖBHAWA SHUDDHA SARWA DHARMA SÖBHAWA
    SHUDDHO HAM
Everything becomes emptiness.

From the state of emptiness, from KAM come skullcup vessels inside which from HUM come offering substances. By nature emptiness, they have the aspect of the individual offering substances and function as objects of enjoyment of the six senses to bestow special, uncontaminated bliss.

OM AHRGHAM AH HUM
OM PADÄM AH HUM
OM VAJRA PUPE AH HUM
OM VAJRA DHUPE AH HUM
OM VAJRA DIWE AH HUM
OM VAJRA GÄNDHE AH HUM
OM VAJRA NEWIDE AH HUM
OM VAJRA SHAPTA AH HUM

Blessing the tormas

OM KHANDAROHI HUM HUM PHAT
OM SÖBHAWA SHUDDHA SARWA DHARMA SÖBHAWA
   SHUDDHO HAM
Everything becomes emptiness.

From the state of emptiness, from YAM comes wind, from RAM comes fire, from AH a grate of three human heads. Upon this from AH appears a broad and expansive skullcup. Inside from OM, KHAM, AM, TRAM, HUM come the five nectars; from LAM, MAM, PAM, TAM, BAM come the five meats, each marked by these letters. The wind blows, the fire blazes, and the substances inside the skullcup melt. Above them from HUM there arises a white, upside-down khatanga which falls into the skullcup and melts whereby the substances take on the color of mercury. Above them three rows of vowels and consonants, standing one above the other, transform into OM AH HUM. From these, light rays draw the nectar of exalted wisdom from the hearts of all the Tathagatas, Heroes, and Yoginis of the ten directions. When this is added the contents increase and become vast.
OM AH HUM   (3x)

Inviting the guests of the torma

PHAIM
Light rays radiate from the letter BAM at my heart and invite Venerable Vajrayogini surrounded by the assembly of Gurus, Yidams, Buddhas, Bodhisattvas, Heroes, Dakinis, and both Dharma and mundane Protectors to come from Akanishta to the space before me. From a HUM in the tongue of each guest there arises a three-pronged vajra through which they partake of the essence of the torma by drawing it through straws of light the thickness of only a grain of barley.

Offering the principal torma

Offer the torma while reciting three or seven times:

OM VAJRA AH RA LI HO: DZA HUM BAM HO: VAJRA DAKINI
SAMAYA TÖN TRISHAYA HO

Offering the torma to the mundane Dakinis

Offer the torma while reciting twice:

OM KHA KHA, KHAHI KHAHI, SARWA YAKYA RAKYASA, BHUTA,
TRETA, PISHATSA, UNATA, APAMARA, VAJRA DAKA, DAKI NÄDAYA,
IMAM BALING GRIHANTU, SAMAYA RAKYANTU, MAMA SARWA
SIDDHI METRA YATZANTU, YATIPAM, YATETAM, BHUDZATA,
PIWATA, DZITRATA, MATI TRAMATA, MAMA SARWA KATAYA,
SÄDSUKHAM BISHUDHAYE, SAHAYEKA BHAWÄNTU, HUM HUM
PHAT PHAT SÖHA

Outer offerings

OM VAJRA YOGINI SAPARIWARA AHRGHAM, PADÄM, PUPE, DHUPE,
ALOKE, GÄNDHE, NEWIDE, SHAPTA AH HUM

Inner offering

OM VAJRA YOGINI SAPARIWARA OM AH HUM

Praise

O Glorious Vajrayogini,
Chakravatin Dakini Queen,
Who have five wisdoms and three bodies,
To you Savior of all I prostrate.

To the many Vajra Dakinis,
Who as Ladies of worldly actions,
Cut our bondage to preconceptions,
To all of you Ladies I prostrate.

Prayer to Behold the Beautiful Face of Vajrayogini

Bliss and emptiness of infinite Conquerors who, as if in a drama,
Appear as so many different visions in samsara and nirvana;
From among these you are now the beautiful, powerful Lady of
    Dakini Land,
I remember you from my heart, please care for me with your
    playful embrace.

You are the spontaneously born Mother of the Conquerors in the
    land of Akanishta,
You are the field-born Dakinis in the twenty-four places,
You are the action mudras covering the whole earth,
O Venerable Lady, you are the supreme refuge of myself, the Yogi.

You who are the manifestation of the emptiness of the mind itself,
Are the actual BAM, the sphere of EH, in the city of the vajra.
In the land of illusion you show yourself as a fearsome cannibal
And as a smiling, vibrant, fair young maiden.

But no matter how much I searched, O Noble Lady,
I could find no certainty of your being truly existent.
Then the youth of my mind, exhausted by its elaborations,
Came to rest in the forest hut which is beyond expression.

How wonderful, please arise from the sphere of the Dharmakaya
And care for me by the truth of what it says
In the Glorious Heruka, King of Tantras,
That attainments come from reciting the supreme close essence
    mantra of the Vajra Queen.

In the isolated forest of Odivisha
You cared for Vajra Ghantapa, the powerful Siddha,
With the bliss of your kiss and embrace and he came to enjoy the
    supreme embrace;
O, please care for me in the same way.

Just as the venerable Kusali was led directly
From an island in the Ganges to the sphere of space,
And just as you cared for the glorious Naropa,
Please lead me also to the city of the joyful Dakini.

Through the force of the compassion of my supreme root and
    lineage Gurus,
The especially profound and quick path of the ultimate, secret,
    great Tantra,
And the pure superior intention of myself, the Yogi,
May I soon behold your smiling face, O Joyful Dakini Lady.

Requesting fulfillment of wishes

O Venerable Vajrayogini, please lead me and all sentient beings
to the Pure Land of the Dakinis. Please bestow on us every single
mundane and supramundane attainment.   (3x)

*If you wish to make a tsog offering you should include it at this
point. The tsog offering starts on page 370.*

Offering the torma to the general Dharma Protectors

OM AH HUM HA HO HRIH   (3x)

HUM
From your pure palace of great bliss in Akanishta,
Great powerful one emanating from Vairochana's heart,

Dorje Gur, chief of all the Protectors of the doctrine,
O Glorious Mahakala come here please and partake of this offering
and torma.

From Yongdui Tsel and Yama's palace
And from the supreme place of Devikoti in Jambudipa,
Namdru Remati, chief Lady of the desire realm,
O Palden Lhamo come here please and partake of this offering and
torma.

From the mandala of the bhaga sphere of appearance and existence,
Mother Yingchugma, principal Lady of all samsara and nirvana,
Chief of Dakinis and demons, fierce female protector of the
mantras,
O Great Mother Ralchigma come here please and partake of this
offering and torma.

From Silwa Tsel and Haha Gopa,
From Singaling and the Ti Se snow mountain,
And from Darlungnay and Kaui Dragdzong,
O Zhingkyong Wangpo come here please and partake of this offer-
ing and torma.

From the eight charnel grounds and Risul in the south,
From Bodhgaya and glorious Samye,
And from Nalatse and glorious Sakya,
O Legon Pomo come here please and partake of this offering and
torma.

From the charnel grounds of Marutse in the north-east,
From the red, rocky hills of Bangso in India,
And from the supreme places of Darlung Dagram and so forth,
O Yakya Chamdrel come here please and partake of this offering
and torma.

Especially from Odiyana, Land of the Dakinis,
And from your natural abode,
Completely encircled by mundane and supramundane Dakinis,
O Father-Mother Lord of the Charnel Grounds come here please
  and partake of this offering and torma.

From the supreme places such as Tushita, Keajra, and so forth,
Great Protector of the doctrine of the second Conqueror,
Dorje Shugden, five lineages, together with your retinues,
Come here please and partake of this offering and torma.

I request you, I make offerings to you, O Host of Protectors of the
  Conqueror's doctrine,
I propitiate you and rely upon you, O Great Protectors of the
  Guru's words,
I cry out to you and beseech you, O Host of Destroyers of the
  obstructors of Yogis,
Please come here quickly and partake of this offering and torma.

I offer a torma adorned with red flesh and blood.
I offer drinks of alcohol, medicine nectars, and blood.
I offer the sound of large drums, thigh-bone trumpets, and
  cymbals.
I offer large, black silk pennants that billow like clouds.

I offer breath-taking attractions equal to space.
I offer loud chants that are powerful and melodious.
I offer an ocean of outer, inner, and secret commitment substances.
I offer the play of the exalted wisdom of inseparable bliss and
  emptiness.

May you protect the precious doctrine of Buddha.
May you increase the renown of the Three Jewels.
May you further the deeds of the glorious Gurus,
And may you fulfill whatever requests I make of you.

Requesting forbearance

Now recite the hundred-letter mantra of Heruka:

OM VAJRA HERUKA SAMAYA, MANU PALAYA, HERUKA TENO PATITA, DRIDHO ME BHAWA, SUTO KAYO ME BHAWA, SUPO KAYO ME BHAWA, ANURAKTO ME BHAWA, SARWA SIDDHI ME PRAYATZA, SARWA KARMA SUTZA ME, TZITAM SHRIYAM KURU HUM, HA HA HA HA HO BHAGAWÄN, VAJRA HERUKA MA ME MUNTSA, HERUKA BHAWA, MAHA SAMAYA SATTÖ AH HUM PHAT

Request forbearance by reciting:

Whatever mistakes I have made
Through not finding, not understanding,
Or not having the ability,
Please, O Protector, be patient with all of these.

OM VAJRA MU The wisdom beings, guests of the torma, dissolve into me and the worldly beings return to their own places.

Dedication prayers

By this virtue may I quickly
Accomplish the actual Dakini,
And then lead every living being
Without exception to that ground.

At my deathtime may the Protectors, Heroes, Heroines, and so
     forth,
Bearing flowers, parasols, and victory banners,
And offering the sweet music of cymbals and so forth,
Lead me to the Land of the Dakinis.

By the truth of the valid Goddesses,
Their valid commitments,

And the supremely valid words they have spoken,
May [my virtues] be the cause for me to be cared for by the
Goddesses.

Extensive dedication

*If you have the time and the wish you can finish with these prayers,
which were composed by Tsarpa Dorjechang:*

In the great ship of freedom and endowment,
Flying the white sail of mindfulness of impermanence,
And blown by the favorable wind of accepting and abandoning
actions and effects,
May I be delivered from the fearsome ocean of samsara.

Relying upon the crown-jewel of the non-deceptive objects of
refuge,
Taking to heart the great purpose of migrators, my mothers,
And cleansing my stains and faults with the nectar of Vajrasattva,
May I be cared for by the compassionate, venerable Gurus.

The beautiful Mother of the Conquerors is the outer Yogini,
The letter BAM is the supreme inner Vajra Queen,
The clarity and emptiness of the mind itself is the secret Dakini
Mother;
May I enjoy the sport of seeing the self-nature of each.

The worldly environment is the celestial mansion of the letter EH,
And its inhabitants, the sentient beings, are the Yoginis of the letter
BAM;
Through the concentration of the great bliss of their union,
May whatever appearance arises be pure appearance.

Thus, through the yogas [numbering] the directions and the moon,
May I eventually be led directly to the city of Knowledge Holders

By the coral-colored Lady of joy
With freely hanging vermilion hair and orange, darting eyes.

Having practiced in a place of corpses with sindhura and a langali
    stem,
And having wandered throughout the land,
May the beautiful Lady to whom the swirl at my forehead transfers
Lead me to the Land of the Dakinis.

When the inner Varahi has destroyed the creeping vine of appre-
    hender and apprehended,
And the dancing Lady residing in my supreme central channel
Has emerged through the door of Brahma into the sphere of the
    pathway of clouds,
May she embrace and sport with the Hero, Drinker of Blood.

Through the yoga of unifying [the two winds], meditating single-
    pointedly
On the tiny seed of the five winds at the lotus of my navel,
May my mental continuum be satiated by a supreme bliss
From the fragrant drops pervading the channels of my body-mind.

When, through the laughing and smiling play of the beautiful Lady
Of blazing light tummo within my central channel,
The youthful letter HAM has been completely softened,
May I attain the ground of the great bliss of union.

When the reddish-black RAM residing in the center of the three
    channels at my navel
Has been set ablaze by my upper and lower winds,
And its cleansing fire has burned away the seventy-two thousand
    impure elements,
May my central channel be completely filled with pure drops.

When the five-colored drop between my eyebrows has gone to my
crown,
And the stream of moon-liquid originating from it
Has reached the stamen of my secret lotus,
May I be satiated by the four joys of descending and ascending.

When, through being struck by the rays of five lights radiating
from that drop,
All stable and moving phenomena, my body and so forth,
Have been transformed into a mass of brilliant, clear rainbows,
May I once again enter the natural abode, the sphere of bliss and
emptiness.

When the Yogini of my own mind, the union beyond intellect,
The primordial state of inexpressible emptiness and clarity,
The original nature free from arising, ceasing, and abiding,
Recognizes its own entity, may I be forever nourished.

When my channels, winds, and drops have dissolved into the
sphere of EVAM,
And the mind itself has attained the glory of the Truth Body of
great bliss,
May I care for these migrators as extensive as space
With immeasurable manifestations of countless Form Bodies.

Through the blessings of the Conquerors and their marvelous Sons,
The truth of non-deceptive dependent relationship,
And the power and force of my pure, superior intention,
May all the points of my sincere prayers be fulfilled.

Auspicious prayers

May there be the auspiciousness of swiftly receiving the blessings
Of the hosts of glorious, sacred Gurus,

Vajradhara, Pandit Naropa, and so forth,
The glorious Lords of all virtue and excellence.

May there be the auspiciousness of the Dakini Truth Body,
Perfection of wisdom, the supreme Mother of the Conquerors,
The natural clear light, free from elaboration from the beginning,
The Lady who emanates and gathers all things stable and moving.

May there be the auspiciousness of the Complete Enjoyment Body,
    spontaneously born,
A body, radiant and beautiful, ablaze with the glory of the major
    and minor marks,
A speech proclaiming the supreme vehicle with sixty melodies,
And a mind of non-conceptual bliss and clarity possessing the five
    exalted wisdoms.

May there be the auspiciousness of the Emanation Body, born from
    the places,
Ladies who with various Form Bodies, in various places,
Fulfill by various means the aims of various ones to be tamed
In accordance with their various wishes.

May there be the auspiciousness of the supreme Dakini, mantra-
    born,
A venerable Lady with a color similar to that of a ruby,
With a smiling, wrathful manner, one face, two hands holding
    curved knife and skullcup,
And two legs in bent and outstretched positions.

May there be the auspiciousness of your countless millions of
    emanations
And the hosts of the seventy-two thousand [Dakinis]
Eliminating all the obstructions of practitioners
And bestowing the attainments that are longed for.

THE TSOG OFFERING

Blessing the tsog offering

OM KHANDAROHI HUM HUM PHAT
OM SÖBHAWA SHUDDHA SARWA DHARMA SÖBHAWA
   SHUDDHO HAM
Everything becomes emptiness.

From the state of emptiness, from AH comes a broad and expansive skullcup inside which the five meats, the five nectars, and the five exalted wisdoms melt and there arises a vast ocean of the nectar of exalted wisdom.
OM AH HUM HA HO HRIH   (3x)

Contemplate that it becomes an inexhaustible ocean of exalted wisdom nectar.

Offering medicine nectars

I offer this supreme nectar
That far transcends vulgar objects;
The supreme commitment of all the Conquerors,
And the foundation of all attainments.

May you be pleased with the great bliss
Of the unsurpassed bodhichitta,
Purified of all stains of obstructions,
And completely free from all conceptions.

Making the tsog offering

HO This ocean of tsog offering of uncontaminated nectar,
Blessed by concentration, mantra, and mudra,
I offer to please the assembly of root and lineage Gurus.

OM AH HUM
Delighted by enjoying these magnificent objects of desire,
EH MA HO
Please bestow a great rain of blessings.

HO This ocean of tsog offering of uncontaminated nectar,
Blessed by concentration, mantra, and mudra,
I offer to please the divine assembly of powerful Dakinis.
OM AH HUM
Delighted by enjoying these magnificent objects of desire,
EH MA HO
Please bestow the Dakini attainment.

HO This ocean of tsog offering of uncontaminated nectar,
Blessed by concentration, mantra, and mudra,
I offer to please the divine assembly of Yidams and their retinues.
OM AH HUM
Delighted by enjoying these magnificent objects of desire,
EH MA HO
Please bestow a great rain of attainments.

HO This ocean of tsog offering of uncontaminated nectar,
Blessed by concentration, mantra, and mudra,
I offer to please the assembly of Three Precious Jewels.
OM AH HUM
Delighted by enjoying these magnificent objects of desire,
EH MA HO
Please bestow a great rain of sacred Dharmas.

HO This ocean of tsog offering of uncontaminated nectar,
Blessed by concentration, mantra, and mudra,
I offer to please the assembly of Dakinis and Dharma Protectors.
OM AH HUM
Delighted by enjoying these magnificent objects of desire,

EH MA HO
Please bestow a great rain of virtuous deeds.

HO This ocean of tsog offering of uncontaminated nectar,
Blessed by concentration, mantra, and mudra,
I offer to please the assembly of mother sentient beings.
OM AH HUM
Delighted by enjoying these magnificent objects of desire,
EH MA HO
May suffering and mistaken appearance be pacified.

Outer offerings

OM VAJRA YOGINI SAPARIWARA AHRGHAM, PADÄM, PUPE, DHUPE,
   ALOKE, GÄNDHE, NEWIDE, SHAPTA AH HUM

Inner offering

OM VAJRA YOGINI SAPARIWARA OM AH HUM

Eight lines of praise to the Mother

OM I prostrate to Vajravarahi, the Blessed Mother HUM HUM PHAT
OM To the Superior and powerful Knowledge Lady unconquered
   by the three realms HUM HUM PHAT
OM To you who destroy all fears of evil spirits with your great vajra
   HUM HUM PHAT
OM To you with controlling eyes who remain as the vajra seat
   unconquered by others HUM HUM PHAT
OM To you whose wrathful fierce form desiccates Brahma HUM
   HUM PHAT
OM To you who terrify and dry up demons, conquering those in
   other directions HUM HUM PHAT

OM To you who conquer all those who make us dull, rigid, and
    confused HUM HUM PHAT

OM I bow to Vajravarahi, the Great Mother, the Dakini consort
    who fulfills all desires HUM HUM PHAT

Making the tsog offering to the Vajra Master

Vajra Holder please listen to me,
This special tsog offering of mine,
I offer to you with a mind of faith;
Please partake as is your pleasure.

EH MA, great peace.
This great, blazing tsog offering burns up delusions
And in that way brings great bliss.
AH HO Everything is great bliss.
AH HO MAHA SUKHA HO

Concerning this, all phenomena are seen as pure,
Of this the assembly should have no doubt.
Since brahmins, outcasts, pigs, and dogs
Are of one nature, please enjoy.

The Dharma of the Sugatas is priceless,
Free from the stains of attachment and so forth,
The abandonment of apprehender and apprehended;
Respectfully I prostrate to thatness.
AH HO MAHA SUKHA HO

Song of the Spring Queen

HUM All you Tathagatas,
Heroes, Yoginis,
Dakas, and Dakinis,

To all of you I make this request:
O Heruka who delight in great bliss,
You engage in the Union of spontaneous bliss,
By attending the Lady intoxicated with bliss
And enjoying in accordance with the rituals.
AH LA LA, LA LA HO, AH I AH, AH RA LI HO
May the assembly of stainless Dakinis
Look with loving affection and accomplish all deeds.

HUM All you Tathagatas,
Heroes, Yoginis,
Dakas, and Dakinis,
To all of you I make this request:
With a mind completely aroused by great bliss
And a body in a dance of constant motion,
I offer to the hosts of Dakinis
The great bliss from enjoying the lotus of the mudra.
AH LA LA, LA LA HO, AH I AH, AH RA LI HO
May the assembly of stainless Dakinis
Look with loving affection and accomplish all deeds.

HUM All you Tathagatas,
Heroes, Yoginis,
Dakas, and Dakinis,
To all of you I make this request:
You who dance with a beautiful and peaceful manner,
O Blissful Protector and the hosts of Dakinis,
Please come here before me and grant me your blessings,
And bestow upon me spontaneous great bliss.
AH LA LA, LA LA HO, AH I AH, AH RA LI HO
May the assembly of stainless Dakinis
Look with loving affection and accomplish all deeds.

HUM All you Tathagatas,
Heroes, Yoginis,
Dakas, and Dakinis,
To all of you I make this request:
You who have the characteristic of the liberation of great bliss,
Do not say that deliverance can be gained in one lifetime
Through various ascetic practices having abandoned great bliss,
But that great bliss resides in the center of the supreme lotus.
AH LA LA, LA LA HO, AH I AH, AH RA LI HO
May the assembly of stainless Dakinis
Look with loving affection and accomplish all deeds.

HUM All you Tathagatas,
Heroes, Yoginis,
Dakas, and Dakinis,
To all of you I make this request:
Like a lotus born from the center of a swamp,
This method, though born from attachment, is unstained by the
    faults of attachment.
O Supreme Dakini, through the bliss of your lotus,
Please quickly bring liberation from the bonds of samsara.
AH LA LA, LA LA HO, AH I AH, AH RA LI HO
May the assembly of stainless Dakinis
Look with loving affection and accomplish all deeds.

HUM All you Tathagatas,
Heroes, Yoginis,
Dakas, and Dakinis,
To all of you I make this request:
Just as the essence of honey in the honey source
Is drunk by swarms of bees from all directions,
So through your broad lotus with six characteristics
Please bring satisfaction with the taste of great bliss.

AH LA LA, LA LA HO, AH I AH, AH RA LI HO
May the assembly of stainless Dakinis
Look with loving affection and accomplish all deeds.

Blessing the offerings to the spirits

OM KHANDAROHI HUM HUM PHAT
OM SÖBHAWA SHUDDHA SARWA DHARMA SÖBHAWA
    SHUDDHO HAM
Everything becomes emptiness.

From the state of emptiness, from AH comes a broad and expansive
skullcup inside which the five meats, the five nectars, and the five
exalted wisdoms melt and there arises a vast ocean of the nectar of
exalted wisdom.
OM AH HUM HA HO HRIH   (3x)

Actual offering to the spirits

PHAIM
UTSIKTRA BALINGTA BHAKYÄSI SÖHA

HO This ocean of remaining tsog offering of uncontaminated
    nectar,
Blessed by concentration, mantra, and mudra,
I offer to please the assembly of oath-bound guardians.
OM AH HUM
Delighted by enjoying these magnificent objects of desire,
EH MA HO
Please perform perfect actions to help practitioners.

*Send out the remainder of the tsog offering to the accompaniment
of music.*

May I and other practitioners
Have good health, long life, power,
Glory, fame, fortune,
And extensive enjoyments.
Please grant me the attainments
Of pacifying, increasing, controlling, and wrathful actions.
You who are bound by oaths please protect me
And help me to accomplish all the attainments.
Eradicate all untimely death, sicknesses,
Harm from spirits, and hindrances.
Eliminate bad dreams,
Ill omens, and bad actions.

May there be happiness in the world, may the years be good,
May crops increase, and may Dharma flourish.
May all goodness and happiness come about,
And may all wishes be accomplished.

By the force of this bountiful giving
May I become a Buddha for the sake of living beings;
And through my generosity may I liberate
All those not liberated by previous Buddhas.

Prayers for the Virtuous Tradition

So that the tradition of Je Tsongkhapa,
The King of the Dharma, may flourish,
May all obstacles be pacified
And may all favorable conditions abound.

Through the two collections of myself and others
Gathered throughout the three times,
May the doctrine of Conqueror Losang Dragpa
Flourish for evermore.

The nine-line Migtsema prayer

Tsongkhapa, crown ornament of the scholars of the Land of the
Snows,
You are Buddha Shakyamuni and Vajradhara, the source of all
attainments,
Avalokiteshvara, the treasury of unobservable compassion,
Manjushri, the supreme stainless wisdom,
And Vajrapani, the destroyer of the hosts of maras.
O Venerable Guru-Buddha, synthesis of all Three Jewels,
With my body, speech, and mind, respectfully I make requests:
Please grant your blessings to ripen and liberate myself and others,
And bestow the common and supreme attainments.

(3x)

Colophon: This sadhana was translated under the compassionate
guidance of Venerable Geshe Kelsang Gyatso. The verse to Venerable
Geshe Kelsang Gyatso in *Requesting the lineage Gurus* was composed by
the glorious Dharma Protector, Duldzin Dorje Shugden, and included
in the sadhana at the request of Geshe Kelsang's faithful disciples. The
verse to Dorje Shugden in *Offering the torma to the general Dharma
Protectors* was composed by Venerable Geshe Kelsang Gyatso and
included in the sadhana at the request of his faithful disciples.

Appendix VIII

The nada
(Please note that the nada should be visualized at the size of a small pea.)

Glossary

Absorption of cessation An uncontaminated wisdom focused single-pointedly on emptiness in dependence upon the actual absorption of peak of samsara. See *Ocean of Nectar*.

Action mudra A Highest Yoga Tantra consort who assists in developing great bliss. See *Clear Light of Bliss* and *Tantric Grounds and Paths*.

Affirming negative See glossary entry "Negative phenomenon."

Aggregate In general, all functioning things are aggregates because they are an aggregation of their parts. In particular, a person of the desire realm or form realm has five aggregates: the aggregates of form, feeling, discrimination, compositional factors, and consciousness. A being of the formless realm lacks the aggregate of form but has the other four. A person's form aggregate is his or her body. The remaining four aggregates are aspects of his mind. See also glossary entry "Contaminated aggregate." See *Heart of Wisdom*.

Akshobya The manifestation of the aggregate of consciousness of all Buddhas. He has a blue-colored body.

Alertness A mental factor that is a type of wisdom which examines our activity of body, speech, and mind, and knows whether or not faults are developing. See *Understanding the Mind* and *Meaningful to Behold*.

Amitabha The manifestation of the aggregate of discrimination of all Buddhas. He has a red-colored body. See *Eight Steps to Happiness*.

Amoghasiddhi The manifestation of the aggregate of compositional factors of all Buddhas. He has a green-colored body.

Arya Tara/Tara A female Buddha who is a manifestation of the ultimate wisdom of all the Buddhas. *Arya* means "Superior" and *Tara* means "Liberator." Because she is a wisdom Buddha, and a manifestation of the completely purified wind element, Tara is able to help us very quickly.

Aryadeva A third century AD Indian Buddhist scholar and meditation master, who was a disciple of Nagarjuna.

Attachment A deluded mental factor that observes its contaminated object, regards it as a cause of happiness, and wishes for it. See *Understanding the Mind* and *Joyful Path of Good Fortune*.

Attention A mental factor that functions to focus the mind on a particular attribute of an object. See *Understanding the Mind*.

Bardo See glossary entry "Intermediate state."

Basis of imputation All phenomena are imputed on their parts, therefore any of the individual parts, or the entire collection of the parts, of any phenomenon is its basis of imputation. A phenomenon is imputed by mind in dependence upon its basis of imputation appearing to that mind. See *Heart of Wisdom* and *Ocean of Nectar*.

Beginningless time According to the Buddhist world view, there is no beginning to mind, and so no beginning to time. Therefore, all living beings have taken countless previous rebirths.

Blessing The transformation of our mind from a negative state to a positive state, from an unhappy state to a happy state, or from a state of weakness to a state of strength, through the inspiration of holy beings such as our Spiritual Guide, Buddhas, and Bodhisattvas.

Bodh Gaya The place where Buddha Shakyamuni showed the way to attain enlightenment; near the modern city of Gaya in the north Indian state of Bihar.

Brahma A worldly god who resides in the first form realm. See *Ocean of Nectar*.

Changing suffering For beings within samsara every experience of happiness or pleasure that arises from samsara's enjoyments is changing suffering. This is because these experiences are contaminated and have the nature of suffering.

Commitments Promises and pledges taken when engaging in certain spiritual practices.

Compositional factors The aggregate of compositional factors comprises all mental factors except feeling and discrimination, as well as non-associated compounded phenomena. See *Heart of Wisdom* and *Understanding the Mind*.

Concentration A mental factor that makes its primary mind remain on its object single-pointedly. See *Joyful Path of Good Fortune*, *Understanding the Mind*, and *Meaningful to Behold*.

Consciousness The six consciousnesses, or primary minds, are the eye consciousness, ear consciousness, nose consciousness, tongue consciousness, body consciousness, and mental consciousness. See *Understanding the Mind*.

Conqueror Buddha A Buddha is called a *Conqueror* because he or she has conquered all the obstructions to attaining liberation and enlightenment, or maras. See also glossary entry "Mara."

Conscientiousness A mental factor that, in dependence upon effort, cherishes what is virtuous and guards the mind from delusion and non-virtue. See *Meaningful to Behold* and *Understanding the Mind*.

Contact A mental factor that functions to perceive its object as pleasant, unpleasant, or neutral. See *Understanding the Mind*.

Contaminated aggregate Any of the aggregates of form, feeling, discrimination, compositional factors, and consciousness of a samsaric being. See also glossary entry "Aggregate." See *Heart of Wisdom*.

Dakinis Female Tantric Buddhas and those women who have attained the realization of meaning clear light. Dakas are the male equivalent. See *Guide to Dakini Land*.

Dakini Land The Pure Land of Heruka and Vajrayogini. *Keajra* (in Sanskrit) and *Dagpa Khacho* (in Tibetan). See *Guide to Dakini Land*.

Damaru A small hand-drum used in Tantric rituals. Playing the damaru symbolizes the gathering of the outer Dakinis into our body, and the manifestation of the inner Dakini (the mind of clear light) within our mind through the blazing of inner fire. It is also used as a music offering to the Buddhas.

Deity (*Yidam* in Tibetan.) A Tantric enlightened being.

Delusion A mental factor that arises from inappropriate attention and functions to make the mind unpeaceful and uncontrolled. There are three main delusions: ignorance, desirous attachment, and anger. From these all the other delusions arise, such as jealousy, pride, and deluded doubt. See also glossary entries "Innate delusions," and "Intellectually-formed delusions." See *Joyful Path of Good Fortune* and *Understanding the Mind*.

Demi-god A being of the demi-god realm, the second highest of the six realms of samsara. Demi-gods are similar to gods but their bodies, possessions, and environments are inferior. See *Joyful Path of Good Fortune*.

Desire realm The environment of hell beings, hungry ghosts, animals, human beings and demi-gods, and the gods who enjoy the five objects of desire.

Dharma Protector An emanation of a Buddha or a Bodhisattva whose main functions are to avert the inner and outer obstacles that prevent Dharma practitioners from gaining spiritual realizations, and to arrange all the necessary conditions for their practice. Also called *Dharmapala* in Sanskrit. See *Heart Jewel*.

Discrimination A mental factor that functions to apprehend the uncommon sign of an object. See *Understanding the Mind*.

Dorje Shugden A Dharma Protector who is an emanation of the Wisdom Buddha Manjushri. His main functions are to avert the inner and outer obstacles that prevent practitioners from gaining spiritual realizations, and to arrange all the necessary conditions for their spiritual development. See *Heart Jewel*.

Dromtonpa (AD 1004–1064) Atisha's foremost disciple. See *Joyful Path of Good Fortune*.

Elements, four These are earth, water, fire, and wind. These elements are not the same as the earth of a field, the water of a river, and so forth. Rather, the elements of earth, water, fire, and wind in broad terms are the properties of solidity, liquidity, heat, and movement respectively.

Example clear light A mind of clear light that realizes emptiness by means of a generic image. See *Clear Light of Bliss* and *Tantric Grounds and Paths*.

Faith A naturally virtuous mind that functions mainly to oppose the perception of faults in its observed object. There are three types of faith: believing faith, admiring faith, and wishing faith. See *Transform Your Life*, *Joyful Path of Good Fortune*, and *Understanding the Mind*.

Feeling A mental factor that functions to experience pleasant, unpleasant, or neutral objects. See *Understanding the Mind*.

Field of Merit Generally, this refers to the Three Jewels. Just as external seeds grow in a field of soil, so the virtuous internal seeds produced by virtuous actions grow in dependence upon Buddha Jewel, Dharma Jewel, and Sangha Jewel. Also known as the *Field for Accumulating Merit*.

Form aggregate Includes all the objects of the five sense awarenesses— all colors and shapes (visual form), sounds, smells, tastes, and tactile objects. A person's form aggregate is his or her body.

Form realm The environment of the gods who possess form and who are superior to desire realm gods. So-called because the gods who inhabit it have subtle form. See *Ocean of Nectar*.

Functioning thing A phenomenon that is produced and disintegrates within a moment. Synonymous with impermanent phenomenon, thing, and product.

Gelug The tradition established by Je Tsongkhapa. The name *Gelug* means "Virtuous Tradition." A Gelugpa is a practitioner who follows this tradition. The Gelugpas are sometimes referred to as the "new Kadampas." See *Heart Jewel*.

Generic image The appearing object of a conceptual mind. A generic image, or mental image, of an object is like a reflection of that object. Conceptual minds know their object through the appearance of a generic image of that object, not by seeing the object directly. See *Heart of Wisdom* and *Understanding the Mind*.

Geshe A title given by Kadampa monasteries to accomplished Buddhist scholars. A contracted form of the Tibetan *ge wai she nyen*, literally meaning "virtuous friend."

Geshe Chekhawa (AD 1102–1176) A great Kadampa Bodhisattva who composed the text *Training the Mind in Seven Points*, a commentary to Bodhisattva Langri Tangpa's *Eight Verses of Training the Mind*. He spread the study and practice of training the mind throughout Tibet. See *Universal Compassion*.

Ghantapa A great Indian Mahasiddha and a lineage Guru in the Highest Yoga Tantra practices of Heruka and Vajrayogini. See *Guide to Dakini Land*.

Gods Beings of the god realm, the highest of the six realms of samsara. There are many different types of god. Some are desire realm gods, while others are form or formless realm gods. See *Joyful Path of Good Fortune*.

Gungtang Gungtang Konchog Tenpai Dronme (AD 1762–1823), a Gelug scholar and meditator famous for his spiritual poems and philosophical writings.

Guru A Sanskrit word for "Spiritual Guide."

Heroes and Heroines A Hero is a male Tantric Deity embodying method. A Heroine is a female Tantric Deity embodying wisdom. See *Guide to Dakini Land*.

Hevajra A principal Deity of Mother Tantra. See *Great Treasury of Merit*.

Hinayana Sanskrit term for "Lesser Vehicle." The Hinayana goal is to attain merely one's own liberation from suffering by completely abandoning delusions. See *Joyful Path of Good Fortune*.

Hungry ghosts Beings of the hungry ghost realm, the second lowest of the six realms of samsara. Also known as "hungry spirits." See *Joyful Path of Good Fortune*.

Imprint(s) There are two types of imprint: imprints of actions and imprints of delusions. Every action we perform leaves an imprint on the mental consciousness, and these imprints are karmic potentialities to experience certain effects in the future. The imprints left by delusions remain even after the delusions themselves have been abandoned, like the smell of garlic lingers in a container after the garlic has been removed. Imprints of delusions are obstructions to omniscience, and are completely abandoned only by Buddhas.

Imputation, mere According to the highest school of Buddhist philosophy, the Madhyamika-Prasangika school, all phenomena are merely imputed by conception in dependence upon their basis of imputation. Therefore, they are mere imputations and do not exist from their own side in the least. See *Heart of Wisdom* and *Ocean of Nectar*.

Imputed object An object imputed by the mind in dependence upon its basis of imputation. See *Heart of Wisdom* and *Ocean of Nectar*.

Indra A worldly god. See *Heart of Wisdom*.

Inferential cognizer A completely reliable cognizer whose object is realized in direct dependence upon a conclusive reason. See *Understanding the Mind*.

Inner fire (*Tummo* in Tibetan.) An inner heat located at the center of the navel channel wheel. See *Clear Light of Bliss*.

Intellectually-formed delusions Delusions that arise as a result of relying on incorrect reasoning or mistaken tenets. See *Understanding the Mind*.

Intention A mental factor that functions to move its primary mind to the object. It functions to engage the mind in virtuous, non-virtuous, and neutral objects. All bodily and verbal actions are initiated by the mental factor intention. See *Understanding the Mind*.

Intermediate state (*Bardo* in Tibetan.) The state between death and rebirth. It begins the moment the consciousness leaves the body, and ceases the moment the consciousness enters the body of the next life. See *Joyful Path of Good Fortune* and *Clear Light of Bliss*.

Je Phabongkhapa (AD 1878–1941) A great Tibetan Lama who was an emanation of Heruka. Phabongkha Rinpoche was the holder of many lineages of Sutra and Secret Mantra. He was the root Guru of Kyabje Trijang Dorjechang (Kyabje Trijang Rinpoche).

Je Tsongkhapa (AD 1357–1419) An emanation of the Wisdom Buddha Manjushri, whose appearance in fourteenth-century Tibet as a monk, and the holder of the lineage of pure view and pure deeds, was prophesied by Buddha. He spread a very pure Buddhadharma throughout Tibet, showing how to combine the practices of Sutra and Tantra, and how to practice pure Dharma during degenerate times. His tradition later became known as the *Gelug*, or *Ganden, Tradition*. See *Heart Jewel* and *Great Treasury of Merit*.

Kapala A skullcup used or visualized in Tantric meditation, symbolizing the indivisible union of great bliss and emptiness.

Kyabje Trijang Rinpoche (AD 1901–1981) A special Tibetan Lama of the twentieth century who was an emanation of Buddha Shakyamuni, Heruka, Atisha, Amitabha, and Je Tsongkhapa. Also known as "Trijang Dorjechang" and "Losang Yeshe."

Lineage A line of instruction that has been passed down from Spiritual Guide to disciple, with each Spiritual Guide in the line having gained personal experience of the instruction before passing it on to others.

Living being Synonymous with sentient being (*sem chen* in Tibetan). Any being who possesses a mind that is contaminated by delusions or their imprints. Both *living being* and *sentient being* are terms used to distinguish beings whose minds are contaminated by either of these two obstructions from Buddhas, whose minds are completely free from these obstructions.

Lord of Death Although the mara, or demon, of uncontrolled death is not a living being, it is personified as the Lord of Death, or *Yama*. The Lord of Death is depicted in the diagram of the Wheel of Life clutching the wheel between his claws and teeth. See *Joyful Path of Good Fortune*.

Losang Dragpa (*Sumati Kirti* in Sanskrit.) The ordained name of Je Tsongkhapa. See *Great Treasury of Merit*.

Mahamudra A Sanskrit term, literally meaning "great seal." According to Sutra, this refers to the profound view of emptiness. Since emptiness is the nature of all phenomena, it is called a "seal," and since a direct realization of emptiness enables us to accomplish the great purpose—complete liberation from the sufferings of samsara—it is also called "great." According to Tantra, or Vajrayana, Mahamudra is the union of spontaneous great bliss and emptiness. See *Mahamudra Tantra*, *Great Treasury of Merit*, and *Clear Light of Bliss*.

Mahayana Sanskrit term for "Great Vehicle," the spiritual path to great enlightenment. The Mahayana goal is to attain Buddhahood for the benefit of all living beings by completely abandoning delusions and their imprints. See *Joyful Path of Good Fortune* and *Meaningful to Behold*.

Maitreya The embodiment of the loving kindness of all the Buddhas. At the time of Buddha Shakyamuni he manifested as a Bodhisattva disciple in order to show Buddha's disciples how to be perfect Mahayana disciples. In the future, he will manifest as the fifth founding Buddha.

Mala A set of prayer beads used to count recitations of prayers or mantras, usually with one hundred and eight beads. See *Guide to Dakini Land*.

Mandala offering An offering of the entire universe visualized as a Pure Land, with all its inhabitants as pure beings. See *Guide to Dakini Land* and *Great Treasury of Merit*.

Mara A Sanskrit word for "demon," referring to anything that obstructs the attainment of liberation or enlightenment. There are four principal types of mara: the mara of the delusions, the mara of contaminated aggregates, the mara of uncontrolled death, and the Devaputra maras. Of these, only the last are actual living beings. The principal Devaputra mara is wrathful Ishvara, the highest of the desire realm gods, who inhabits the Land of Controlling Emanations. A Buddha is called a "Conqueror" because he or she has conquered all four types of mara. See *Heart of Wisdom*.

Marpa (AD 1012–1096) Marpa Lotsawa, or Marpa the translator, was a great lay Tantric Yogi and the Spiritual Guide of Milarepa. See *Joyful Path of Good Fortune*.

Meaning clear light A mind of clear light that realizes emptiness directly without a generic image. Synonymous with inner Dakini Land and with Mahamudra Tantra. See *Clear Light of Bliss*.

Meditation A mind that concentrates on a virtuous object, and a mental action that is the main cause of mental peace. There are two types of meditation—analytical meditation and placement meditation. When we use our imagination, mindfulness, and powers of reasoning to find our object of meditation, this is analytical meditation. When we find our object and hold it single-pointedly, this is placement meditation. There are different types of object. Some such as impermanence or emptiness, are objects apprehended by the mind. Others such as love, compassion, and renunciation, are actual states of mind. We engage in analytical meditation until the specific object that we seek appears clearly to our mind or until the particular state of mind that we wish to generate arises. This object or state of mind is our object of placement meditation. See *The New Meditation Handbook.*

Meditation break See glossary entry "Subsequent attainment."

Mental continuum The continuum of a person's mind that has no beginning and no end.

Mental factor A cognizer that principally apprehends a particular attribute of an object. There are fifty-one specific mental factors. Each moment of mind comprises a primary mind and various mental factors. See *Understanding the Mind.*

Mental image See glossary entry "Generic image."

Mere appearance All phenomena are mere appearance because they are imputed by mind in dependence upon a suitable basis of imputation appearing to mind. The word "mere" excludes any possibility of inherent existence. See *Ocean of Nectar.*

Merit The good fortune created by virtuous actions. It is the potential power to increase our good qualities and produce happiness.

Migrator A being within samsara who migrates from one uncontrolled rebirth to another. See also *Living being.*

Milarepa (AD 1040–1123) A great Tibetan Buddhist meditator and disciple of Marpa, celebrated for his beautiful songs of realization.

Mindfulness A mental factor that functions not to forget the object realized by the primary mind. See *Understanding the Mind, Meaningful to Behold,* and *Clear Light of Bliss.*

Nagarjuna A great Indian Buddhist scholar and meditation master who revived the Mahayana in the first century AD by bringing to light the teachings on the *Perfection of Wisdom Sutras*. See *Ocean of Nectar*.

Nalanda Monastery A great seat of Buddhist learning and practice in ancient India.

Naropa (AD 1016–1100) An Indian Mahasiddha and a lineage Guru in the Highest Yoga Tantra practice of Vajrayogini. See *Guide to Dakini Land*.

Negative phenomenon An object that is realized through the mind explicitly eliminating a negated object. There are two types of negative phenomenon: affirming negatives and non-affirming negatives. An affirming negative is a negative phenomenon realized by a mind that eliminates its negated object while realizing another phenomenon. A non-affirming negative is a negative phenomenon realized by a mind that merely eliminates its negated object without realizing another phenomenon. See *Ocean of Nectar*.

Non-affirming negative See glossary entry "Negative phenomenon."

Object of negation An object explicitly negated by a mind realizing a negative phenomenon. In meditation on emptiness, or lack of inherent existence, it refers to inherent existence. Also known as *negated object*.

Obstructions to liberation Obstructions that prevent the attainment of liberation. All delusions, such as ignorance, attachment, and anger, together with their seeds, are obstructions to liberation. Also called *delusion-obstructions*.

Obstructions to enlightenment The imprints of delusions, which prevent simultaneous and direct realization of all phenomena. Also known as *obstructions to omniscience*. Only Buddhas have overcome these obstructions.

Offering That which delights the holy beings.

Phabongkha Rinpoche See glossary entry "Je Phabongkhapa."

Perfection of Wisdom Sutras Sutras of the second turning of the Wheel of Dharma, in which Buddha revealed his final view of the ultimate nature of all phenomena—emptiness of inherent existence. See *Heart of Wisdom* and *Ocean of Nectar*.

Pratimoksha vow *Pratimoksha* is the Sanskrit term for "personal liberation," and so a Pratimoksha vow is a vow that is motivated mainly by the wish to attain personal liberation. There are eight types of Pratimoksha vow. See *The Bodhisattva Vow*.

Primary mind A cognizer that principally apprehends the mere entity of an object. Synonymous with consciousness. There are six primary minds: eye consciousness, ear consciousness, nose consciousness, tongue consciousness, body consciousness, and mental consciousness. Each moment of mind comprises a primary mind and various mental factors. A primary mind and its accompanying mental factors are the same entity but have different functions. See *Understanding the Mind*.

Pure Land A pure environment in which there are no true sufferings. There are many Pure Lands. For example, Tushita is the Pure Land of Buddha Maitreya, Sukhavati is the Pure Land of Buddha Amitabha, and Dakini Land (or Keajra), is the Pure Land of Buddha Vajrayogini and Buddha Heruka. See *Living Meaningfully, Dying Joyfully*.

Ratnasambhava The manifestation of the aggregate of feeling of all Buddhas. He has a yellow-colored body.

Realization A stable and non-mistaken experience of a virtuous object that directly protects us from suffering.

Sadhana A ritual prayer that is a special method for attaining spiritual realizations, usually associated with a Tantric Deity.

Saraha One of the first Mahasiddhas, and the Teacher of Nagarjuna. See *Essence of Vajrayana*.

Shantideva (AD 687–763) A great Indian Buddhist scholar and meditation master. He composed *Guide to the Bodhisattva's Way of Life*. See *Meaningful to Behold* and *Guide to the Bodhisattva's Way of Life*.

Shepherd-like bodhichitta The wish to lead all living beings to Buddhahood in the way that a shepherd leads his sheep to safety. Just as shepherds first supply all the needs of their flock and attend to their own needs last of all, so some Bodhisattvas want to lead all living beings to Buddhahood first and then attain enlightenment for themselves last of all. See *Joyful Path of Good Fortune*.

Stupa A symbolic representation of Buddha's mind.

Subsequent attainment The period between meditation sessions; also known as "meditation break." See *Joyful Path of Good Fortune*.

Superior being (*Arya* in Sanskrit.) A being who has a direct realization of emptiness. There are Hinayana Superiors and Mahayana Superiors.

Sutra The teachings of Buddha that are open to everyone to practice without the need for an empowerment. These include Buddha's teachings of the three turnings of the Wheel of Dharma.

Torma offering A special food offering made according to either Sutra or Tantra. See *Essence of Vajrayana* and *Guide to Dakini Land*.

Tranquil abiding A concentration that possesses the special bliss of physical and mental suppleness that is attained in dependence upon completing the nine mental abidings. See *Joyful Path of Good Fortune* and *Meaningful to Behold*.

Transference of consciousness (*Powa* in Tibetan.) A practice for transferring the consciousness to a Pure Land at the time of death. See *Living Meaningfully, Dying Joyfully* and *Great Treasury of Merit*.

Tsog offering An offering made by an assembly of Heroes and Heroines. See *Essence of Vajrayana* and *Guide to Dakini Land*.

Vaibhashika The lower of the two schools of Hinayana tenets. This school does not accept self-cognizers and asserts external objects to be truly existent. See *Meaningful to Behold* and *Ocean of Nectar*.

Vairochana The manifestation of the aggregate of form of all Buddhas. He has a white-colored body.

Vajra and bell A vajra is a ritual object resembling a scepter and symbolizing great bliss, and a bell is a ritual hand-bell symbolizing emptiness. See *Guide to Dakini Land* and *Tantric Grounds and Paths*.

Vajradhara The founder of Vajrayana, or Tantra. He appears directly only to highly realized Bodhisattvas to whom he gives Tantric teachings. To benefit other living beings with less merit, he manifested in the more visible form of Buddha Shakyamuni. He also said that in degenerate times he would appear in an ordinary form as a Spiritual Guide. See *Great Treasury of Merit*.

Vajradharma The manifestation of the speech of all Buddhas. He looks like Conqueror Vajradhara, except that his body is red. There are three ways we can visualize him: in his outer aspect as Hero Vajradharma, in his inner aspect as Buddha Vajradharma, or in his secret aspect as Buddha Vajradharma with consort. See *Guide to Dakini Land*.

Vajrasattva Buddha Vajrasattva is the aggregate of consciousness of all the Buddhas, appearing in the aspect of a white-colored Deity specifically in order to purify the negativity of living beings. He is the same nature as Buddha Vajradhara, differing only in aspect. The practice of meditation and recitation of Vajrasattva is a very powerful method for purifying our impure mind and actions. See *Guide to Dakini Land*.

Vinaya The moral discipline of the Pratimoksha, and in particular the moral discipline of the ordained Sangha.

Vow A virtuous determination to abandon particular faults that is generated in conjunction with a traditional ritual. The three sets of vows are the Pratimoksha vows of individual liberation, the Bodhisattva vows, and the Secret Mantra or Tantric vows. See *The Bodhisattva Vow* and *Tantric Grounds and Paths*.

Wheel of Dharma A collection of Buddha's teachings. Dharma is compared to the precious wheel, one of the possessions of a legendary chakravatin king. This wheel could transport the king across great distances in a very short time, and it is said that wherever the precious wheel traveled the king reigned. In a similar way, when Buddha revealed the path to enlightenment he was said to have "turned the Wheel of Dharma," because wherever these teachings are present, deluded minds are brought under control.

Wisdom A virtuous, intelligent mind that makes its primary mind realize its object thoroughly. A wisdom is a spiritual path that functions to release our mind from delusions or their imprints. An example of wisdom is the correct view of emptiness. See *Heart of Wisdom*, *Ocean of Nectar*, and *Understanding the Mind*.

Wisdom being An actual Buddha, especially one who is invited to unite with a visualized commitment being.

Wrong awareness A cognizer that is mistaken with respect to its engaged, or apprehended, object. See *Understanding the Mind*.

Yidam See glossary entry "Deity."

Yoga A term used for various spiritual practices that entail maintaining a special view, such as Guru yoga and the yogas of sleeping, rising, and experiencing nectar. *Yoga* also refers to "union," such as the union of tranquil abiding and superior seeing. See *Guide to Dakini Land*.

Yogi/Yogini Sanskrit terms usually referring to a male or a female meditator who has attained the union of tranquil abiding and superior seeing.

Bibliography

*G*eshe Kelsang Gyatso is a highly respected meditation master and scholar of the Mahayana Buddhist tradition founded by Je Tsongkhapa. Since arriving in the West in 1977, he has worked tirelessly to establish pure Buddhadharma throughout the world. Over this period he has given extensive teachings on the major scriptures of the Mahayana. These teachings are currently being published and provide a comprehensive presentation of the essential Sutra and Tantra practices of Mahayana Buddhism.

Books

The following books by Geshe Kelsang Gyatso are all published by Tharpa Publications.

The Bodhisattva Vow. A practical guide to helping others. (2nd ed., 1995)

Clear Light of Bliss. A Tantric meditation manual. (2nd ed., 1992)

Eight Steps to Happiness. The Buddhist way of loving kindness. (1st American ed. 2010)

Essence of Vajrayana. The Highest Yoga Tantra practice of Heruka body mandala. (1997)

Great Treasury of Merit. How to rely upon a Spiritual Guide. (1992)

Guide to Dakini Land. The Highest Yoga Tantra practice of Buddha Vajrayogini. (2nd ed., 1996)

Guide to the Bodhisattva's Way of Life. How to enjoy a life of great meaning and altruism. (A translation of Shantideva's famous verse masterpiece.) (2002)

Heart Jewel. The essential practices of Kadampa Buddhism. (2nd ed., 1997)

Heart of Wisdom. An explanation of the *Heart Sutra.* (4th ed., 2001)

How to Solve Our Human Problems. The four noble truths. (1st American ed. 2007)

Introduction to Buddhism. An explanation of the Buddhist way of life. (1st American ed. 2008)

Joyful Path of Good Fortune. The complete Buddhist path to enlightenment. (2nd ed., 1995)

Living Meaningfully, Dying Joyfully. The profound practice of transference of consciousness. (1999)

Mahamudra Tantra. The supreme Heart Jewel nectar. (2005)

Meaningful to Behold. The Bodhisattva's way of life. (5th ed., 2007)

Modern Buddhism. The Path of Compassion and Wisdom. (2011)

The New Meditation Handbook. Meditations to make our life happy and meaningful. (1st American ed. 2009)

Ocean of Nectar. The true nature of all things. (1995)

Tantric Grounds and Paths. How to enter, progress on, and complete the Vajrayana path. (1994)

Transform Your Life. A blissful journey. (1st American ed. 2007)

Understanding the Mind. The nature and power of the mind. (3rd ed., 2002)

Universal Compassion. Inspiring solutions for difficult times. (4th ed., 2002)

Sadhanas and Other Booklets

Geshe Kelsang Gyatso has also supervised the translation of a collection of essential sadhanas, or prayer booklets.

Avalokiteshvara Sadhana. Prayers and requests to the Buddha of Compassion.

The Bodhisattva's Confession of Moral Downfalls. The purification practice of the *Mahayana Sutra of the Three Superior Heaps.*

Condensed Essence of Vajrayana. Condensed Heruka body mandala self-generation sadhana.

Dakini Yoga. Six-session Guru yoga combined with self-generation as Vajrayogini.

Drop of Essential Nectar. A special fasting and purification practice in conjunction with Eleven-faced Avalokiteshvara.

Essence of Good Fortune. Prayers for the six preparatory practices for meditation on the stages of the path to enlightenment.

Essence of Vajrayana. Heruka body mandala self-generation sadhana according to the system of Mahasiddha Ghantapa.

Feast of Great Bliss. Vajrayogini self-initiation sadhana.

Great Liberation of the Father. Preliminary prayers for Mahamudra meditation in conjunction with Heruka practice.

Great Liberation of the Mother. Preliminary prayers for Mahamudra meditation in conjunction with Vajrayogini practice.

The Great Mother. A method to overcome hindrances and obstacles by reciting the *Essence of Wisdom Sutra* (the *Heart Sutra*).

A Handbook for the Daily Practice of Bodhisattva Vows and Tantric Vows

Heartfelt Prayers. Funeral service for cremations and burials.

Heart Jewel. The Guru yoga of Je Tsongkhapa combined with the condensed sadhana of his Dharma Protector.

The Kadampa Way of Life. The essential practice of Kadam Lamrim.

Liberation from Sorrow. Praises and requests to the Twenty-one Taras.

Mahayana Refuge Ceremony and Bodhisattva Vow Ceremony.

Medicine Buddha Prayer. A method for benefiting others.

Medicine Buddha Sadhana. A method for accomplishing the attainments of Medicine Buddha.

Meditation and Recitation of Solitary Vajrasattva.

Melodious Drum Victorious in all Directions. The extensive fulfilling and restoring ritual of the Dharma Protector, the great king Dorje Shugden, in conjunction with Mahakala, Kalarupa, Kalindewi, and other Dharma Protectors.

Offering to the Spiritual Guide (*Lama Chopa*). A special way of relying upon a Spiritual Guide.

Path of Compassion for the Deceased. Powa sadhana for the benefit of the deceased.

Pathway to the Pure Land. Training in powa—the transference of consciousness.

Powa Ceremony. Transference of consciousness for the deceased.

Prayers for Meditation. Brief preparatory prayers for meditation.

A Pure Life. The practice of taking and keeping the eight Mahayana precepts.

Quick Path to Great Bliss. Vajrayogini self-generation sadhana.

The Root Tantra of Heruka and Vajrayogini. Chapters One and Fifty-one of the *Condensed Heruka Root Tantra*.

Treasury of Wisdom. The sadhana of Venerable Manjushri.

Union of No More Learning. Heruka body mandala self-initiation sadhana.

Vajra Hero Yoga. A brief essential practice of Heruka body mandala self-generation, and condensed six-session yoga.

The Vows and Commitments of Kadampa Buddhism.

Wishfulfilling Jewel. The Guru yoga of Je Tsongkhapa combined with the sadhana of his Dharma Protector.

The Yoga of Buddha Amitayus. A special method for increasing lifespan, wisdom, and merit.

The Yoga of Buddha Heruka. The brief self-generation sadhana of Heruka Body mandala.

The Yoga of Buddha Maitreya. Self-generation sadhana.

The Yoga of Buddha Vajrapani. Self-generation sadhana.

The Yoga of Enlightened Mother Arya Tara. Self-generation sadhana.

The Yoga of Great Mother Prajnaparamita. Self-generation sadhana.

The Yoga of Thousand-armed Avalokiteshvara. Self-generation sadhana.

The Yoga of White Tara, Buddha of Long Life.

To order any of our products, please visit www.tharpa.com or request a catalog by contacting your nearest Tharpa office (see page 411).

NKT – IKBU

Study Programs of Kadampa Buddhism

Kadampa Buddhism is a Mahayana Buddhist school founded by the great Indian Buddhist Master Atisha (AD 982–1054). His followers are known as *Kadampas*. *Ka* means "word" and refers to Buddha's teachings, and *dam* refers to Atisha's special Lamrim instructions known as "the stages of the path to enlightenment." By integrating their knowledge of all Buddha's teachings into their practice of Lamrim, and by integrating this into their everyday lives, Kadampa Buddhists are encouraged to use Buddha's teachings as practical methods for transforming daily activities into the path to enlightenment. The great Kadampa Teachers are famous not only for being great scholars, but also for being spiritual practitioners of immense purity and sincerity.

The lineage of these teachings, both their oral transmission and blessings, was then passed from Teacher to disciple, spreading throughout much of Asia, and now to many countries throughout the Western world. Buddha's teachings, which are known as *Dharma*, are likened to a wheel that moves from country to country in accordance with changing conditions and people's karmic inclinations. The external forms of presenting Buddhism may change as it meets with different cultures and societies, but its essential authenticity is ensured through the continuation of an unbroken lineage of realized practitioners.

Kadampa Buddhism was first introduced into the West in 1977 by the renowned Buddhist Master Venerable Geshe Kelsang Gyatso. Since that time, he has worked tirelessly to spread Kadampa Buddhism throughout the world by giving extensive teachings, writing many profound texts on Kadampa Buddhism, and founding the New Kadampa Tradition–International Kadampa Buddhist Union (NKT-IKBU), which now has over a thousand Kadampa Buddhist Centers and branches worldwide. Each Center offers study programs on Buddhist psychology, philosophy, and meditation instruction, as well as retreats for all levels of practitioner. The emphasis is on integrating Buddha's teachings into daily life to solve our human problems and to spread lasting peace and happiness throughout the world.

The Kadampa Buddhism of the NKT-IKBU is an entirely independent Buddhist tradition and has no political affiliations. It is an association of Buddhist Centers and practitioners that derive their inspiration and guidance from the example of the ancient Kadampa Buddhist Masters and their teachings, as presented by Geshe Kelsang Gyatso.

There are three reasons why we need to study and practice the teachings of Buddha: to develop our wisdom, to cultivate a good heart, and to maintain a peaceful state of mind. If we do not strive to develop our wisdom, we will always remain ignorant of ultimate truth—the true nature of reality. Although we wish for happiness, our ignorance leads us to engage in non-virtuous actions, which are the main cause of all our suffering. If we do not cultivate a good heart, our selfish motivation destroys harmony and good relationships with others. We have no peace, and no chance to gain pure happiness. Without inner peace, outer peace is impossible. If we do not maintain a peaceful state of mind, we are not happy even if we have ideal conditions. On the other hand, when our mind is peaceful, we are happy even if our external conditions are unpleasant. Therefore, the development of these qualities is of utmost importance for our daily happiness.

Geshe Kelsang Gyatso, or *Geshe-la* as he is affectionately called by his students, has designed three special spiritual programs for the systematic study and practice of Kadampa Buddhism that are especially suited to the modern world—the General Program (GP), the Foundation Program (FP), and the Teacher Training Program (TTP).

GENERAL PROGRAM

The General Program provides a basic introduction to Buddhist view, meditation, and practice that is suitable for beginners. It also includes advanced teachings and practice from both Sutra and Tantra.

FOUNDATION PROGRAM

The Foundation Program provides an opportunity to deepen our understanding and experience of Buddhism through a systematic study of six texts:

1. *Joyful Path of Good Fortune*—a commentary to Atisha's Lamrim instructions, the stages of the path to enlightenment.
2. *Universal Compassion*—a commentary to Bodhisattva Chekhawa's *Training the Mind in Seven Points*.
3. *Eight Steps to Happiness*—a commentary to Bodhisattva Langri Tangpa's *Eight Verses of Training the Mind*.
4. *Heart of Wisdom*—a commentary to the *Heart Sutra*.
5. *Meaningful to Behold*—a commentary to Bodhisattva Shantideva's *Guide to the Bodhisattva's Way of Life*.
6. *Understanding the Mind*—a detailed explanation of the mind, based on the works of the Buddhist scholars Dharmakirti and Dignaga.

The benefits of studying and practicing these texts are as follows:

(1) *Joyful Path of Good Fortune*—we gain the ability to put all Buddha's teachings of both Sutra and Tantra into practice. We can easily make progress on, and complete, the stages of the path to the

supreme happiness of enlightenment. From a practical point of view, Lamrim is the main body of Buddha's teachings, and the other teachings are like its limbs.

(2) and (3) *Universal Compassion* and *Eight Steps to Happiness*—we gain the ability to integrate Buddha's teachings into our daily life and solve all our human problems.

(4) *Heart of Wisdom*—we gain a realization of the ultimate nature of reality. By gaining this realization, we can eliminate the ignorance of self-grasping, which is the root of all our suffering.

(5) *Meaningful to Behold*—we transform our daily activities into the Bodhisattva's way of life, making every moment of our human life meaningful.

(6) *Understanding the Mind*—we understand the relationship between our mind and its external objects. If we understand that objects depend on the subjective mind, we can change the way objects appear to us by changing our own mind. Gradually we will gain the ability to control our mind and in this way solve all our problems.

TEACHER TRAINING PROGRAM

The Teacher Training Program is designed for people who wish to train as authentic Dharma Teachers. In addition to completing the study of fourteen texts of Sutra and Tantra, which include the six texts mentioned above, students are required to observe certain commitments with regard to behavior and way of life, and to complete a number of meditation retreats.

All Kadampa Buddhist Centers are open to the public. Every year we celebrate Festivals in many countries throughout the world, including the USA and England, where people gather from around the world to receive special teachings and empowerments and to enjoy a spiritual vacation. Please feel free to visit us any time!

For further information, please contact:

NKT-IKBU (Central Office)
Conishead Priory
Ulverston
Cumbria, LA12 9QQ
England

Tel: 01229-588533
Fax: 01229-587775

Email: info@kadampa.org
Website: www.kadampa.org

NKT-IKBU (US Office)
Kadampa Meditation Center New York
47 Sweeney Road
Glen Spey, NY 12737
USA

Phone: 845-856-9000
Toll free: 877-523-2672
Fax: 845-856-2110

Email: info@nkt-kmc-newyork.org
Website: www.nkt-kmc-newyork.org

Tharpa Publications Worldwide

Books from Tharpa Publications are currently available in English (American and British), Chinese, French, German, Italian, Japanese, Portuguese, and Spanish. Most languages are available from any Tharpa Publications office listed below.

Visit us at www.Tharpa.com or contact your local office for more information.

United States of America
Tharpa Publications US
47 Sweeney Road
Glen Spey, NY 12737
Phone: 845-856-5102
Toll-free: 888-741-3475
Fax: 845-856-2110
E-mail: info.us@tharpa.com

United Kingdom
Tharpa Publications UK
Conishead Priory
Ulverston
Cumbria, LA12 9QQ
Phone: +44 (0)1229 588 599
Fax: +44 (0)1229 483 919
E-mail: info.uk@tharpa.com

Australia
Tharpa Publications Australia
25 McCarthy Road (PO Box 63)
Monbulk VIC 3793
Phone: +61 (3) 9752 0377
E-mail: info.au@tharpa.com

Brazil
Editora Tharpa Brasil
Rua Fradique Coutinho, 701
Vila Madalena
CEP 05416-011 São Paulo - SP
Phone/Fax: +55 (11) 3812 7509
E-mail: info.br@tharpa.com

Canada
Tharpa Publications Canada
631 Crawford St.
Toronto, ON M6G 3K1
Phone: 416-762-8710
Toll-free: 416-762-2267
Fax: 905-274-1714
E-mail: info.ca@tharpa.com

France
Editions Tharpa
Château de Segrais
72220 Saint-Mars-d'Outillé
Phone: +33 (0)2 43 87 71 02
Fax : +33 (0)2 76 01 34 10
E-mail: info.fr@tharpa.com

Germany
Tharpa Verlag Deutschland
Sommerswalde 8
16727 Oberkrämer OT Schwante
Phone: +49 (0)33055 222135
Fax: +49 (0)33055 222139
E-mail: info.de@tharpa.com

Hong Kong
Tharpa Asia
2nd Fl., 21 Tai Wong St. East
Wanchai
Phone: +852 25205137
Fax: +852 25072208
E-mail: info.hk@tharpa.com

Japan
Tharpa Japan
Dai 5 Nakamura Kosan Biru #501
Shinmachi 1-29-16
Nishi-Ku, Osaka, 550-0013
Phone: +81 6-6532-7632
E-mail: info.jp@tharpa.com

Mexico
Editorial Tharpa Mexico
Enrique Rébsamen No. 406
(entre Xola y Diagonal de San
   Antonio)
Col. Narvate, C.P. 03020
México, D.F.
Phone: +01 (55) 56 39 61 86
Phone/Fax: +01 (55) 56 39 61 80
E-mail: info.mx@tharpa.com

Republic of South Africa
Tharpa South Africa
c/o Mahasiddha Kadampa
   Buddhist Centre
2 Hollings Road
Malvern, Durban, 4093
Phone: +27 31 464 0984
E-mail: info.za@tharpa.com

Spain
Editorial Tharpa España
Camino Fuente del Perro s/n
29120 Alhaurín el Grande
   (Málaga)
Phone: +34 952 596808
Fax: +34 952 490175
E-mail: info.es@tharpa.com

Switzerland
Tharpa Verlag AG
Mirabellenstrasse 1
8048 Zürich
Phone: +41 44 401 02 20
Fax: +41 44 461 36 88
E-mail: info.ch@tharpa.com

Index

M